D0269687

Au

T

A. R. C. LEANEY

THE RULE OF QUMRAN
AND ITS MEANING

new
test
ament
lib
rary

A. R. C. LEANEY

THE RULE
OF QUMRAN AND
ITS MEANING

Introduction, translation and commentary

SCM PRESS LTD
BLOOMSBURY STREET LONDON

FIRST PUBLISHED 1966
© SCM PRESS LTD 1966
PRINTED IN GREAT BRITAIN BY
W. & J. MACKAY & CO LTD, CHATHAM

CONIUGI DILECTISSIMAE
QUAE QUAMVIS SE SCIENTIA
PRAEDITAM ESSE DISSIMULET
COTIDIANAM DEMONSTRAT
SAPIENTIAM

A speech of Antigone, a single sentence of Socrates, a few lines that were inscribed on an Indian rock before the Second Punic War, the footsteps of a silent yet prophetic people who dwelt by the Dead Sea, who perished in the fall of Jerusalem, come nearer to our lives than the ancestral wisdom of barbarians who feed their swine on the Hercynian acorns.

Lord Acton,
Inaugural Lecture on the Study of History,
given at Cambridge, 11 June 1895

CONTENTS

THE RULE OF QUMRAN

PREFACE

THIS WORK HAS been written with at least five objects. The first is to try to show, especially to all those interested in the Bible, how the *Rule* of Qumran fits into its historical setting between the Old and New Testaments and thereby illuminates the history of religious ideas in the intertestamental period.

The second derives from the first: to show the relevance of the work for students of both Testaments, but especially of the New Testament. The third is to demonstrate how deeply into the past we must plunge in order to discover the ultimate sources of the thought of this remarkable body of men; the fourth to bring out as far as possible the characteristics of that thought as it is revealed in this writing. In this sphere their intellectual limitations are from a modern point of view obvious. Indeed, the modern reader might regard their moral convictions as equally narrow; it is certain that the men of Qumran would regard the absence of moral conviction in the modern world with the same horror and contempt as that with which they regarded their contemporaries. It is possible, then, that in this sphere, despite or even because of their limitations, the men of Qumran can teach us something; and accordingly an effort has been made to reveal some of those intellectual and moral virtues which excited at once the opposition and the admiration of their contemporaries. For this reason both introduction and commentary discuss fairly fully the ideas and doctrines expressed in the *Rule*, especially in relation to their causes and to those to which they gave rise. It is hoped that some assistance has hereby been given towards an appreciation of the thought of Qumran considered for its own sake as well as for its historical interest.

The fifth aim can be properly stated only with great diffidence; it is by revealing the character of a work typical of that intensely troubled and intensely formative period, which saw the gradual but inevitable and relatively swift physical destruction of one of the great sources of our civilization, to contribute towards the ultimate healing of the tragic breach between Judaism and Christianity.

Department of Theology
The University
Nottingham
25 February 1965

ROBERT LEANEY

ACKNOWLEDGEMENTS

My sincere thanks are due to Professor C. F. D. Moule and to Professor H. H. Rowley for valuable suggestions for improvement; especially to the latter for much hard work on the typescript. I wish also to thank most sincerely Miss M. J. Cunningham of the SCM Press, and Mrs Brenda Hall for her valiant work on the indexes.

A.R.C.L.

ABBREVIATIONS

SCROLLS

1QS	*The Rule of the Community* or *Manual of Discipline*
1QSa, 1QSb	Mss. associated with the *Rule*
4QSa, b, etc.	Fragmentary mss. of the *Rule* from Cave 4
1QH	*Psalms of Thanksgiving*
1QpHab	*The Commentary on Habakkuk*
1QIsa(a)	Scroll of Isaiah from Cave 1
4QPs37	Fragment of a commentary on Ps. 37 from Cave 4
4QFl	Fragment of a Florilegium, i.e. a collection of messianic passages with comments, from Cave 4
CD	Cairo *Damascus Document* or *Zadokite Document*
DSW	*The War Scroll* (often referred to by scholars as 1QM)

GENERAL ABBREVIATIONS

Ant.	*Antiquities* of Josephus
AP	*Apocrypha and Pseudepigrapha of the Old Testament*, 2 vols., ed. R. H. Charles, Clarendon Press, Oxford, 1913
BDB	Francis Brown, S. R. Driver and C. A. Briggs, *Hebrew and English Lexicon of the Old Testament*, Clarendon Press, 1907, corrected impression, 1952
BJ	*De Bello Judaico*, i.e. *The Jewish War* of Josephus
ERE	*Encyclopaedia of Religion and Ethics*, 13 vols., ed. J. Hastings, T. and T. Clark, Edinburgh, 1908–26
HDB	Hastings's *Dictionary of the Bible*, 5 vols., T. and T. Clark, 1908–9
HE	*Historia Ecclesiastica* of Eusebius
HN	*Historia Naturalis* of Pliny
HUCA	*Hebrew University College Annual*, Cincinnati

Jastrow	M. Jastrow, *Dictionary of Talmud Babli, Yerushalmi, Midrashic Literature and Targumim*, Pardes, New York, 1950
JBL	*Journal of Biblical Literature*, Philadelphia
JE	*Jewish Encyclopedia*, ed. I. Singer, 12 vols., Funk and Wagnalls, New York, 1906
JTS	*Journal of Theological Studies*, Oxford
JSS	*Journal of Semitic Studies*, Manchester
LXX	The Septuagint
MT	Masoretic Text
NEB	New English Bible
NT	New Testament
NTS	*New Testament Studies*, Cambridge
OT	Old Testament
PL	Migne, *Patrologia Latina*, Paris
Praep. Ev.	*Praeparatio Evangelica* of Eusebius
RB	*Revue Biblique*, Paris
RQ	*Revue de Qumrân*, Paris
RSV	Holy Bible, Revised Standard Version of 1952, Nelson, Edinburgh, 1957
RV	The Holy Bible, English Revised Version of 1885
SH	*Scripta Hierosolymitana*, Jerusalem
TWNT	*Theologisches Wörterbuch zum Neuen Testament*, ed. G. Kittel, Stuttgart, 1932 ff.

THE WORLD OF QUMRAN

I

MAN AND THE UNIVERSE

1. ASTRONOMY

THE *Rule of Qumran* is one of the most important of the Dead Sea Scrolls. Some indication of its origin and nature is given in the commentary which constitutes a large section of this book and attempts to show the connexions between the thought of its author or authors and that of the Old Testament and Judaism on the one hand and that of the New Testament and early Christianity on the other. But to appreciate the thought of the *Rule* fully we must take account of an unusual and characteristic element in it. This is a sense of obligation to live according to the divinely ordained structure of the universe. To understand this we must therefore begin—rather unexpectedly—with astronomy.

The earth and the other planets revolve round the sun. This fact is one of several which constitute our view of the universe which has developed since Copernicus, who wrote his *De Revolutionibus Orbium Coelestium* in 1543. This view might have been held by mankind for many centuries before that date; for Aristarchus of Samos, who in 279 BC observed the summer solstice at Alexandria, suggested that the earth revolved on its axis and round the sun; but the view which placed the earth at the centre and regarded the heavenly bodies as revolving round it in their spheres seemed far less difficult in the state of knowledge at that time. It was a view which—in one form or another—had not only prevailed from a time of unknown antiquity but dominated much of man's thinking on many subjects during these formative centuries. A developed form of the 'revolving spheres' view was set out by the Alexandrian Claudius Ptolemaeus (AD 90–168) in his *Almagest*. His system incorporated certain refinements which complicated the simple notion (usually associated with Aristotle) of concentric spheres revolving round the earth, allowing for the observed fact that the apparent paths of the planets, unlike that of the 'fixed' stars, did not follow a continuous circle.

These refinements are unimportant: the main point so far is that the system according to which the structure of the universe was understood was based on observation of the apparent facts.

Science is quite rightly proud of basing itself upon facts. The gradual development of astronomy justifies this claim, and refutes the mistaken formulation of it which would say that science was based on observation alone. The modern astronomer explains the apparent facts in ways which alone explain them satisfactorily, but which cannot be derived from simple observation of the heavens. The hypothesis of the rotation of the earth round the sun illustrates this: once it was suspected, it could be shown by an experiment, but it could not be seen by direct observation of the heavenly bodies. Foucault (1851), who suspended a heavy iron ball from the dome of the Panthéon in Paris, observed the steady deviation of the plane of its swing. The explanation was already known: the plane of swing remains fixed in space, whereas the earth is rotating. This was to confirm by observation, but by observation of significant behaviour already built into what was being observed.

Such observation is not that of pre-scientific man. He saw the sun rise in the east, trace a path through the sky and set in the west every day. It appeared therefore to revolve round the earth, although not all observers were interested even in this much of theory. Again, the moon puzzled her observers, and her phases were attributed to many fanciful causes. These are not important, but the observed behaviour of the sun and moon, partly in relation to the stars, determined much of the activity of ancient man; for the sun exhibits to systematic observation a pattern of behaviour additional to its daily course through the sky. It moves its position against the background of the stars which, were they visible in the daytime, would appear to casual observation to move with it. Ancient astronomers were not casual. They marked which constellations were nearest to the sun as soon as they could be seen after sunset, and familiarity with the heavens enabled them to place it in a neighbouring constellation. By continuous watching it became clear that in contrast to its daily course from east to west the sun moved slowly from west to east relative to the stellar background. This apparent path of the sun is known as the ecliptic, and may be imagined as a line drawn across the sky on the circumference of the celestial sphere which seems to arch over any

observer who stands on the face of the earth. It does not coincide
with the celestial equator but (owing to the tilt of the earth's axis
at an angle of 23½°) it changes gradually during a year from a
position 23½° north of the celestial equator to one 23½° south of it,
and back again. Twice in a year therefore the ecliptic coincides with
the celestial equator and these times are the spring and the autumn
equinoxes. The summer solstice, such as Aristarchus observed,
occurs three months later, when the sun reaches its most northerly
position.

The ecliptic passes through a number of constellations forming a
belt round the heavens known as the zodiac, an area divided into
twelve equal portions, each distinguished by one of the famous
constellations of the zodiac. This belt includes 8° on either side of the
ecliptic, and against this background the seven heavenly bodies move;
they are the five planets ('wanderers') which can be seen with the
naked eye and were therefore visible to the ancients—Mercury,
Venus, Mars, Jupiter and Saturn—the moon, and the sun. The sun's
apparent path westward, the plane of the ecliptic, is the norm from
which the other bodies deviate but slightly. They deviate only within
the zodiacal belt, the moon as much as 5° from the ecliptic. At any
particular time of the year the sun occupies a position in—or against
the background of—one of these constellations, staying in each for
about a month; and its entry into Aries, or the Ram, is held to
coincide with the spring equinox. This place in the heavens is called
the First Point of Aries and from this spot the positions of stars are
conventionally measured. In reality at the spring equinox the sun
in our era stands in Pisces: astronomically, therefore, the signs of the
zodiac must be distinguished from its constellations. The constellations
form the observed background; the signs, in which the sun is said
conventionally to be according to the date (Aries 21 March to
19 April; Taurus 20 April to 20 May and so on), move through the
constellations westward. The sun's position in Aries as marking the
beginning of the year dates from the reign of Nabonassar, an eighth-
century king of Babylon; and the alteration illustrates the fact that
the sun is not found in exactly the same position at each recurring
equinox. It is then *said* to be at the first point of the sign Aries; but it
is not in that actual constellation. In seventy-two years the displacement amounts to one day, in 2,200 years to about an entire zodiacal
sign. It therefore requires 12 × 2,200 years for the sun to be found
standing in each of the constellations of the zodiac successively at the

spring equinox. This displacement of the sun's position, called the precession of the equinoxes, was observed by Hipparchus of Nicaea in the second century BC. It was confirmed by Ptolemy (Claudius Ptolemaeus) and explained by Newton in his *Principia* (1687). It is due to the equinox occurring at a different point in the earth's orbit each year owing to the behaviour of its axis, which describes a small circle as it spins instead of revolving in a fixed position. It appears to have been known already to ancient Babylonians, for they divided antiquity into ages characterized by the sun's place in the zodiac at the equinox. The period of the Ram was preceded by those of the Twins and of the Bull. The Age of the Bull may have been inaugurated simply by the ascendancy of Babylon, whose god Marduk was symbolized by the Bull: we find that the king was invested with his office in the month Iyyar, when the sun was in the sign and actual constellation of the Bull (Taurus). Thus the calendar year was arbitrarily made to begin with this month without regard to the equinox. But Nabonassar was an unimportant king during a period when Babylon was without influence; it seems likely, therefore, that the dating of the period of the Ram from his reign was due to astronomical observation only.

The Babylonian system of belief, worship, chronology and calendar was more complicated than is implied by even the able observations involved in the facts so far given. The seasons of the year, conceived of as directed by the relative positions of the sun, moon and Venus (Ishtar), and to a subordinate degree by the planets Jupiter, Mars, Mercury and Saturn, were thought to have their counterparts in epochs of a vast span of time, the Great Year. The year was measured by the monthly passage of the sun through the zodiacal signs (though correlated with the thirteen lunations of the moon), the Great Year by the sun's more gradual shift of position in the equinoctial precession, along with the changing relative positions of the planets. The alignment of these in Cancer (the 'summer' of the Great Year) portended a cosmic conflagration, in Capricorn (the 'winter' of this vast era) a cosmic flood, the latter of which it was believed had already once taken place. Myths of the time before this Flood told of great sages and of their contemporary kings, one of whom was Emmeduranki, favourite of the great gods, who taught his son the secret of heaven and earth. We shall find him reappearing in the Bible as Enoch.[1]

[1] P. 66.

Ancient Babylon had an immense influence on the way in which man in antiquity regulated his life and interpreted the world in which he lived. Some of the ways in which this influence was spread will become clear later: it seems that the influence upon Israel was both direct and indirect, the latter being the influence mediated through Hellenism. The Greek world had learnt from Babylon both through the early Ionian philosophers and through Berosus, a Babylonian priest who taught in Cos in the third century and to whose astrological teaching the Stoics paid attention.

It will be necessary to trace in some detail both the direct influence of Babylon and that of Hellenism at various points in Israel's history, in order to appreciate the 'vocabulary' of the *Rule*; but for the present it is enough to show that Israel no less than Babylon assumed the duty of living according to the universe, although interpreting this duty characteristically in accordance with her monotheism. The men of the Old Testament did not doubt the importance of the heavenly bodies and of their observed behaviour, and to understand their outlook we must put ourselves in the place of those who really believed the earth to be more or less flat and the apparent celestial sphere to be an actual sphere. In its majestic turning, carrying the sun, moon and stars on their wheeling motion through the heavens, they saw the direct hand of God who had made these things. 'The heavens declare the glory of God, and the firmament showeth his handiwork' (Ps. 19.1; see vv. 1-6)—these words are meant literally and with a directness which we can hardly imagine. For us they still carry meaning, more awe-inspiring than for the psalmist, since we have to conceive of a God whose 'handiwork' is far vaster and far more subtle, and of which we speak with more consciousness of the word 'handiwork' being a metaphor than would enter the psalmist's mind. Similarly, when we read Amos 5.8, 'Seek him that maketh Pleiades and Orion', we should understand that the prophet is recalling his fellow countrymen from false gods to the true creator, and not atheists to acknowledge that God exists.

The visible structure of the universe was then immediately relevant: it contained its own regulators of the seasons and was its own calendar and clock. Moreover, since God had made it, this calendar itself must regulate worship. When such a grand and simple notion first became articulate in Israel it is difficult to say, but it appears that thoughts on this matter crystallized as a result of the Exile and the sojourn in Babylonia, when probably educated Israelites learnt astronomy and where we know that they adopted the names of the months which they still use for their religious calendar. Certainly Gen. 1 is post-exilic, and there in v. 14 we read that God set luminaries in the firmament (the celestial sphere of which we have spoken) to divide the day from the night; and to be 'for signs, and for seasons, and for days and years'; not until v. 15 is their function 'to give light upon the earth' mentioned.

Rashi, the great medieval commentator (Troyes, 1040–1105), comments on the word *mo'adim* translated 'seasons': '(This is written) with a view to the future when Israel would receive command regarding the festivals which would be calculated from the time of the lunar conjunction.' (The conjunction or *mo'ad* is equivalent to the new moon.) We do not share Rashi's belief in the Mosaic authorship of Gen. 1 and we hold that it does not refer to the future, but is a direct message to the writer's contemporaries. S. R. Driver comments on the same word, 'seasons': 'not the four seasons of the year (though these may be included), but fixed times, whether secular or sacred: . . . and also sacred seasons—the festivals and other sacred days in the Jewish calendar being fixed for definite days in the week, month, or year (see esp. Lev. 23), and the same word *mo'adim* being frequently applied to them'. The word is used frequently in these different senses in the *Rule* (e.g. 1.9,15; 3.18; 10.3 ff.).

The emphasis laid above upon regulation of the religious calendar by observation, without interpreting the data by theory, is justified when we consider the evidence lately discovered from Babylonia itself, where the astronomy of the Old Testament seems to have been learnt. Among the baked-clay tablets inscribed with cuneiform writing discovered in the ruins of the ancient cities of Ur, Babylon and Uruk are a group containing planetary observations, tables to predict the motions and eclipses of the moon, and so forth. The careful recording of times of earthquakes and plagues of locusts suggests that the compilers hoped to be able to predict these also; for they were remarkably successful in predicting the behaviour of the heavenly bodies. Their method was to amass data over a number of years, reducing irregularities by making fresh tables of what seemed to be exceptions in tables so far kept, until even apparent anomalies fell into a pattern. When the periods of eclipses, conjunctions, apparent retrograde motions of planets and the like had been thus determined, it was easy to assume that the pattern would repeat itself regularly in the future, and successful experiment confirmed the soundness or led to correction of the method used in each particular case, until sheer observation provided an entirely reliable corpus of knowledge. The Babylonians failed to interpret this knowledge so as to acquire understanding of the universe because they neither desired nor needed it: they wished simply to regulate their religious festivals and to maintain an accurate calendar for the needs of the state. In the course of their work they evolved considerable mathematical skill, using a numerical system based on 1 to 60 (a rebuke to contemporaries who wish to simplify monetary calculations by confining us to the decimal system); but this wonderful store of knowledge was used all in the service of the calendar as the regulator of the national and social life, based on and intricately bound up with their religious beliefs. (Names of heavenly bodies were also names of gods, though a god need not be identified with star or planet.)

We can point to no evidence which suggests that any Israelites learnt the entire knowledge of astronomy available in Babylonia, and indeed it would be neither feasible nor permissible for any unqualified person to learn it; but there are certain indications which show Israelite awareness of the Babylonian system. The most obvious is the adoption of the names of the months from Babylon from the time of the Exile onwards, namely Nisan, Iyyar, Sivan, Tammuz, Ab, Elul, Tishri, Marcheshvan, Kislev, Tebet, Shebat, Adar. These names do not occur in any book dating from before the exile and the Jews themselves affirm their Babylonian origin.

2. THE CALENDAR

In the Pentateuch and in the books of Joshua, Judges and Ruth numbers are used for the months except for the first, whose ancient pre-exilic (i.e. Canaanite) name of Abib appears at Ex. 13.4; 23.15; 34.18; Deut. 16.1. In the last three references it is characterized as the month in which Passover occurs, and must therefore be a spring month. It has indeed been assumed by some that Abib means 'spring' (although the use at Lev. 2.14 suggests other possibilities) and the modern town of Tel-Abib (or Tel-Aviv) was given its name to mean 'Hill of Spring'. Of the other Canaanite month names the Bible preserves for us Zif for the second (I Kings 6.1, 37), Ethanim for the seventh (I Kings 8.2) and Bul for the eighth (I Kings 6.38). Whether in the pre-exilic calendar they were so numbered is doubtful.

At first sight more important than the derivation of the names of the months is the fact that both the Babylonian and the orthodox Jewish calendar are lunar. This means that the calendar was regulated by the observation of the moon, or by calculations which provided the date of the new moon if it could not be observed; it does not mean that the sun played no part, but that it was subordinate to the moon. The Bible implies the great importance of determining the beginning of Nisan (the first month) so that Passover and Weeks could be kept correctly, and of Tishri (the seventh month) for the other feasts. This can be seen best in Lev. 23, the chapter usually referred to by Jews for authority for festivals. Verse 5 gives instructions for Passover, vv. 15 and 16 for Weeks (counted from Passover, though exactly how was a matter of controversy—see p. 96). Verse 24 is about the 'old' New Year (see p. 243) which is still the traditional Jewish New Year's Day. To see this the verse must be compared with Num. 29.1. Verse 27 gives the date for the Day of Atonement, v. 34 that for the Feast of Booths or Tabernacles. All the last three dates are in Tishri.

Besides this famous chapter, Ex. 23 and Deut. 16 give the scheme of feasts at earlier stages of history, and Num. 28–29 gives a more detailed and probably later schedule. Num. 28.11–15 gives careful instructions for sacrifices at the beginning of every month in the year and a number of other passages refer to these days as specially observed. Col. 2.16 shows that the custom of keeping them was still prevalent in New Testament times.

Despite the evident importance of knowing when any month began, and the special importance for Nisan and Tishri, the Bible does not give any hint of how the new moon was to be observed or anticipated. For this we must turn to the Mishnah tractate, *R'osh Hashshanah*, the first half of which describes in detail the method of observation and the testing of witnesses who reported to the Sanhedrin that they had seen the new moon. The Talmud knows the length of a lunar month, the time between one appearance of the moon and its reappearance at the beginning of the next month. The figure is very nearly accurate: 29 days, 12 hours, $44\frac{1}{18}$ minutes ($\frac{1}{18}$ minute is $3\frac{1}{3}$ seconds, the true figure being $2\frac{1}{2}$ seconds if expressed in the nearest fraction). It is certain that in Mishnaic times it was known that no month could be longer than thirty or shorter than twenty-nine days. In the absence of witnesses, therefore, the thirty-first day after the previous new moon automatically became the first day of the new month.

Twelve such months, half containing twenty-nine, half thirty days, make up the year of a lunar calendar. This gives only 354 days, and if it is desired to co-ordinate the lunar with the solar year one rough-and-ready way of doing this is to intercalate an extra month from time to time. We know that the Jews adopted this method (when is not known) and still use it; they base their intercalations on a nineteen-year cycle, for nineteen solar years differ by only about half a day from 235 lunar months. Their reason for wishing to co-ordinate the solar and lunar years is probably that the Passover is not only a lunar festival but is in particular held at the full moon nearest to the spring equinox. The sacrificial lamb seems to be a substitute for a firstborn son (Ex. 12), and may have been originally a firstborn offering to the moon deity at the time near the spring equinox when the flocks bear their young. This would account for the persistence of the tradition that the Passover is a spring festival (Deut. 16.1).

The orthodox calendar is therefore lunar—based on the moon, but with consciousness of the importance of the sun. Other indications of the influence of the solar year lie in the agricultural feasts which were absorbed into the calendar when the Israelites settled in Canaan. These are Unleavened Bread, which is associated with Passover, Weeks (the beginning of harvest) and Tabernacles (the completion of harvest).

It is a natural deduction that the original calendar (no doubt in a primitive form and without details) not only of the Israelites but of kindred nomadic tribes was lunar. While the Israelites learned the names of the months from the Babylonians at the time of the exile, they did not owe entirely to them the idea of the moon as the basis of the calendar, having preserved this from very early times. They may well owe to Babylonia their methods of observation and calculation, but, as we shall see, the lunar calendar in its developed form came by way of Greek civilization (p. 87).

Whatever the origin of the calendar used by orthodox Judaism, it serves as an excellent example of an all-important fact: insistence on keeping festivals not only in the manner but on the dates enjoined by God shows a desire—almost compulsive—to live according to the structure of the universe which God has created. This was a powerful element in the religious psychology of the Qumran sect which we shall see well attested by their conscientious adherence to a special calendar different from that of orthodox Judaism.

This special calendar of the sect and its significance are discussed in Chapter II, Section 6; we are concerned here to make a claim more fundamental to our way of interpreting the *Rule*: that the desire to live according to the structure of the universe is found everywhere in the ancient world, differing only in the forms which it takes; philosophy itself takes its rise from it.

3. PHILOSOPHY

A claim such as that made at the end of the previous section may well seem exaggerated; it would be hard to prove, and however true and important is best given illustration rather than an attempted full vindication. We have already touched and need not enlarge upon the subject of the influence of Babylon on Israel. It will suffice to refer to the fact that study of Old Testament ideas and their history has now for many years involved the study of Near Eastern cultures in general. It is perhaps less well known that these same cultures had a decisive influence on the early thinking which immediately preceded classical Greek philosophy and provided so much of its vocabulary. For example, according to a tradition preserved by the tenth-century lexicographer usually known as Suidas, Pherecydes of Syros (*fl.* about the middle of the sixth century BC) used Phoenician secret books. Kirk and Raven[1] comment to the effect that the exact form of this tradition is no doubt wrong, but that it must have some foundation; thus it provides one indication of the dispersal of oriental ideas at least as far as the Aegean. The case of Thales is clearer: the cause of the solar eclipse predicted by him in 585 BC was unknown to his successors. It seems that he did not know the reason for it, but predicted it on the basis of empirical observations. 'It is overwhelmingly probable that Thales' feat depended on his access to . . . Babylonian records',[2] or possibly to similar observations made in Egypt, for ancient mentions of him connect him with that country; but to connect ancient Greek sages with Egypt was a literary fashion and history would suggest that Thales' city Miletus, in the Ionian sea-board of Asia Minor, the birthplace of western philosophy, was more certainly influenced by countries from the eastern horn of the fertile crescent. The famous Nebuchadrezzar, the destroyer of Jerusalem in 598 and 587, intervened to check the successful western exploits of

---

[1] G. S. Kirk and J. E. Raven, *The Presocratic Philosophers*, p. 52.
[2] *Op. cit.*, p. 80.

Cyaxares, king of Media, and helped to fix the boundary between the
territory which the latter had won and that of Alyattes, king of
Lydia, on the river Halys in Asia Minor in the very year which saw
Thales' eclipse (585). Wars bring a mingling of cultures and the
exchange of ideas. Here is the historical possibility of such an exchange
between Babylon and Ionia.

Again, if we turn from cosmology to the first adumbrations of
philosophy, we find an affinity between the Greek mind and the
Semitic while the former is still at the level of using a concrete
vocabulary for what later ages would regard as abstract ideas.
Anaximenes (Miletus, *c.* 500 BC) will provide an excellent example.
He is reported to have said, 'As our soul (*psyche*), being air, holds us
together, so does wind (*pneuma*) and air enclose the whole world.'[1]
Kirk and Raven show that this is no isolated example of a belief
which related the soul to the universe[2] and the *psyche* to *pneuma*. It is
true that Gen. 2.7 implies a Hebrew psychology with a conception of
what constitutes the life of a man fundamentally different from the
Greek notion of an immortal *psyche* in a mortal *soma*, but the 'breath
of life' of Gen. 2.7 in the early tradition (J) becomes the wind, or
spirit, of life (the *ruach* of life) in the priestly recension (P) at Gen. 6.17
and 7.15, while at 7.22 (P) the composite phrase 'the breath of the
spirit (*ruach*) of life' appears. The *ruach* is the wind or breath of nature,
or the spirit of God. Sometimes it is quite obviously both; not only
do the P passages of Genesis just cited show this but it is inescapably
clear in the famous vision of Ezekiel in Ezek. 37.1–14, where the
'breath' which is to come from the four winds is the *ruach* from four
ruchoth (plural of *ruach*); and it is also the life-giving power of God.

It is true that the paramount importance of a sovereign God in
the Hebraic view of the world and of man distinguishes this outlook
essentially from that of the philosophers and their forerunners, and
this point will be emphasized later. For the moment it is enough to
show the affinity in certain basic ideas.

The same scripture, Gen. 2.7, which provided a starting-point for
the brief comparison of the biblical *ruach* and the Greek *pneuma* will
serve also to show a parallel in primitive ideas about matter; for
Gen. 2.7 suggests that to the primitive thinking mind earth and water
were the sole primary constituents of matter. This is roundly stated,
directly and without mythical form, by Xenophanes (perhaps *c.* 570
to *c.* 475 BC, first in Ionia, later in Sicily).

[1] *Op. cit.*, no. 163.   [2] *Op. cit.*, pp. 9, 95 ff., 158 ff., 200, 205 ff., 360.

Approaching the kind of statement which seems nearer the conceptual thinking of developed philosophy, we find that the Logos of Heraclitus (who flourished in Ephesus about 504 BC) means something like the divine order of the cosmos,[1] although it is doubtful if Justin (*c.* AD 100 to 165) was right to connect it with the Logos of the Fourth Gospel. It is interesting that Heraclitus conceived of himself as revealer of a secret and was even accused by a later biographer of having written with deliberate obscurity.[2] He regarded religious rites as illogical yet sometimes enshrining truth and guiding men indirectly to apprehend the Logos.[3] Diogenes Laertius (third century AD), the biographer just mentioned, credits Heraclitus with the cryptic statement that 'the wise thing is one: to understand true judgment, how all things are guided through all'; this seems to mean that the life of man is by the very plan and structure of the universe bound up with his environment which is expressed in that structure.

We are attempting no more than to show how in spheres where conceptual thinking began a dominant theme was the desire to live according to the structure of the universe. We cannot do better, therefore, than to quote a judgment of Kirk and Raven on Pythagoreanism: 'The central notions, which held together the two strands that were later to fall apart, seem to have been those of *theoria* (contemplation), *kosmos* (an orderliness found in the arrangement of the universe) and *katharsis* (purification). By contemplating the principle of order revealed in the universe—and especially in the regular movements of the heavenly bodies—and by assimilating himself to that orderliness, man himself was progressively purified until he eventually escaped from the cycle of birth and attained immortality.'[4] The conception of liberation from 'the wheel of becoming'[5] in the last part of this quotation is certainly poles apart from the Hebraic belief about man's personal destiny, but other elements, notably the duty of man to assimilate himself to a cosmic orderliness principally revealed in the movements of the heavenly bodies and his duty to purify himself, will be seen to be held in common with Israel, especially as represented in the sect at Qumran.

In the commentary upon the word 'order' (1.16) it is claimed that the word here translated (*serek*) expresses the structure of the com-

---

[1] *Op. cit.*, fragments 197 and 199.
[2] *Op. cit.*, fragment 195.
[3] *Op. cit.*, p. 212.
[4] *Op. cit.*, p. 228.
[5] Cf. James 3.6.

munity at Qumran and also that it has something in common with
the Greek word κόσμος. In the *Gorgias* 508 Plato eloquently claims,
'The wise, Callicles, say that heaven and earth and gods and men
are held together by communion and by friendliness and orderliness
and temperance and justice, and this whole for this reason they call
κόσμος.' In his commentary on the *Gorgias*, Prof. E. R. Dodds has a
most interesting note discussing the evidence for the early philosophical use of the word in this sense of 'universe', and concludes that it
may well go back to Heraclitus and Empedocles.[1] It is this merely
adumbrated and wholly unsophisticated conception of living according to the structure of the universe that seems most characteristic of
Qumran; but it would be impossible to deny the feasibility of the
influence of the later and more articulate development of the conception as it is found in Stoicism upon the lonely community by the
Dead Sea. The acceptance of asceticism as self-discipline and the
doctrine of harmony *(ὁμολογία)* in God, universe and man suggest
at least that the Stoics had much in common with the Jewish
sect; but not only is the way of Qumran less sophisticated, it is
distinguished by its profound sense of the transcendence of God.
It would not belong to the Jewish tradition if it were not. St Paul
may be reported as quoting the Stoic Aratus at Acts 17.28, but he
could not have shared his idea of God. The ideal defined by Chrysip-
pus (280–206 BC) as 'to live according to scientific knowledge of the
phenomena of nature, doing nothing which the Universal Law
forbids, which is the Right Reason which pervades all things, and is
the same as Zeus, the Lord of the ordering of this world', has only
to be quoted to show the elements which would need radical change
before an Israelite could accept it. Nevertheless, the common idea is
the determination to live according to a law discoverable in the
structure of the universe, whether this is discoverable by man's
intellectual quest or discovered to man by a transcendent God.

However much there is, therefore, which we can see in common
between Qumran and the Stoa, it remains clear that the communion
(κοινωνία) which according to Plato the wise believe to hold together
the universe (the cosmos) was something felt rather than arrived at
by reason in the minds of the men of Qumran, the structure of whose
community expressed for them the structure of the universe.[2]

This evolution of the meaning of κόσμος as 'order' into its widespread use as 'universe' or 'world' can be seen also in the way in which

[1] E. R. Dodds, *Plato: Gorgias*, p. 338.   [2] P. 69.

the OT was translated into Greek. In the LXX 'the host of heaven' in Deut. 4.19; 17.3 becomes 'the κόσμος of heaven' (cf. Gen. 2.1), as it does most instructively in Isa. 40.26. In these instances κόσμος is the array or order of the stars, but by the time the Book of Wisdom is written κόσμος is clearly the 'world' or 'universe', the object of God's creation.[1]

In insisting on the importance of the transcendence of God for the men of Qumran no less than for Judaism as a whole we have introduced the most essential element in the account which we must give of the way in which the community strove to live according to the universe: it was a universe constituted by God, and he communicated with man by his spirit. This factor will occupy us more fully in the following pages, especially pp. 34–37.

[1] Even in the NT a few passages betray the fact that κόσμος originally meant 'order': Gal. 4.3; Col. 2.8, 20; while in II Peter 2.5 we could substitute 'order' for 'world'. I Peter 3.3 carries the associated meaning of 'ornament'. The passages from Luke and Hebrews illustrate a usage of τάξις which could be covered by *serek*, but which is represented by a different term in Hebrew—'order' near to the sense in which we speak of the order of priesthood, but in Luke 1.8 nearer to 'division'.

II

THE TEACHING OF QUMRAN

IN CHAPTER I we have tried to show that the men of Qumran, like many other thoughtful men of antiquity, sought to live according to the universe. We are now ready to look more closely at their teaching and to see how they believed God was calling them to live according to the universe which he had made, how he enabled them to obey him, and how he revealed the ways which they must follow if they were to obey him.

We begin with a preliminary section on the relation of the sect at Qumran to the Essenes. The discussion here does not attempt to settle this important question, but only to explain the view taken in this work that the sect at Qumran was part of that large movement which Josephus calls the Essenes.

1. QUMRAN AND THE ESSENES

The article by Moffatt on Essenes in the *ERE* (V. 396) published in 1912 is a model of the way in which what was then known of the order might properly be set out. At the end of the most useful display of the main passages from Philo (*Quod omnis probus liber*, 12–13, and the passage from the lost *Apology for the Jews* preserved by Eusebius in *Praep. Ev.* 8.11) and from Josephus (*BJ* 2.8.2 ff.[1] and *Ant.* 18.1.5) there is a brief mention of Christian references which is followed by an even shorter closing paragraph of this section which reads:

> A solitary notice occurs in Latin literature, which is interesting rather than important. Pliny (*HN* 5.15), after describing the Dead Sea, continues: 'On the West side the Essenes avoid the baleful shoreline.

---

[1] This is conveniently accessible to the modern reader in the Penguin Classic, *The Jewish War*, translated by G. A. Williamson, as Excursus I, p. 371.

They are a race by themselves, more remarkable than any other in the wide world; they have no women, they abjure sexual love, they have no money, and they live among palm-trees. Still their membership . . . is steadily recruited from the large number of people who resort to their mode of existence because they are wearied of life's struggle with the waves of adversity. In this way the race has lasted (strange to say) for thousands of ages, though no one is born within it; so fruitful for them is the dissatisfaction with life . . . which others feel. Below them lay the town of En-gedi, once second only to Jerusalem in fertility and palm-groves, now simply a second sepulchre. Then comes the rock-fort of Masada, which also is not far from the Dead Sea.'

From 1947, with the discovery of Cave 1 (which yielded the *Rule* among other mss.), these lines of Pliny the Elder have become as important as they are interesting, justifying Moffatt's inclusion of the passage rather than his judgment of it, which in 1912 could hardly have been otherwise.

Certainly difficulties still remain: the sombre reference to En-gedi and Jerusalem—giving as grim an impression of the latter as of the former—reflects the fact that Pliny wrote after the appalling destruction which visited Jerusalem in 70, Masada in 73—and Qumran, as the archaeological evidence so clearly tells us, in 68. No community can have been flourishing at Qumran when Pliny wrote. Again, graves on the edge of the cemetery reveal that women had dwelt there.

The correspondence of the site with that now excavated is too impressive to allow these difficulties to cancel the importance of the passage. No doubt Pliny had himself not visited the site and was carried away by his literary enthusiasm into blurring past and present. He would hardly be interested enough to distinguish types of Essenes; if he had been, he could have learnt from Philo (in his *De vita contemplativa*) of the Therapeutae, an order like the Essenes who admitted to their ranks and celibate life both men and women; he was still less likely to encounter someone who had read the *Damascus Document* and who could therefore have persuaded him that many ascetics of the time did not all live in withdrawn communities, but in various towns and villages, where some were evidently married (CD 7.6 f.; 11.11 f.; 12.1, 11; 13.17; 14.10, 16; 15.5 f.; 16.10). Josephus was still to write his account of the Essenes when Pliny composed his book. In the passage in *BJ*, at 2.8.13 he concludes his description of the Essenes by modifying his opening statement that among them there is contempt of marriage by telling us that 'There is a second order of Essenes, which agrees with the other in its way of life, customs and rules, and differs only in its view on marriage. They think that the biggest thing in life—the continuance of the race—is forfeited by men who do not marry, and further, if everyone followed their example mankind would rapidly disappear . . .'[1]

It seems not only reasonable but demanded by the evidence to conclude that the men of Qumran were some kind of Essenes. Scholars have tended on the whole to accept this view, frankly acknowledging the difficulty of squaring all the external evidence with the documents found in the caves. The differences between the *Rule* and Josephus' account of the regulations for admission are discussed in the commentary *ad loc.* (6.13–23).

Other views fail in the end to carry conviction. Likeness to Pharisees is surely to be expected, since the movements share the same inheritance; but the men of Qumran appear to be both as like as and as different from Pharisees as were the Essenes. Again, to conclude that the sect had affinities with Sadducees is to rely too much on their title, 'sons of Zadok', and to fail to perceive that it is precisely in claiming to be the true Zadokites that they took issue with the more worldly families who surrounded the high priest and who formed the group usually known as Sadducees. It seems impossible for them to have been Zealots: their withdrawn way of life and their condemnation of violence (1QS 10.19 and 11.2) show them far removed both in practice and in ideals. Their willingness to fight was confined absolutely to the eschatological war to which in their belief God would summon them. This fact may well explain, as Yadin has suggested,[2] the discovery at the Zealot stronghold of Masada of a fragment identical with a liturgical scroll from Cave 4.

It is this majority view, the identity of the men of Qumran with some order of Essenes, which is accepted as the basis for the following discussion of Qumran doctrine. It is also part of the position adopted in this book that internal evidence shows the community at Qumran to be a special form of a movement which originally existed in different branches in various towns and villages of Palestine. This movement may well have been identical with or part of that which Josephus calls the Essenes. In such a case his description of the regulations for admission may belong to the order in general, while 1QS 6.13–23 describes those of the sect which derived from it.

---

[1] Williamson, *op. cit.*, p. 375.
[2] *The Observer*, 12 April, 1964.

R.Q.M.–C

2. SPIRIT

A starting-place for our understanding of this conception is provided by the paragraph on p. 27 in which a number of important passages are cited. The breath of life or 'breath of living things' in Gen. 2.7 is a conception absorbed into that of the spirit (*ruach*) of life.[1] The fact that this absorption can take place is instructive, for it enables us to see how one notion of *ruach*, primitive and pluralistic, can be held alongside another, which is highly developed and monistic. The primitive conception is easily illustrated by famous passages in the OT: to take but one or two examples, the spirit of the LORD may come upon Gideon (Judg. 6.34) but God sent an evil spirit upon Abimelech (Judg. 9.23); perhaps most obvious example of a defiant pluralism, 'the spirit of the LORD abandoned Saul and there tormented him an evil spirit from the LORD' (I Sam. 16.14). At this stage what God sends, whether good or bad, is abnormal and temporary.

The more developed conception of spirit is that which sees it as the source of all life and therefore as that by which (not until the NT can we say 'by *whom*') God bestows on man all the powers which man possesses. Ezek. 37.1–14 expresses perfectly the notion of the spirit of God as the source of all life, and so under the influence of this idea the act of creation is reconceived and the breath of life is identified with the spirit of God (Gen. 6.17; 7.15, 22). While this idea of spirit has been developing a parallel change has come about in man's feeling about the holiness of God. No longer is God unapproachable mainly because of unpredictable danger in the inscrutable source of power, but because of his moral holiness (Isa. 6.5); to use modern terms, God is great because of his goodness.

This refinement in the ideas of God and of his spirit, this monistic tendency, enabled men to think of God as the origin not primarily of inexplicable phenomena (though that notion survived, as Amos 4.7–8 shows) but of moral qualities. He will bestow on a chosen one his spirit, which is the spirit of wisdom, understanding, counsel and might (Isa. 11.2).

---

[1] This absorption may be illustrated by the *ruach* idea being expressed at least once in later literature by the word used for breath (*neshamah*) in Gen. 2.7. This occurs in the very well-known saying in Prov. 20.27: 'The spirit of man is the candle of the LORD', but the expression is surprising, the reading and especially the meaning of the text having been much discussed.

The doctrine of the spirit of God held by the Qumran sect is of this kind. God can give a man a spirit of true counsel and of uprightness and humility (1QS 3.6, 8), but it is a holy spirit (or hallowed spirit) by which he gives these virtues (3.7; cf. 8.16; 9.3; 1QH 16.2, 3, 7). The holiness of God's spirit is emphasized again and again: only God's spirit is holy and only he can bestow it upon a man (1QH 7.6; 9.32; 12.11, 12; 13.19; 14.15; 16.11, 12; 17.17). The similarity of phraseology may easily mislead us into imagining that the doctrine here implied is identical with that in the New Testament, especially as in CD 2.12 God will grant his Messiah the power to make the spirit of his holiness known to the 'remnant'. But it is vital to true understanding of the Qumran way to remember that what its members desire, and so often make the subject of their writing, is not the Holy Spirit, but a spirit of holiness; and this must be interpreted in the contexts in which it occurs. Possession of such a spirit certainly implies possession of moral qualities, but the context of the passage of the *Rule* quoted above (3.6–8) is significant and typical. The subject is purification from moral and ceremonial defilement (see commentary *ad loc.*), and it is a remarkable tenet of the sect that moral failure necessitates both repentance and bodily purification. God will finally 'purify for himself some from mankind' . . . 'removing all blemishes of his flesh and purifying him with a spirit of holiness from all deeds of evil. He will sprinkle upon him a spirit of truth like waters for purification' (1QS 4.20 f.). It is the spirit of holiness in this combined moral and levitical sense that is the acme of a sectarian's desire. This is clear not only from the *Rule* but also from DSW 7.5 and many passages in 1QH, e.g. 16.12 ('to cleanse me with a spirit of holiness'). In the NT the phrase Holy Spirit, of course, means much more than this; and passages which express the NT equivalent of the Qumran ideal (a holiness now thought of as entirely moral, and from which the idea of ceremonial holiness has fallen away) are easily forgotten because of the prevalence of the doctrine of the personal Holy Spirit. But the idea of personal holiness occurs at II Cor. 1.12; 7.1; I Thess. 3.13 and Heb. 12.10, the last being specially interesting since it speaks of sharing the holiness of God. It is also relevant that Christians are often called ἅγιοι, a word which means 'holy ones' more obviously than 'saints', by which it is usually translated. Paul curiously uses the vocabulary appropriate in this realm of ideas on one occasion to express what is normally expressed by 'Holy Spirit', viz. at Rom. 1.4, where he uses the phrase not found elsewhere in the NT but common in the Scrolls, 'spirit of holiness'.[1]

It is a natural concomitant of the doctrine so far explained that the qualities bestowed on man by God through his spirit are attributes of God. That is their origin. 1QH 7.6; 17.26; frgt. 2.9 show that the idea of God imparting his holiness by his spirit is derived from the picture of Gen. 1.2; and when he makes his spirit to hover over the obedient it is to impart a real gift based on his own nature. Thus God shows mercy in a spirit of holiness, according to 1QSb 2.24.

Although holiness can be acquired only as it is given by God, yet the belief is steadfast that God chose Israel as a nation holy, or set apart, for himself (Ex. 19.6). The psalmist believes that as an Israelite he has the spirit of God's holiness and asks of God, 'take not the spirit of thy holiness from me' (Ps. 51.11, Hebrew 51.13). This passage —in EVV Ps. 51.9–12—comprises a prayer such as members of the sect might properly have uttered to express their aspirations and ideals.

It is doubtful whether the men of Qumran, probably an Essene sect, would themselves have expressed their doctrine in the manner in which Josephus represents that of the Essenes in *BJ* 2.8.11. It is argued elsewhere[2] that Josephus' report of the Essene belief in the immortality of the soul is not likely to be fundamentally wrong; but the passage needs only to be read to make clear that Josephus is writing there for a Hellenistic public. Betz indeed claims[3] that the Essene notion of souls as composed, according to Josephus, from λεπτότατος αἰθήρ (Whiston, 'most subtile air'; Williamson, 'most rarefied ether') might aid the men of Qumran in believing that God's holy gift could enter a defiled man so that he became once again united with God. That they believed in some unity with himself as God's final gift to his chosen is no doubt true, but it seems that this unity is rather of moral purpose than of actual being. It is rather to the status of spirits in the sense of angels that the redeemed portion of mankind will be raised.

Josephus' λεπτότατος αἰθήρ reminds us of the description of Wisdom in Wisd. 7.22 f.: in her there is a spirit described by many epithets and as διὰ πάντων χωροῦν πνευμάτων . . . λεπτοτάτων. For that author wisdom, for the sect at Qumran the spirit is a gift of God, but not God

---

[1] For the sake of completeness it will be well to observe that the plural, 'spirits of holiness', occurs 1QH 8.12; cf. 11.13; 13.8. These are simply angels as in Ps. 104.4. In DSW 7.6 we find the phrase 'angels of holiness'.

[2] Pp. 69 f.

[3] O. Betz, *Offenbarung und Schriftforschung in der Qumransekte*, p. 131.

himself. Josephus' vocabulary is of ancient lineage; see p. 27 for references in presocratic philosophers in which the soul is related to the universe and the *psyche* to πνεῦμα. There can be little doubt that he has accommodated his account too thoroughly to his public; in any case there is no evidence in the scrolls of belief in an ontological union of God and man. The general description of a gift to the disciple (1QH 12.12) and the highly poetical 'pouring within' of the holy spirit (1QH 7.6 f.; 17.26; frgt. 2.9, 13) do not amount to this.

3. THE TWO SPIRITS

A.   THE DOCTRINE

When spirit is understood both as the creative function of God and as the means by which he bestows on man all the powers which man possesses, it is easy to understand the rise of the doctrine of the two spirits of mankind as it is found in 1QS 3.13–4.26. This passage is given a heading (3.13 ff.) which shows its fundamental importance to the men of the sect. Then 3.17 ff. claims that God 'created man for dominion over the earth; and he set in him two spirits for him to set his course by them until the set time of his visitation. They are the spirits of truth and perversity. In a dwelling of light are the generations of truth and from a well of darkness come the generations of perversity.' If we attend carefully to the last two sentences of this remarkable passage we see the language change into metaphor. It is not easy to show the logical connexion between the spirits 'set in' man and the sources ('dwelling' and 'well') from which the two 'generations' of men respectively arise. Perhaps there is here an example of thinking which at the logical level is confused; and the reason for this confusion is that the writer is not clear whether he wishes to teach that man as such is a combination of a good and a bad spirit or that mankind is divisible into the good (arising from light) and the bad (arising from darkness). The main doctrine at Qumran appears to have been that every individual man is a mixture of the two spirits (see the commentary on 3.13–4.26, especially on 4.16), but the thought certainly oscillates between two sets of terms, truth/perversity, light/darkness; and from the metaphorical and inexact way of writing when the latter set is used, as from the fact that light/darkness seems to provide a fundamental antithesis in all poetry, religion and primitive philosophy, it is safe to assume that this set of terms is the more fundamental; it will therefore be described first.

Before this task is undertaken it may be interesting to compare very briefly and in a general way the famous prologue to the Fourth Gospel with the poetical way of thinking betrayed in the *Rule* at this point. It is obvious that the writers have in common the fact that they are meditating on what is true 'in the beginning' (John 1.1; 1QS 3. 15: '. . . before they came to be he prepared all their pattern'; 3.17: 'he created man for dominion over the earth'). For Israelites this must mean that they are meditating upon Genesis, as indeed is already obvious. That book begins with God, spirit, and light. These are the great archetypes of thought and imagery with which the author of the *Rule* deals here. The Fourth Gospel begins with Logos, God and life, and then almost abruptly equates life with light, about which he then goes on to say a great deal. It is not always observed that in this progression of concepts and images life (John 1.4) represents the spirit of Genesis, which enables us to say that in his own way the author of the Gospel also is using the archetypes (Logos-)God, spirit, light. He intellectualizes the creative spirit into Logos, reassures us that the Logos is the source of life (he has not forgotten this profound pre-logical concept), and then equates life with light.

This comparison is enough to show that for writers in the Hebrew tradition—as probably for those in almost every tradition—light is an image or concept which must make its way into the exposition where the author attempts to deal with the sources of life and behaviour. We proceed to pay some attention to the terms light and darkness before we expound the doctrine of the two spirits.

A work of great industry, patience and insight happily exists upon this subject, written by S. Aalen; and the following exposition and discussion will be based upon his book,[1] although it cannot be claimed as an adequate summary of even one strand in it, nor should it be taken as expressing Aalen's views.

It seems beyond question that man as such is deeply affected, albeit unconsciously, by his involuntary, inevitable, and repeated experience of the alternation of light and darkness in the form of day and night. This is the most striking aspect of his environment. In the earliest evidence from the OT it is this which determines man's imagery and thinking rather than any association of sun with day

---

[1] S. Aalen, *Die Begriffe 'Licht' und 'Finsternis' im alten Testament, im Spätjudentum und im Rabbinismus.*

or moon and stars with night. The sun indeed is associated with the day, but since it appears after daylight is not conceived as the source of light nor, therefore, of day. The day brings the sun, rather than the sun brings the day. This attitude is preserved in the prayer habit of the Jew, who associates morning-prayer not with sunrise but with the appearance of light, with the time 'from the rise of dawn to sunrise', in a proverbial phrase.[1] Aalen regards it as a principle that 'the structure of Judaism's teaching on God, Israel, sin, etc., is cosmologically orientated', so that changes in the form of doctrine and the development of new doctrines are alike inevitable when in later Judaism observation of the heavenly bodies in space provides the concept of time. The main concept of time in the Old Testament had been an expression of man's existence ('eine Bestimmung des menschlichen Daseins'),[2] but it now became mechanical, a correlative of the movements of the heavenly bodies. Nevertheless, such is the peculiar nature of the Hebrew genius, morality keeps breaking in: the orderly behaviour of the heavenly bodies is expressed in ethical terms, beautifully exemplified by *II Baruch* 48.9, 'Thou instructest created things in the understanding of thee, and thou makest wise the spheres so as to minister in their orders.'[3]

At this point there becomes most explicit the need felt by man in antiquity to live according to the structure of the universe, a *motif* which we have insisted is operative in the men of Qumran and enters into many aspects of their life, their constitution as a corporate body, their observance of a solar calendar and, if they are to be identified with the Essenes, their reverence for the sun.[4] In *I Enoch* 2–5 the orderly and predictable behaviour of the heavenly bodies is set up as an example to man. Here indeed the feeling of the necessity of being in harmony with the universe and its behaviour in one's innermost being gives place to an ethical exhortation based on example. It is not as odd as it appears if we remember the notion of cosmos, of order pervading the universe which lies behind this pious-sounding passage. *Test. Naphtali* 3.2 sums up admirably: 'Sun and moon and stars change not their order; so do ye also change not the law of God in the disorderliness of your doings.'

---

[1] Cf. J. Schechter, *Mabo' Lassiddur*, p. 17.
[2] Aalen, *op. cit.*, p. 159.
[3] Cf. *Pss. Sol.* 18.12; *I Enoch* 41.5; 43.2; 69.20 ff. These are but a few of the passages from later Judaism which illustrate this important point. The last is perhaps the most eloquent.
[4] See pp. 77 ff. below.

It is not surprising that heavenly bodies are treated as personal beings. Indeed, in *I Enoch* 18.14 ff. it appears that some stars after all failed to set the required example of orderliness and are punished 'because they did not come forth at their appointed times' (cf. 21.1–6; 80.6). It might be fascinating for a modern astronomer to conjecture what celestial phenomena led to this short way with cosmic dissenters. Aalen is uncertain whether these errant stars are to be identified with angels, but this is taken to be the case by Charles and seems very likely in view of the language used and the concept of the punishment of angels. *II Enoch* (*The Secrets of Enoch*) 29.3–5 (AD 1–50) confirms this in an interesting way. Here a rebellious angel is punished by being set in a continuous orbit above the abyss. If elsewhere identity is not direct, it is clear that to each angel there corresponds a star (*I Enoch* 43.2; 82.10, the latter giving to angels the task of presiding over the correct behaviour of the stars).

The crystallization of the parts of the cosmic structure into comprehensible and relatively clear-cut images of angels is balanced by a systematization of the ideas of light and darkness. *II Enoch* 25–27 exemplifies the manner in which the image-thinking of Genesis 1–2 becomes more conceptual and nearer to philosophical speculation. A comparison of 27.3 f. with Gen. 1.4 is particularly instructive, for here light has become identified with day, and darkness with night, in a manner which assigns places to light and darkness, so that when the place of light comes round it is day. Light and darkness, as Aalen says, have become absorbed into a static world-construction. The division made between light and darkness in Gen. 1.4 now runs between heaven and earth, between the light of heaven and the darkness of the depth. The light created by God in Gen. 1.3 is the light of heaven, of heavenly origin, and in sharp contrast to the darkness of the depth. The world is a compound of what is above (light) and what is below (darkness), but the heavenly light of Gen. 1.3 is now quite clearly distinguished from the light of morning in the terrestrial daily round.

There has emerged therefore a concept of *Urlicht* or heavenly light, and this is expounded fully in IV Ezra 6.38–40 and other passages. According to *II Enoch* 29.1 (B) the sun is formed from this light. In 24.4 God seems to think of himself as the 'sun' of the invisible world, and the original Hebrew version of Ecclus. 42.16 by its parallelism suggests that the sun is the glory of the invisible God: 'The shining sun appears upon all; and the glory of the LORD upon all his works.'

We are thus well prepared for the fact that in the Qumran *Psalms of Thanksgiving* the *Urlicht* is identified even with God himself, at least in a poetic way, although it is uncertain how far this commits the author to a firm quasi-metaphysical conception. For him God is an eternally shining light (1QH 7.25; cf. 9.26 f.) or shines like a perfect light[1] on the countenance of his pious ones (1QH 4.5 f.). Light as *Urlicht* seems therefore to be regarded as conveying the presence of God, like the pillar of fire or luminous cloud in the story of Moses and the exodus,[2] the garment of God (Ps. 104.2) or the unapproachable light in which he dwells (Ex. 33.20; I Tim. 6.16; Rev. 21.23; 22.5);[3] but the main effect and function of the light which surrounds God is to reveal the truth to man. The truth belongs to the light, falsehood to darkness (1QS 3.19 ff.; cf. 1Q27 1.5 f.). This doctrine has affected the form of the priestly blessing at 1QS 2.3 and appears fully in 11.3 ff.

These doctrines explain the rise of characteristic elements in the life and teaching of Qumran, their solar calendar and, if they are to be identified with the Essenes, their daily veneration of the sun.[4] The relatively late work *III Baruch* (its assignment to the beginning of the second century by Hughes does not remove it far from the activity of the Qumran sect) in ch. 8 represents the sun as being defiled by the unrighteousness of men so that its crown has to be renewed by angels every day.[5]

Behind these apparently curious fantasies lay a long development of ideas which were a serious attempt to explain the nature of man and his relation to God and his universe. The attempt does not issue in a consistent solution of the problem of good and evil coexisting in one universe, but provides a number of expressive formulations of the problem itself in image form. Thus in *I Enoch* 41–48 we find the division of light from darkness applied even to the spirits of men. Here the language is too poetic for us to extract a metaphysical doctrine from the passage, but when we reach IV Ezra 4.4 ff. we find a clear illustration of the fact that Judaism as a rule does not entertain

---

[1] Betz, *Offenbarung*, p. 112, remarks that 1QH 4.5 f. depends on Hos. 6.3, where the same kind of language is used.

[2] E.g. Ex. 19.9; 24.18; 33.9; 34.5; 40.34 ff.; cf. Lev. 16.2; II Chron. 5.13 f. See W. K. Lowther Clarke, *Divine Humanity*, pp. 9–40.

[3] John 12.41, interpreting Isaiah's vision (Isa. 6.1) as of the Son rather than as of the Father, may well reflect a contemporary tendency in Judaism to believe that all theophanies are of God's glory, not of God himself, whom no man has ever seen (John 1.18); cf. Col. 1.15.

[4] See p. 77.

[5] Hughes observes (in *AP* II, p. 528), that the notion reappears in the *Acta Pauli* 4.

the notion of original sin. So common is the use of the light/darkness
metaphor that it is a justifiable guess that had Jewish thinkers entertained this notion seriously they would somewhere have expressed it
by suggesting that man contained within him something of the
heavenly light and something of the darkness of the depth, that is of
the strongest opposition to the divine light. Such a conception would
have represented moral evil as that fearsome irrational entity which
it must appear to be to the sufferer of torture and to the creator of
Iago. However strongly circumstances might have influenced the
Israelite mind in such a direction, the temptation so to express the
matter was resisted; in man there was an inclination to good and an
inclination to evil and sin is not an irrational entity but an opposition
to the limited good in man, an opposition which, like the forces of
chaos within creation, must be kept within certain limits. The angelic
answer to the puzzled question, 'Whence comes the evil heart?' in
IV Ezra 4.4 ff. reflects Job 28.20 ff., where the question is morally
neutral. IV Ezra uses a cosmological puzzle to suggest an answer to
a moral difficulty: the measured power which God has given to
cosmic forces he has given to forces within man. 'Sin must itself be
judged and treated as analogous to the powers of nature.'[1] On this
view, which is identical with the view of the discourse on the two
spirits in 1QS 3.13–4.26, 'the division of the good and evil inclination in man and the allegiance of man to the good or to the evil
way is a special case of the division of light and darkness which
man knew from Gen. 1.4'.[2]

The doctrine of the inclinations in man need not detain us long.
It expresses in moderate terms characteristic of rabbinic thought the
facts of human nature, with a reference to the way in which God
created man in the universe, but with the minimum of speculation
and with strictly controlled imagination. It seems likely that the idea
of the evil inclination or impulse was conceived first, and that of the
good impulse resulted in contrast to it. Schechter[3] points out nevertheless that the two impulses are known in the Mishnah *Berakoth*
9.5. The notion of the evil inclination (*yeṣer haraʿ*) probably arose
from Gen. 6.5 and 8.21.[4] It appears that from the Tannaim onwards

---

[1] Aalen, *op. cit.*, p. 172.
[2] *Ibid.*
[3] S. Schechter, *Some Aspects of Rabbinic Theology*, ch. 15, pp. 242 ff.
[4] For further references see, e.g., Schechter, *ibid.*; *JE* XII, p. 601; Strack-Billerbeck,
'Der gute und der böse Trieb', Exkursus 19 in *Kommentar zum Neuen Testament aus Talmud
und Midrasch* IV, p. 1; C. G. Montefiore and H. Loewe, *A Rabbinic Anthology*, ch. 11,
pp. 295 ff.; and Roy A. Stewart, *Rabbinic Theology*, pp. 77 ff.

(i.e. from some time in the first century of our era) interpretations of various scriptures whether targumic or midrashic expounded the theology of the *yeṣer haraʿ* and discussed its function and power, usually holding that the inclination was not itself sin and that man could and sometimes had successfully overcome it.

The doctrine of the two spirits in man, allied one to light the other to darkness, clearly owes more both to speculation and to poetic imagination. Again, while the rabbis debated with caution what they took to be the permanent truth about human nature independently of the course of events in history or in the cosmos itself, the thinkers with whom we are concerned, the apocalyptists and authors of cosmic speculation, effectively related their doctrine of man to their views about the march of history and the unfolding of God's purpose in this history, which was not mere secular history but the story of the whole of creation. Thus the opposition of light and darkness expresses that of the strife of order with disorder in the universe, a radical feature presented also as war between God and Belial. More, 'the struggle in the heart of man is inseparable from the cosmic array of powers (1QS 4.18)'.[1] The war for which the men of Qumran were prepared they therefore regarded as part of the cosmic struggle. The war of the sons of light against the sons of darkness, itself the subject of a surviving work, is but the terrestrial and visible part of a war in the whole universe, a part spatially continuous with the celestial war, so that it can even be said that angels are in the company of the sons of light[2] and men's behaviour must be such as follows from recognition of their presence.

The tendency to personify as angels the powers which control the stars and to identify God himself with the *Urlicht* may be paralleled by the identification of the two spirits with personal supernatural beings. O. Betz argues[3] that the men of Qumran identified not only the Angel of Darkness with Belial but also the Angel of Truth with Michael: he compares 1QS 1.17 f. with 3.20–24, for in this latter passage the dominion by Belial extends over the righteous (though here in a moral or metaphysical sense rather than in the political sense, as at 1.17 f.); he refers also to CD 5.18, where the Prince of Light and Belial are opposed, and to DSW 13.10 f., where the Prince of Light and Belial are opposed, their creation being attri-

---

[1] U. Simon, *Heaven in the Christian Tradition*, p. 173.
[2] For references see on 11.7 f.
[3] *Der Paraklet*, p. 66.

buted to God. Again, the concept *mastema* is attached at 1QS 3.23 and
at DSW 13.11 to Belial. The identification of Michael with the
Prince of Light is made more indirectly: CD 5.17–19 and DSW 13.10
represent the latter as a helper; and in DSW 17.6 the angel helper is
named Michael. In the first two passages and at 1QS 3.20 his title *šar*
or Prince associates him with Michael in Daniel, where he is 'one of
the *šarim*' (10.13) and 'the great *šar*' (12.1).

Inconsistent with this dualism but dependent on the fundamental
belief that man is a creature of God who is the creator of all, there
is found at the same time the belief that God created both the
warring spirits in man,[1] a belief much more in harmony with the
later rabbinic doctrine of the two inclinations or impulses in man.
Inconsistent it may be; it is certainly inevitable, since it reflects the
unsolved problem for all theism, the presence of evil, which seems to
negate God, in a universe where he is held to reign supreme. It is
therefore not in the least surprising that this inconsistency should
emerge in the later speculations of a people who could regard their
important concept of *ruach* as both monistic and pluralistic. If God
can bestow upon Saul his own spirit but also send into him an evil
spirit, it is not surprising that in time good and evil should be thought
of as alike due to God's ordinance. The nettle is sometimes firmly
grasped: in *Test. Naphtali* 2.7 ff. right conduct means acting according to the order which God has ordained, and the argument that he
has made various organs of the body each to perform its own function
ends with 'For if thou bid the eye to hear it cannot; so neither while
ye are in darkness can ye do the works of light' (2.10). The question
which suggests itself, 'may it be sometimes right to act according to
the evil inclination, since that too is part of God's creation?' appears
to be in the mind of Ben Sirach at Ecclus. 33.7–15; but he solves the
problem which it poses no better than Paul when it arises in Rom.
9–11 (see esp. 9.14 ff. and cf. Wisd. 15.7). It is clear that in the
Ecclesiasticus passage good and evil are constituent parts of creation,
although the author does not express the matter exactly thus. The
tradition persists and later authors, following the way of gnosticism
and perhaps at least when in this mood less sensitive to the paramount
claims of righteousness, set good and evil in the midst of an apparently
purely physical account of their cosmic structure. Thus the *Sepher
Yeṣirah* in the third or fourth century[2] constructs the universe in part

---

[1] Cf. Isa. 45.7; 1QH 4.38; and DSW 13.10 f. mentioned above.
[2] See *JE* XII, pp. 602 ff.

of ten *sephiroth* without limit, arranged in pairs: 'depth of beginning and depth of end, depth of good and depth of evil, depth of above and depth of beneath, depth of east and depth of west, depth of north and depth of south' (1.5).

The doctrine apparently affected the very text of the Scriptures used by the Qumran sect. In Isa. 45.7 the Masoretic Text reads 'the former of light and creator of darkness, the maker of peace (*shalom*) and creator of ill (*ra'*), I the LORD am the doer of all these' but the text found in Cave 1 reads 'the former of light and creator of darkness, maker of good (*tob*) and creator of evil (*ra'*), I the LORD am the doer of all these'. In the latter the substitution for *shalom* (peace, welfare, wealth, prosperity, ease) of *tob* (good generally, but including the moral sense) justifies a sharper rendering of *ra'*. In the MT this means evil in contrast to physical and social welfare, in the scrolls version its contrast with 'good' makes it mean moral and cosmic evil.

This absorption of light and darkness, or good and evil, equally into the structure of the universe is one strand of thought. The other, logically opposed but in practice mingled with it, is that which exalts light above all else and seeks to make this attitude at least momentarily consistent with the other by giving this reverence only to the heavenly light. Such a move might have had a better chance of logical defence if the heavenly light had been regarded always and consistently as the wisdom of God, inalienable and unattainable. This wisdom is indeed 'fairer than the sun, and above all the constellations of the stars'; it is said of her that 'to the light of day succeedeth night, but against wisdom evil doth not prevail' (Wisd. 7.29 f.). But this power of the universe is also identified with the wisdom which the author seeks for himself and which he commends to his readers, and which Ben Sirach had already identified with Torah (Ecclus. 24.1–12, esp. v. 8, and 39.1–8).

It is not so easy to show that the Law, although identified with wisdom, was thought of in the Wisdom literature as light; but this is suggested by Ps. 119.105 (where God's word is the Law), perhaps by Ecclus. 32.16 and the LXX of 50.29. In apocalyptic this simile or metaphor is much clearer, as at Bar. 4.2; IV Ezra 14.20 f. is unequivocal, as also are certain passages in the *Test. XII Patr.*, e.g. *Reub.* 3.8; *Levi* 14.3 f.; 19.1 and *Asher* 5.1–6.3, as well as others in *II Baruch*.

Those who keep the Law for the people are called shepherds and sometimes lights or lamps (*II Bar.* 46.2; 45.2; 77.13, 15; *Pss. Sol.* 18.12). Those who do not keep it cease to know it and to understand it. Thus sin is the radical cause of ignorance. 'To know the truth' is a state of mind parallel with the action, 'to keep the Law'; and 'to practise the truth' (1QS 1.5 and note in commentary) means 'to keep the Law'. So Paul holds that a practical moral life is a necessary qualification for teaching and derives concrete sins from the fundamental fault of idolatry (Rom. 2.19 ff.). Small wonder that the Qumran sect, an elder brother to the Christian Church within the family of Judaism, combined the ideals of a strict ethic with study of the Law and called themselves 'sons of light', possessors of the spirit of truth and opposed by and to those who were possessed by and of a spirit of perversity.

The combination of ethic with study meant that in their own eyes the sect were enabled to reveal the hidden secrets of the scriptures. They were constituted for it both outwardly and inwardly. Their conception of revelation is discussed elsewhere (p. 63); it suffices here to point to the aptness of the term 'spirit of truth' to describe the power resident in those who were able to discern what was revealed from time to time from within the Scriptures.

B. ORIGINS AND AFFINITIES

In view of the account of the doctrine of the two spirits already given, it may be claimed that the outlook which it represents must be that of all mankind, since we all share the experience of the alternation of day and night and come to associate light with good, and darkness with evil. How this experience came to be expressed within Judaism both in the metaphors of light and darkness and in the form of a doctrine of spirit has been explained in such a way as to render a detailed discussion of the possible influence of doctrines from outside Judaism in one sense unnecessary: such discussion is needed to explain neither the meaning nor the development of the doctrine. Nevertheless, it is part of our argument that many different streams of ideas flowed into Judaea from Babylon, Egypt, Ionia and Hellas, and it would be idle to deny that history makes it probable that Persia also influenced this tiny country at the crossroads of the ancient world; such influence, if it existed, seems to have been of like upon like, and not that of an opposite point of view modifying an existing notion. For this very reason we cannot be certain that the older is the origin of the younger. It is rather a matter of indicating affinities.

The Mazdean dualism of Persia, strongly influenced by the Iranian reformer Zarathustra (or Zoroaster), who lived in the seventh or sixth century BC, taught the existence of two principles opposed to

one another. The evil spirit Ahriman, spirit of darkness, who arose
from the abyss,[1] wars with the light and with the creatures of Ahura
Mazda or Ormazd. A period during which there exists a balance of
forces will end with the final victory of the good spirit, and the whole
world is constituted by its division into the hosts which support one
the evil, the other the good spirit. By good deeds, thoughts and words
man can fight for the victory of Ormazd, a victory made logically
possible by regarding the evil spirit as a negative entity, and thus
approximating the system very closely to monotheism. It is therefore
natural at least to contemplate the possibility that Isa. 45.1–7, uttered
by a prophet in a Babylon in process of being conquered by Cyrus
the Persian, reflects the Iranian dualism already so close to Judaic
monotheism.[2]

How tempting and yet how tenuous are apparent parallels in
quite other cultures may be illustrated from early Greek philosophy;
Kirk and Raven[3] quote Aristotle's *Metaphysics* A 5. 985b 23 ff. to
support the brief reference in Diogenes Laertius 8.83 to the dualism
of Alcmaeon of Croton.[4] Aristotle's account reminds us of the strange
mixture of physical and moral elements in the account of creation in
the *Sepher Yeṣirah* (pp. 44 f.): 'Other members of this same school (the
Pythagoreans) say there are ten principles, which they arrange in
two columns of cognates—limit and unlimited, odd and even, one
and plurality, right and left, male and female, resting and moving,
straight and curved, light and darkness, good and bad, square and
oblong. In this way Alcmaeon of Croton seems also to have conceived
the matter . . .'

Once again the influence of the long-lasting Pythagorean 'school'
on Judaism might be argued, but in this instance it is clearly more
judicious to draw attention to a parallel than to a possible explanation
of origin.[5] With such caution it is perhaps allowable lightly to indicate
the monistic influence of Parmenides (born about 515–510 BC) as
exerting an influence parallel to the monotheistic tendency of Persia
and Judaea.

[1] It is impossible not to compare 1QS 3.19: 'from a well of darkness', but the well
is the source not of the single spirit but of the generations of perversity; the similarity of
expression is probably accidental.
[2] In the OT an embryonic form of dualism appears in such passages as Deut. 30.15–20;
Jer. 21.8; Ps. 1; Prov. 2.13; 7–8.
[3] *The Presocratic Philosophers*, pp. 236 ff.
[4] *Ibid.*, p. 232. Alcmaeon is dated to early in the fifth century BC.
[5] On the other hand, later Greek knowledge of Zoroastrianism is illustrated by
Plutarch, *De Iside et Osiride*, 46–47.

We can be more definite—but no more dogmatic—about affinities with later literature. It seems that in the passage 1QS 3.13–4.26 we have stumbled upon an ancestor of a work known to scholars as the *Two Ways* whose independent existence had been justifiably deduced from an examination of the *Epistle of Barnabas*, especially when this was compared with the *Didache* 1–6. The facts are these: *Ep. Barn.* 18–21 consists of a treatise in which the ways of light and of darkness are expounded according to Christian ethics derived from the Old and New Testaments. The *Epistle* appears to date from the period AD 70–100. A similar treatise is comprised in *Didache* 1–6, but the date of this work is much disputed; perhaps we may assign it to the early second century. One of the Latin versions of the *Didache*, but a version containing only chs. 1–5 (known as the *Doctrina Apostolorum*) seems to represent a document very like *Ep. Barn.* 18–21 and suggests once more the independent existence of the *Two Ways*. J. A. Robinson believed that the author of *Ep. Barn.* was himself the author of the *Two Ways* (identified with chs. 18–21 of the *Epistle*) but this is a view attacked by Audet[1] and in any case not now widely held. Audet's own view in the article referred to is that *Ep. Barn.* 18–21, *Didache* 1–6 and the *Doctrina Apostolorum* all derive from a work which we may call the *Two Ways* composed in a Christian milieu but ultimately based on a Jewish source like 1QS 3.13–4.26 and to which the *Rule* passage was related. B. C. Butler contests the simplicity of this view on the ground that *Didache* 1–6 has been influenced by the Gospel according to St Matthew and that the *Doctrina Apostolorum* shares most of the features due to these influences.[2] Butler's full argument involves an impossibly early date for Matthew and we may take Audet's view as set out in the *Revue Biblique* as reasonable and probable.[3]

In an article continuing the same investigations[4] Audet arrives after careful investigation at even more interesting conclusions with regard to the *Shepherd* of Hermas which he dates along with most scholars on the authority of the Muratorian fragment of the canon to *c.* AD 140–150, a time when Christian links with Judaism were already broken. Nevertheless, although the work is certainly Christian, 'when

---

[1] J.-P. Audet, 'Affinités littéraires et doctrinales du Manuel de Discipline', *RB* 59, 1952, pp. 219 ff.

[2] B. C. Butler, 'The "Two Ways" in the Didache', *JTS* (NS) 12, 1961, pp. 27-38.

[3] In his edition *La Didachè*, Audet develops a much more elaborate theory with regard to the whole of the *Didache*. For a brief and clear account of the relation to one another of the documents so far mentioned, Audet's view and a criticism of the latter see R. P. C. Hanson, *Tradition in the Early Church*, pp. 172 ff.

[4] *RB* 60, 1953, pp. 41 ff.

one reads the *Shepherd*, at every step one meets Judaism'—a Judaism detached from nation and Law, but still unmistakable. The writer's faith is strictly monotheistic in the Jewish sense. The term 'Lord' when used—as often—absolutely, denotes God and not Jesus. Textual emendation in some of the manuscripts in a 'Christian' direction serves only to enhance this impression of a Jewish Christianity, very clearly illustrated in the Fifth Parable. In the explanation of this parable *Sim.* 5.5.2 betrays an unusual order of Spirit and Son, justified by the theology which appears at *Sim.* 5.6.5, a passage clearly based on Gen. 1.2. The Holy Spirit is the agent of creation and Hermas speaks of him in much the same way as, for example, Prov. 8.22–36 speaks of Wisdom. The position of the Holy Spirit in regard to the Son of God is more striking still: *Sim.* 5.5.2 shows the Holy Spirit as the son of the owner of the vineyard, and the servant who cultivates the vineyard is clearly subordinate to him, though this servant is called Son of God, a paradox of which Hermas is aware. This 'Son of God', or servant, is a messianic figure and falls short ontologically of the Son in the Christian Trinity. He is indeed commended because he has not defiled the Holy Spirit given to him. Other men have been defiled by the action of the evil spirit in spite of their possession of the Holy Spirit, a doctrine set out in *Mand.* 5.1–2; Audet remarks that 'the idea that the Holy Spirit could be defiled in us by a fault is so far from current that it would suffice to give rise to the probability of literary connexion, direct or indirect, between the writings where it occurs'. The passages in the scrolls to which he appeals are CD 5.11; 7.4,[1] but he adds that this notion is part of an exposition of the moral life integral to the whole work of the *Shepherd* which recalls 'avec une étonnante similitude' the teaching of the *Rule*. This teaching is that the whole moral life of man is subject to the mutually opposed action of angels and spirits, good against bad, from the first prompting to good or bad action until the final rewards or punishments which are their eventual outcome. In support of this claim Audet compares *Sim.* 5.5.6 with 1QS 4.18–22.

The arguments of Audet on the *Shepherd* of Hermas are impressive. In spite of the Christian milieu from which it sprang the work evinces extraordinary proof of more than literary affinities with the *Rule* passage on the two spirits (3.13–4.26) with which we are concerned. In this instance we have an early Christian work whose very theology is strikingly different from that of its contemporaries (e.g.

---

[1] Rabin compares the Hebrew of *Test. Napht.* 10.9; *Test. Asher* 2.7.

Ignatius, Justin), and different by those features which are most readily explained by ascribing them to Jewish influences represented best among surviving literature by the *Testaments of the Twelve Patriarchs* and above all by the *Damascus Document* and the *Rule*. Such a statement avoids with Audet the boldness of deriving material in the *Shepherd* directly from the *Rule*, while suggesting nevertheless that the kind of teaching found in the latter found its way into Christian thought and even into a work which almost gained a permanent place in the canon of the New Testament despite its unusual theology.

O. J. F. Seitz has followed Audet in examining the doctrine of the two spirits, its roots in the Bible and its appearance in both late Judaistic and early Christian literature.[1] With the help of Audet and Seitz it is possible to draw up a table (pp. 51 f.) showing parallels between 1QS 3.13–4.26, OT sources, Judaistic writings roughly contemporary with the *Rule*, the NT and finally other early Christian works.

The concept of the two spirits seems to reach full development, at least in one form, in the Johannine literature. Here, as elsewhere in the New Testament, we find a contrast with the uncritical acceptance of the existence of both good and bad spirits under the rule of God: uneasiness is felt about the plurality of spirits and suspicion of their being evil attends recognition of their presence. I John 4.1–6, providing a remarkable reminiscence of 1QS 3.18 (see esp. I John 4.6), reckons with the reality of spirits which do not proceed from God and which inspire false prophets. It seems probable that while for this writer there is one spirit of truth, the spirit of perversity (or spirit of error, as the New English Bible justly translates τὸ πνεῦμα τῆς πλάνης) is regarded as divisible, just as there is but one Christ but many antichrists (I John 2.18); and it is a sign of belonging to falsity to adopt a gnostic multiplication of beings which allows among other things belief in a Jesus who is separable from the Christ, as Cerinthus taught (I John 2.22; cf. 4.3, esp. with the reading λύει for μὴ ὁμολογεῖ). The idea of a spirit of error which is the source of moral as well as doctrinal defect may also lie behind Paul's claim in I Thess. 2.3.

The idea of a multiplicity of spirits as probably portending spiritual evil may well have been shared by Jesus himself, as the famous logion Matt. 12.43–45; Luke 11.24–26 illustrates, and by his contemporaries (Mark 5.9; Luke 8.30). St Paul's insistence on the one spirit no doubt owed much to this fear (I Cor. 12.1–13).

[1] O. J. F. Seitz, 'Two Spirits in Man: an Essay in Biblical Exegesis', in *NTS* 6, 1959–60, pp. 82–94.

Rule (1QS) (and other scrolls)	Old Testament and Apocrypha	Late Judaism	New Testament	Other Christian writings
3.18 (cf. 4.23) (two spirits) cf. CD 2.7 ff.; 2.11; 1QH 4.38; 14.15; 15.13–21; 15.23; 17.21 DSW 13.10 ff.	Cf. Isa. 11.2	*T. Levi* 2.3; 18.7; 19.1 f.; *T. Jud.* 20.1; *T. Reub.* 2.1 f. ('seven spirits of error'); *II Enoch* 30.15 *T. Asher* 1.3 ff.; 3–6	I John 4.6; Rev. 4.5; 5.6 ('seven spirits of God'); Matt. 12.45; Luke 11.26 ('seven evil spirits'); 9.55; I John 4.1–6	*Ep. Barn.* 18.1; *Did.* 1.1; *Doct. Ap.* 1.1; *Shepherd Mand.* 6.1.2 ff.; 2.1 ff.
3.20 (light and darkness)	Prov. 4.18 f. cf. Isa. 2.5; 5.20, etc.		Matt. 4.16; 6.23; 27.45 Luke 1.79; 11.35; 22.53; 23.44 John 1.5; 12.35 f., 46; Acts 26.18; Rom. 2.19; II Cor. 6.14; Col. 1.13; I Thess. 5.4 f.	*Ep. Barn.* 18.1
3.21 (Angel of darkness leads righteous astray)	Isa. 50.10 Wisd. 5.6	*T. Gad* 6.2 *Jub.* 7.20 ff.; 10.1–15; 11.4 ff.; 12.20	John 3.19 ff. Rom. 13.12 II Cor. 4.4; 11.14 Eph. 4.30 f.; 5.8 ff.; I Peter 2.9; I John 1.5 f.; 2.8–11	*Mand.* 5.1.2 (ὑσκοτούμενον); 9.11 f.
[Cf. CD 5.11; 7.4]	Lev. 20.25			[*Mand.* 5.2 ff.]
3.24 (spirits of the portion of the angel of darkness)			Eph. 6.12	*Mand.* 6.2.4; 9.11; 11.11

Rule (1QS) (and other scrolls)	Old Testament and Apocrypha	Late Judaism	New Testament	Other Christian writings
3.24 (sons of light)			Luke 16.8; John 12.36; Eph. 5.8; I Thess. 5.5	
4.3 (spirit of humility)	Prov. 25.15 LXX		I Cor. 4.21; Gal. 5.20–23; 6.1; I Peter 3.4	*Mand.* 6.2.3 f.
4.4 (spirit of understanding and wisdom)	Isa. 11.2			*Sim.* 9.15.2
4.9 (cf. 1QH 4.12–16) (a lying spirit)	I Kings 22. 21–23 II Chron. 18.20–22 Ps. 32.2; Hos. 4.12; 5.4			*Doct. Ap.* 5.1–2 *Mand.* 3.1.2, 4; 11
4.10 (shortness of temper)	Prov. 14.17, 29; 16.32	*T. Gad* 4.7; *Pirqe 'Aboth* 4.1	Gal. 5.20, 22	*Mand.* 5.2
4.18–22 (purification by truth)				*Sim.* 5.5.6
4.21 (purification from all deeds of evil) Cf. 3.7; 8.16; 9.3				*Mand.* 5.1–3

Belief in one God is a foundation of morality (Deut. 6.4–6; James 2.8, 11, 19); it was natural that belief in one spirit should come to be felt as equally necessary. Again, where more than one recognizable and reasonable idea seem to a thinker to express much the same reality, it is a natural progression of his thought to identify them, thus arriving at a comprehensive conception which represents an advance in understanding. It is therefore altogether probable that, as Betz urges in *Der Paraklet*, the concept, spirit of truth, was taken over by the author of the Fourth Gospel and deliberately identified by him with the 'other paraclete' promised by Jesus (John 14.16 f.; 15.26; 16.7, 13) and the paraclete with the Holy Spirit (14.26). It is unnecessary to follow Betz (*op. cit.*, pp. 207 ff.) in identifying the paraclete further with the archangel Michael: the main point is already clear: the term 'spirit of truth' is not a mere descriptive phrase in the Johannine literature but an already existing concept with a known meaning which the author has deliberately identified with the Holy Spirit.

Similarly, the author of the Fourth Gospel took over the concept of 'practising the truth' (1QS 1.5; 5.3; 8.2; Tobit 4.6; 13.6; John 3.21; I John 1.6), a natural course for one who saw meaning in the idea of the spirit of truth; but in taking over these concepts he adapted and absorbed them into his Christian gospel: the spirit of truth became the Holy Spirit, the truth as object of practice became Christ himself, who is made to say 'I am the way, the truth and the life' (John 14.6).

The question naturally arises, how far is the passage on the two spirits (3.13–4.26) an isolable work, to be contrasted with the teaching found elsewhere in the scrolls? Betz points out[1] differences between the teaching of this passage and that of other scrolls passages. For example, here the spirit of truth enlightens the heart of man (4.2); elsewhere it is God who does so (2.3; 1QH 4.5 f., 23). Again, he urges that in CD 5.17–19 the Prince of Lights raises up Moses and Aaron, while Belial raises up Jannes and Jambres to oppose them and that this corresponds exactly to the concepts of 1QS 3.13–4.26 (esp. 3.24); but that in CD 1.11; 2.11; 6.2 it is God who raises up the great figures of the sacred history. It is clear therefore from his own examples that elsewhere than in the *Rule* both the pluralistic and monistic doctrines are found. This implicit admission by Betz in contrasting the passages in CD just cited means that his division of *Geisterlehre* (doctrine of

---

[1] *Offenbarung*, p. 144.

spirits), which we have called the pluralistic doctrine, from *Geistlehre* (doctrine of Spirit), our monistic doctrine, is too sharp, since, as we have seen, the two are mingled even in the *Rule* passage which at first seems to be devoted to the pluralistic doctrine. Again Foerster draws attention[1] to parallels between 1QS 3.13–4.26 and the *Psalms of Thanksgiving*. These can be given concisely thus:

1QS:	4.2	1QH:	1.21, 23; 9.23, 34; 12.11 f.
	4.3 f., 6		4.35–37
	4.4 f.		2.7 f.
	4.20 f.		3.21; 6.8; 16.10–12

In addition, 1QS 10.13 may be compared with 1QH 9.31; 1.26; 4.33 f. and 1QS 10.16 with 1QH 6.4–6; 7.29 f.; 11.8 f.

As might be expected, parallels to the doctrine of the two spirits are found in the *War Scroll*, but in the same work other passages exhibit the same monistic inconsistency which is already clear to us in the *Rule*. Yadin on p. 242 of his edition of the *War Scroll* indicates a number of parallels with 1QS 3.13–4.26, and these are again worth listing:

1QS:	3.20	DSW:	13.10 (Prince of Light)
	3.25		13.10 f.
	4.14		14.5; 17.5
	4.22		14.7
	4.26		13.9

But once again reservations must be made. For example, the point of comparing 1QS 4.22 with DSW 14.7 is the common phrase 'the perfect of way'; but the exact expression is found also in 1QS 8.10, 18, 21; 9.5, 6, 8; 1QSa 1.28; 1QH 1.36—that is, not only in the *Rule* outside the 'two spirits' passage but also in other scrolls. A very similar expression, though not exactly the same, is found in 1QS 2.2; 3.9; 9.2, 9; 1QSb 5.22; CD 1.21; 2.15. Conversely, a passage within the 'two spirits' section, i.e. 3.16–18, contrasts with DSW 13.2–6 in that in the former God's plan includes the creation of both the good and evil spirits, but in the latter the plans of God himself—not that of the spirit of truth—and of Belial are opposed.

A fair summary seems to be that in 1QS 3.13–4.26 the 'doctrine of spirits' (the *Geisterlehre* of Betz) is not isolated, but that a strong

---

[1] *NTS* 8, 1961–2, pp. 129 f.

concentration of it is to be found here. This fact along with the compact parallels in later Jewish Christian literature suggest that the passage may have once existed independently of its present context; even though its teaching is not unique in the scrolls, it may be the original statement, or close to the original statement, which inspired the other passages like it.

This view is enhanced by comparing our passage on the two spirits with the *Testament of Asher*. If this work belongs to the second century BC, it is a remarkable testimony to the influence of both the more poetic and imaginative statement of the doctrine and the more 'official' form of it which speaks of two inclinations. Aalen[1] argues that in 5.1–4 the fundamental idea of day/night alternation underlies the whole passage, and that this is clear when the passages not found in the Armenian version are omitted;[2] and the work opens its main discourse at 1.3 with 'Two ways hath God given to the sons of men, and two inclinations', Charles remarking in a note that this is the earliest occurrence in Jewish literature of the phrase 'two ways'.[3] 1QS 3.20 f. speaks of the ways of light and the ways of darkness, but speaks of neither two ways nor two inclinations, although it speaks of two spirits. All this evidence is inconclusive, but suggests that 1QS 3.13–4.26 represents a work older even than the *Testament of Asher* which was originally independent and has exerted a great influence upon the scrolls and subsequent literature.

This conclusion is strengthened if the *Testaments of the Twelve Patriarchs* or elements in them which include the *Testament of Asher* do not date from the second century BC, but belong in their present form to the early Christian era. This question of the date of the whole work is a matter for much contemporary debate; an admirable survey of a number of different views is given by Russell;[4] the almost standard theory is that of Charles, who dated the origin of the *Testaments* to 108 BC, believing that there are many Christian interpolations in the work in its present form. Alternative views regard the work as Jewish, often as emerging from or closely related to Qumran (e.g. Dupont-Sommer);[5] or as essentially Christian though using much Jewish material (de Jonge);[6] or as a work whose

[1] '*Licht*' *und* '*Finsternis*', p. 106.
[2] See *AP* II, p. 344.
[3] *Ibid.*, p. 343.
[4] D. S. Russell, *The Method and Message of Jewish Apocalyptic*, pp. 55 ff.
[5] A. Dupont-Sommer, *The Essene Writings from Qumran*, pp. 301–5, 354–7.
[6] M. de Jonge, *The Testaments of the Twelve Patriarchs*, esp. pp. 117 ff.

composition has been a growth round the original nucleus of the *Testament of Levi* (e.g. van der Woude).[1]

Our discussion of the *Two Ways* has not perhaps been such as to throw any new light on this question, but it may be observed that the combination of 'two ways' with 'two inclinations' in *Test. Asher* 1.3 suggests that it may at least in its present form represent a relatively late rather than early stage of development in the Jewish Christian doctrine of man typical of the documents which we have been considering.

4. GOD AND REVELATION

A. GOD AND HISTORY

The quotation from Anaximenes on page 27 we owe to a certain Aetius[2] of about the second century AD. He follows it with an interesting criticism: 'but he too is wrong in thinking that living things are composed of a single and homogeneous air and breath (*pneuma*);[3] for it is impossible for one single original substance to be the ground of the matter of existents, but it is necessary to postulate the creative cause also; just as silver is not enough for the existence of a cup, without there being something to make it, that is the silversmith . . .'[4] This argument could be adopted by a theistic philosopher; but the idea which prompted it would be taken for granted by the Hebrew mind, for whom the reality of God is such as to require no discussion. We do not need to debate whether he is but to do what he says.

According to the Jews of the time with which we are concerned, who had inherited the Old Testament, God had indeed revealed himself in history; but this does not mean that by means of his actions in history he had revealed that there is a God, but that he had revealed his character—and this revelation is so bound up with his actions that his character is expressed by words which reflect them. The prophet, even where he approaches a little towards the philosophical, does not address God as omniscient, omnipresent, omnipotent (subjecting the living upholder of the universe to the dead hand of intellectual categorization), but asks, 'Art thou not it which dried

---

[1] A. S. van der Woude, *Die messianischen Vorstellungen der Gemeinde von Qumran*, pp. 190–216.

[2] Not the medical writer of the sixth century. For the Aetius intended see Kirk and Raven, *op. cit.*, p. 5.

[3] Aetius has already remarked that for Anaximenes air and breath are synonymous.

[4] H. Diels and W. Kranz, *Die Fragmente der Vorsokratiker* I, p. 95.

up the sea, the waters of the great deep; that made the depths of the sea a way for the redeemed to pass over?' (Isa. 51.10).

God has revealed not only himself in his action in history, but also his will in the Law, given to Moses on Mount Sinai, requiring interpretation and application, but none the less given once for all. To the pious Jew therefore man's duty is to live less according to the structure of the universe than according to the will of God which he has revealed for this purpose. The idea of a God who has revealed himself in the structure and function of the universe (other than by the action, at the beginning of history, of making it) is almost wholly absent from the Bible; and those passages in the Old Testament, such as Ps. 19, which appear to suggest it, emphasize that he has provided in the heavens an illustration of the orderliness in creation of the God of the Law, rather than that his existence and character may be deduced from them. Such passages in any case are rare, and Job 26.14 may be said to pass the Bible's verdict on man's natural knowledge of God: 'Lo, these are but the outskirts of his ways: and how small a whisper do we hear of him! But the thunder of his mighty power who can understand?'

It was therefore altogether foreign to the Hebrew mind to speculate about the character of the universe in order to derive from it an answer to the question, Is there an object worthy of man's worship? Nevertheless, antecedently convinced—indeed not raising the question—of the reality of God, the same mind was necessarily faced with elements in creation which invited explanation: for example, how was the world made, how is man's position, at once with dominion over and hardship under nature, to be accounted for? To these and similar questions were added in course of time questions of a more scientific nature: but they were asked by men who believed already in a God whose supreme revelation of his being was in history and of his will in the Law. Solomon asks for the wisdom to rule rightly and thus shows himself the conventional Israelite, obedient to the Law. This is how I Kings 3.4–15 now presents the matter, although the famous story of the following verses, 16–27, suggests a native wit of an independent kind, such as a later tradition suggests to have been also literary and critical (I Kings 4.29–34).

B. WISDOM AND APOCALYPTIC

The freer movement of the mind described as 'wisdom' is usually associated with the Wisdom of the Near East, exemplified in the Bible and the Apocrypha in Job, Ecclesiastes, Proverbs, certain Psalms, Ecclesiasticus and the Wisdom of Solomon. Such literature is normally contrasted with apocalyptic and many of their characteristics are indeed sharply opposed to one another. Yet an important motive unites them: to bring new knowledge and insights within the compass of authoritative teaching. This was indeed one reason for the birth of apocalyptic, that prophecy had been discredited and driven underground. To this the late passage now found at Zech. 13.1–6 bears witness. Apocalyptic is certainly in part, if not essentially, prophecy re-arising in a modified and anonymous form. Wisdom literature had in essence always been free-lance, the exertion of man's right to think for himself; yet it operated inevitably within the framework of its own local traditions. There is much bold questioning in the book of Job, but it is based on the fundamental belief that righteousness is divinely rewarded, and the author shows his originality by raising the question whether righteousness can be an attribute of man rather than solely of God.[1] Other books reveal the same strand of conservatism. Proverbs insists on the moral character of wisdom; Ecclesiasticus, taking Proverbs as a model in many respects and writing about 180 BC, was the first to make the logical deduction from the moral character of wisdom that the true wisdom was the Law.

The movement of thought which we describe loosely as 'wisdom' had therefore either come amicably to terms with the Law before the rise of the Qumran sect or was tending to do so at that very time (for we cannot date the foundation of Qumran exactly). In parallel fashion apocalyptic reveals the trait of reinterpretation as well as of reincarnation of prophecy in a book written about 165 BC and showing clear affinities with the Qumran literature, especially in its treatment of already established Scripture. This is the book of Daniel, which combines both apocalyptic and wisdom elements.

It has recently been shown that there are important affinities in thought and perhaps sources also in common between Ecclesiasticus and the Qumran literature;[2] this is entirely consistent with the para-

---

[1] This seems to be the real subject of the book; its treatment of the problem of suffering is superficial: Job's prosperity is after all restored and his suffering shown to be but a temporary test. The real problem of suffering is far more mysterious and the author does not raise it. Job does not ask 'Why do I suffer?' but protests 'I can prove my innocence if given a chance!'

[2] M. R. Lehmann, 'Ben Sira and the Qumran literature' in RQ 3, 1961, pp. 103–16; ' "Yom Kippur" in Qumran', ibid., pp. 117–24; J. Carmignac, 'Les rapports entre l'Ecclésiastique et Qumrân' in RQ 3, 1961, pp. 209–18.

doxical association in both of conservatism and new ideas—and, as we have seen, a similar appreciation can be made of apocalyptic as it appears in the book of Daniel.

We shall see that two other works at least, the *Book of Jubilees* and *I Enoch*, which belong wholly or in part to the period (the two centuries before Christ) which concerns us, exhibit the same important characteristic of absorbing new ideas into a conservative matrix. This matrix was, of course, orthodox Judaism, or rather Judaism striving to remain orthodox and loyal to tradition, while the new ideas entered from that very world—the world of Hellenism—against which the authors of these books strove to protect their heritage. The hand was the hand of Esau, the voice Jacob's voice; but in this instance Jacob protested that he was not Esau. Every book which shows Greek influence carries a warning against it.

The influence of Hellenistic ideas, philosophical and religious, upon Judaism needs very little arguing. It is universally conceded in connexion with 'wisdom' literature, especially from 198 BC onwards, when Judaea passed once for all under the sway of the Seleucids, and its presence in the life of the people generally, beginning with the upheaval of Alexander's conquests, from his southward march after the Battle of Issus (331 BC) through Syria and Palestine into Egypt, was immense and continuous.[1]

The apocalyptic literature might seem to be so clearly peculiar to Judaism as to be entitled to resist the claim that it was influenced by new ideas from the Hellenistic world; certainly it would regard itself as so entitled, but even this sphere of Jewish thought was not immune from Greek influence, perhaps not even in that department which seems most Jewish, its eschatological expectations and their expression.[2]

In *I Enoch*, for example, chapters 1–36 relate the patriarch's journeys into unknown parts of the universe, and the description of them may owe much to Greek descriptions of a *Nekuia*, or journey to the abode of the dead. In 22.5–7 Abel takes on the character of an avenging spirit like a Fury in an environment which suggests a Greek Hades rather than a Hebrew *She'ol*. The divisions in *She'ol*

---

[1] See, for example, E. Bevan, *Jerusalem under the High Priests*, ch. II; Tarn and Griffith, *Hellenistic Civilization*, ch. VI (a cautious view inclining to regard apocalyptic at least without Greek influence); W. D. Davies, *Paul and Rabbinic Judaism*, ch. I; C. H. Dodd, *The Interpretation of the Fourth Gospel*, esp. ch. 2 (on Philo).

[2] See T. Francis Glasson, *Greek Influence in Jewish Eschatology*, to which the following paragraphs are indebted.

afford another conception probably borrowed from the Greek Hades. Greek influence upon Jewish belief in the survival of the soul after death (a notion foreign not only to the mainstream of Jewish religious belief but also inconsistent with Hebraic psychology) cannot be disputed when we reach books as late as the Wisdom of Solomon and *IV Maccabees*. The former holds together Hellenistic reverence for the soul, as the immortal element in man (3.1), with Jewish eschatology (3.7–8), apparently unaware of any incongruity. The latter book reveals to the most superficial reader the author's full employment of Greek philosophical ideas derived from Plato through the Stoics to give point to his story of Jewish martyrdom. The martyrs' bravery is firmly founded on belief in immortality; of the doctrine of the resurrection there is no trace whatever. Since with this book we have arrived at the age of Philo, we cannot be surprised at the skill and thoroughness with which a Jewish author uses Greek philosophy to commend Judaism to an educated public; but it is well worth while to urge the reasonableness of supposing these authors to stand at the climax of a long period of interaction of Judaism and Hellenism, even though during this period many Jews who unconsciously borrowed from the other world of learning made loud protests against its influence.

C.   HELLENISM

Throughout the long period of Israelite history represented by the extremes of the time of the J narrative in Genesis and that of the passionate patriotism of *IV Maccabees* expressed in the terms of Hellenistic philosophy there persisted the strong feeling of necessity to live in public and in private, on the large and on the small scale, according to the revealed commands of God who had made the universe and who had set in its overarching vault the great luminaries which determined the religious calendar. It will be our task to show that in the sect at Qumran we possess a striking example of a company of men who deeply felt this strong compulsion, but who as passionately believed themselves to be the inheritors of a special revealed wisdom, which they studiously obeyed and which they ingeniously incorporated into the system derived from the original revelation on Mount Sinai.

If the *Rule* and the other writings discovered at Qumran are regarded as internal evidence for Essene beliefs, the testimony of Philo and Josephus affords valuable external evidence. On pp. 31–33

the evidence of these authors and of Pliny the Elder for the identification of the Qumran sect is discussed. Here it will be used to support
the claim that the Essenes—and therefore the men of Qumran—
incorporated in their system of belief a number of tenets strongly
influenced by Hellenism, while the system remained unquestionably
loyal to that revealed in the Jewish scriptures.

The manner and extent of the absorption of Hellenistic thought
by the Essenes is well summarized by Philo in *Quod omnis probus liber*
12–13: 'Physical science they regard as too lofty for human nature,
and so they leave that to high-flying theorists, except as it includes
the study of God's existence and the formation of the universe.' The
exceptions are expressed in Greek terms and correspond to the Jewish
preoccupation with the self-revelation of God and with obedience to
his injunctions that life is to be conducted in accordance with the
pattern of the universe, a pattern believed to be expressed historically
in terms of divinely ordained chronology, and liturgically in a calendar
related to the sun, greatest of the heavenly bodies set in the firmament
by the creator. Thus for them it would be natural to make one
exception from the science which they regarded as too lofty for
human intellects, that is, the science of astronomy, and it is this
science which we find receiving attention in literature associated with
the Essenes and their beliefs; in this literature, because all must be
included in the great divine law, a special revelation through angels
to a patriarch of unique status is made out to be the means of conveying this knowledge to the sect. This concept of a special revelation
is discussed in the following section and their astronomy on pp.
81–83.

If an interest in physical science is a Hellenistic characteristic, the
Essenes certainly gave it a Jewish form by subsuming it under the
category of revelation. In another respect they are credited by
Josephus with a belief thoroughly Greek in origin and character,
that in the immortality of the soul. In *BJ* 2.8.11 he writes, after
describing the heroism of Essenes under torture in the Roman war,
'For it is their firm opinion that, while the body is corruptible, and
its substance transient, the soul is permanent and immortal; that the
soul comes from the thinnest air by a sort of natural spell to be
imprisoned, as it were, within the body; and that, on being released
from the fetters of the flesh, it joyfully soars away into freedom from
the long bondage.' Josephus proceeds explicitly to identify these and
similar views about the soul with that of 'the Greeks'; it has been

argued that he is here accommodating Jewish belief in the resurrection of the body to his Graeco-Roman readers, but this appears an impossible explanation for this passage in view of two important arguments: 1. As a Jew who had undertaken part of the probationary training as an Essene postulant and later joined the Pharisees[1] Josephus must have understood well both the differences in general between them and the distinctive character of the Pharisaic doctrine of the resurrection of the body. 2. He here quite explicitly compares the Greek and Essene views and delivers it as his judgment that they are the same. This is the very point which he is making. Thus literary accommodation seems excluded. Nor need we be surprised that a Jewish sect entertained so Hellenistic a belief in the midst of their apocalyptic expectations when we recall precisely the same juxtaposition in the book of the Wisdom of Solomon[2] and the description of Jewish martyrs upheld by the same faith in *IV Maccabees*.[3]

These considerations may prompt serious attention to another statement of Josephus, made somewhat in passing, in *Ant.* 15.10.4, that the Essenes live the same kind of life as do those whom the Greeks call Pythagoreans. It would be foolish to ignore Josephus' caution—he does not say that the Essenes derive their manner of life from Pythagoras—but if it appears that the sect had something in common with the widely diffused teachings generally called Pythagorean in his day, it may confirm the impression that they owed more to Hellenism than they would have been willing to admit. We have already claimed[4] that certain general aspirations of Pythagoreans— or one branch of them—to live according to the orderliness of the universe as embodied in a calendar, and to practise purification, were shared with Israel and especially with Qumran; but this was part of the more general claim that mankind in antiquity shared these aspirations without necessarily having borrowed them one from another. Josephus may well therefore have intended to draw attention to a resemblance rather than to a borrowing; but the question remains open, and considerations will later be urged which may lead to the conclusion that Pythagoreanism had real influence upon the Essenes. That the latter accepted Hellenistic influence, even while denying it, in the matter of their special calendar and the principles which lie behind it will be seen presently.[5]

[1] *Vita* 2.
[2] Wisd. 3.1–4; 4.8–10; see p. 60 above.
[3] *IV Macc.* 13.17; 17.18; 18.23; see p. 60 above.
[4] See p. 28 above.   [5] See p. 87 below.

Brief references may be made to other important traces of Hellenistic influence upon Jewish apocalyptic. For example, the strange story in Gen. 6.1–4 is retold with some amplification in *I Enoch* 6 (from the *Book of Noah*) and *Jub.* 5. In Genesis it is implied that the offspring of the union of the 'Sons of God' with the 'daughters of men' were giants. In *I Enoch* 7.2 and *Jub.* 5.1 this is repeated, but according to *I Enoch* 15.9–12 and 16.1 evil spirits proceed from the bodies of these giants when they are destroyed. This is supported by the story in *Jub.* 10 (also from the lost *Book of Noah*). That spirits or demons are the product of gods and women is a Greek idea; once more a Jewish conception is seen to have developed under the influence of prevailing Hellenistic thought without losing its predominant Semitic character. To put it simply, the author of *I Enoch* 15 and 16 and of the lost *Book of Noah* were so imbued with the Greek maxim that gods and women produced demigods or demons that in rewriting Genesis they took this for granted.

D. REVELATION, SCRIPTURE AND TRADITION

The object of all who join the community at Qumran must be to 'do what is good and right before him according to the command which he gave through Moses and through all his servants the prophets'. It is clear therefore at the outset that whatever new knowledge the men of Qumran had absorbed, they held it as part of the divine revelation given through Moses and the Scriptures. To explain how they reconciled the new with the old ostensibly given once for all is a task of some difficulty and complication, and what follows attempts no more than to suggest the lines along which such an explanation may be found.

It has already been argued that a number of ideas, common to thinking men in the ancient world, were impressed into the matrix of the orthodox Judaism of the Qumran sect by the prevalent Hellenism. It now becomes necessary to say more about this matrix and especially the methods by which the original divine revelation was preserved, transmitted, interpreted, applied and—unconsciously—adapted to new knowledge, all within an apparently unchanging frame. In giving some account of this it is necessary to emphasize elements in the concept of revelation which are apparently alien to the main Old Testament claim with regard to it. Amos's belief will illustrate this: 'Surely the LORD God will do nothing, but he revealeth his secret unto his servants the prophets' (3.7). We are familiar both with the notion that God reveals himself, according to the main teaching of the Old Testament, in history, and with the claim that he revealed his will, and what he was about to do, to the prophets; we are apt to regard these two notions as either identical, or two halves of the same truth. Neither judgment is quite accurate. God's self-revelation through history is a concept which can be accepted, propounded and preserved by scholars who study historical records of events long past; but his self-revelation to the prophet's eye or ear, as the book of Amos shows so clearly, is different: it is a direct self-revelation in which the spirit of God is supposed to communicate (albeit in ways which may seem odd and dubious) with the spirit of man. Amos, had he been self-analytical, rather than analytical of what was given to himself, might have anticipated the words of Paul: 'For God has revealed to us through the spirit; for the spirit searches out everything, even the deep mysteries of God' (I Cor. 2.10).

The ways in which the main corpus of revelation was received, transmitted, interpreted and applied must therefore be distinguished from those by which special or new revelations were thought to be made. These two distinct though certainly connected subjects will now occupy us, beginning with the latter, at least in so far as they concern the life and work of the men of Qumran.

First, the manner of special revelation. Study of cultic prophecy in the ancient world and its relevance for understanding of the Old Testament prophets is an established and growing department of the disciplines of theology and of comparative religion. It is unnecessary to give a full account of it here, because the Judaistic understanding of it, such as is presupposed in Qumran, certainly did not include comparison with the form which it took in other cultures. The main features are clear from the Bible: prophets are not confined to prophets of the LORD, and prophets of pagan gods illustrate sharply the type of behaviour necessary to enter into communication with the deity. Thus the prophets of Baal on Mount Carmel work themselves into an ecstasy to try to force their god into communication (I Kings 18.26–29); and prophets perhaps not originally of the LORD seek to compel the divinity's action by drama (I Kings 22.5–12, esp. v. 11). Trance seems to bring no disgrace even to one dedicated to the LORD (I Sam. 19.24) and the ecstatic utterance of Saul implied (though not obvious in English translation) in I Sam. 10.9–13 persists into the New Testament (e.g. Acts 2.1–13; I Cor. 14). The measure of impartation of divine secrets implied in these instances is very varied, and St Paul in his day did not set a high value on the experience. In those earlier days did Saul's trance reveal anything to him? Any attempt to answer this question would no doubt contrast the manifest and demonstrable content received through the 'second sight' and clairaudience of an Amos, Hosea, Isaiah or Jeremiah, but must allow some connexion between the manner of reception of the content exemplified by these giants and that of their less-impressive counterparts. Isaiah, for example, is the subject of compulsion (20.2) and Jeremiah, while scorning the ecstatic prophets, experienced the word of God as fire and a hammer within him (23.29).

Special revelation, as it is pertinent to an understanding of Qumran, involves experiences even more mysterious. It is impossible to read of the deep sleep which 'fell upon' Abraham (Gen. 15.12) without a stir of excitement and a sense of awe. Jacob's—or Israel's—visions of the night (Gen. 46.2) and the famous communication of the LORD with Samuel in the night silence (I Sam. 3) are all occasions when the recipient learns what the LORD will do in the future, and as such may well be regarded as parts of God's self-revelation in history; but later generations are fascinated by other aspects of these apparent visitations. For example, IV Ezra 3.14 makes Abraham the recipient of a revelation of 'the ends of the times'—an apocalyptic reading of the original story; in *II Baruch* 4.4 he even sees the heavenly Jerusalem. These are but two examples of the elaboration to which the famous vision of Abraham 'among the portions of the victims' was subjected in later generations.

Dreams and night-visions seem to be identified, as, for example, in *Jub.* 32.1, 21, but sometimes a writer is evidently interested in the mystery of different levels of consciousness, although he could not formulate such a phrase and must express himself poetically, as in Job 4.12–16. Behind this passage in Job may lie the conception of a 'whisper' (v. 12) from the dead—that is, from another world, and Hooke[1] suggests that this provides a key to the experience of Elijah after his deep sleep in I Kings 19.5–8.

Levels of consciousness through which a man passes when he—as we put it with unnoticed aptness—'goes to sleep', or 'returns to' what we call consciousness are easily confused with apparent journeys to more or less distant places. The most obvious example in the Old Testament is Ezekiel, who provides interpreters with a problem as to whether he is physically in Babylonia and mentally in Jerusalem

[1] S. H. Hooke, *The Siege Perilous*, pp. 57 f.

or whether he visits Jerusalem in actual fact (Ezek. 3.12–15; 8.3; 11.1, 24). The most probable explanation seems to be that he makes long journeys under 'the spirit's' guidance while in what is conveniently called a trance. It is no far cry from such interpretation to a further formalization of such strange experiences: if the subject of them can recount upon awakening what he has seen or learnt in his deep sleep, dream or trance, he may naturally find a ready answer to the question, 'Who communicated these revelations to you?' An older generation had no hesitation in seeing the LORD himself as the one who was revealed either in an unusual state of consciousness or in a strange experience which takes its place. The LORD appears to Abraham in a vision (Gen. 15.1) preparatory to the more important vision in 'deep sleep', the vision 'between the portions' (15.12), and to Moses in full consciousness at the burning bush according to E (Ex. 3.4), although it is the angel of the LORD who calls to him out of it according to J (3.2). Later generations, moved by a profounder sense of awe and of the remoteness of God (philosophical abstraction calls it 'transcendence'), were diligent to insert angels between God and men. A clear and well-known example occurs in Acts 7.53, where the appearance of angels rather than the LORD himself as the imposers of the covenant at Sinai betray the fact that the theology of contemporary Judaism has overlaid Luke's knowledge of Ex. 19, where the LORD's own appearance is emphatically and awesomely narrated.

Angels may indeed be the media of revelation; but the men to whom they reveal the divine secrets must also be appropriate to receive them. Negative support is given to this contention by *I Enoch* 6.1–8 (cf. *Jub*. 5.1 ff.), for it is evil angels who reveal many hitherto hidden skills to men who are not able to use them innocently (cf. *I Enoch* 8.1–9.11). By contrast, the case of Enoch himself lends positive support. The cryptic story in Gen. 5.24 makes him an obvious choice to receive secret revelation.

Enoch, seventh from Adam, is probably the Hebrew version of the seventh of the kings named by Berosus as living in the period before the Flood. His Babylonian name is Emmeduranki, 'favourite of the great gods', who taught his son the secrets of heaven and earth, having been summoned by the sun-god Shamash to be initiated into them. A trace of Enoch's connexion with the sun-god remains in Gen. 5.23, which tells us that Enoch's days were three hundred and sixty-five. Another Babylonian source, the Gilgamesh epic, tells the story of the Babylonian 'Noah', Utnapishtim, whom the gods 'took' because his previous conduct had pleased them. Enoch's 'walking with God' is similarly interpreted by the LXX, which has 'and Enoch pleased God' for this phrase.[1]

In *I Enoch* 1.2 the ways by which knowledge otherwise hidden from men was imparted to Enoch are described: 'Enoch a righteous man, whose eyes were opened by God, saw the vision of the Holy One in the heavens, which the angels showed me, and from them I heard everything, and from them I understood as I saw, but not for this generation, but for a remote one which is for to come.'[2] It is impossible to say with confidence to what stratum of this composite book and therefore to what date this opening chapter belongs, but the passage quoted is sufficient to illustrate the continuing belief in a man who had been given a special position by God, in virtue of which he could obtain and communicate to others secret knowledge. The book, composite as it is, illustrates the two broad categories of revelation—knowledge of the universe, its construction and mechanisms on the one hand, and on the other prescience of future history. Chapter 14 reduces Enoch's translation to heaven to a vision in sleep (v. 2) and relates its course very largely as a fantastic journey (vv. 8 ff.). In many passages it is claimed or implied that the book was written by Enoch himself (e.g. 92.1), implying an even more thoroughgoing act of identification with their guide by the actual authors than that achieved by the final editor of the book of Daniel, who tells the story of Daniel in the first two chapters, but in ch. 4 introduces Nebuchadrezzar as the speaker without preamble, a convention which he maintains for eighteen verses until Daniel appears before a king who is now reported in the third person, at 4.19. In ch. 7 Daniel himself begins to address the reader, introduced by a brief report that 'Daniel had a dream'. The first-person usage continues to the end of ch. 9, a very similar device of third person dissolving into first recurs at the opening of ch. 10, and Daniel continues to address the reader until the end of the book. Very similar but more developed is the remarkable device in the passage already quoted at the beginning of *I Enoch*: 'Enoch . . . saw the vision . . . which angels showed me . . .' Third person becomes first without regard for formal clarity, thus partly concealing and partly revealing the need of the writer (who may or may not be the final editor of the

[1] See J. G. Davies, *He Ascended into Heaven*, pp. 16 ff.
[2] R. H. Charles, *AP* II, p. 188.

book as we have it) to lose himself in the person whose special knowledge he claims to record. This identification of author with guide, of 'medium' with 'control', is not merely a device; an author who was completely convinced of two things apparently quite incompatible has neatly solved a problem. He believes that all knowledge has been already revealed to the patriarchs of old; he believes also with the same religious fervour that he has new and necessary knowledge to impart.[1] A member of a people distinguished by a strong sense of the mutual inherence of the one and the many could in such circumstances feel without insincerity an identity with a representative person of his nation's past. The author *is* Daniel, *is* Enoch, just as in John 1.19 ff. (for example) the thought can be entertained that the Baptist *is* Elijah, or *is* the Prophet.[2]

Not only Enoch but other patriarchs also served as figures with whom an author sufficiently identified himself as to make them the mouthpieces of his revelation. The names which appear as the first examples of faith in Heb. 11.1–12, Abel, Enoch, Noah, Abraham and Sarah, names upon whom considerable comment is lavished and who form a list sealed off by the general comment in vv. 13–16 before Abraham reappears to begin another list in v. 17, are not chosen at random by the author. Abel is the very type of the righteous man, the man who offers the acceptable sacrifice, who therefore anticipates the law given through Moses. It was a rabbinic interpretation of Abraham's righteousness that he, too, kept the Law before it had been given to Moses, and the *Book of Noah*, now lost except for fragments incorporated in *Jubilees* and *I Enoch*, represents Noah as anticipating the Law even to the point of keeping the levitical rule with regard to fruit-trees (*Jub.* 7.36 f.). That Sarah's reputation and honour were exalted along with Abraham's has long been known from many legends springing from their story in Genesis, and the Aramaic *Genesis Apocryphon* found in Cave 1 shows that such an estimate was known and perhaps fostered at Qumran.

Enoch is perhaps the most important of the patriarchs in the study of the Qumran community, since it can be shown that the calendar laid down in *I Enoch* 72–82 was obeyed by the community. It seems

[1] Cf. *The Gospel of Thomas*, logion 88: the disciples already possess in essence what they obtain with the help of angels and indeed can give the angels what is in their own hands. Revelation is a continuous new progressive disclosure of a good already received (Betz, *Der Paraklet*, p. 219).

[2] It is for this reason that so many objections to the theory of pseudonymity of authorship of some New Testament books, on the ground that it involves dishonesty, must be dismissed as based on complete misunderstanding of the author's aims.

clear that his connexion with the sun survived in some form throughout the tradition. It is therefore natural that a sect organized round
a priesthood who maintained a solar calendar should show respect for
writings gathered under the name of Enoch, and it may be that they
accepted as divine revelation writings like *Jubilees*, such elements of
the *Enoch* corpus as already existed, and the *Testaments of the Twelve
Patriarchs* (or, again, such parts of them as were already written), in
which new knowledge and new prophecy could be represented as
revelation which, though now published for the first time, had been
revealed to chosen recipients long ago.

The sect was even more obviously equipped to receive, preserve,
interpret and transmit the Scriptures which it revered in company
with all other Israelites. It was so equipped by its very organization,
revealed in the *War Scroll* by a study of the military banners and
the divisions of the whole sect which they imply. Professor Yadin has
rendered a great service to all who wish to understand the character
of the sect by his painstaking and clear unravelling of the complicated
instructions in the *War Scroll* in his edition of it, and the following
discussion is greatly indebted to his work. It appears that the sect's
organization in its military aspect deliberately expressed the way in
which the sect understood Israel to have been organized in its desert
days. There is a banner for the 'whole congregation' and also separate
banners for the families of Levi as well as for other, non-levitical, units.
Most interestingly, there is a division into four 'camps' at the head of
each of which stands a chief who rules over three tribes. This arrangement 'corresponds exactly to the description of the stars and of the
heavenly host, and the chiefs who *rule over the four seasons* and the
months, in *Enoch*'.[1] Clearly the sect was organized to express in its
very constitution and being the Israel of God from of old, and in
doing so the way in which God had framed the universe and its
regular functions and movement. Within this ingenious structure the
priests and Levites found an appropriate place.

Our concern here is with the function of priests and Levites in
connexion with revelation, in particular with the Torah received
once for all, but requiring preservation, transmission and application.
Reference is made elsewhere[2] to Deut. 17.9–13, where 'the priests the
Levites' give decisions about the Law, and to Deut. 17.18, where it
is revealed that the king would have access to a book in their possession. Moreover, 'the priests the sons of Levi' are according to Deut.

[1] Yadin, p. 47; he refers to *I Enoch* 82.9–15.   [2] P. 92.

31.9–13 to read out the deuteronomic form of the Law of Moses every seventh year, at the Feast of Tabernacles.

In Deuteronomy no apparent distinction is made between priests and Levites,[1] but in Ezekiel, P and Chronicles they are co-operating but distinguishable elements in the hierarchy; while in Chronicles, Levites are accorded a high status.[2] Both orders have an important part to play in the task of receiving the revelation.

The primary task of the priests was certainly to maintain the system of worship and sacrifice in the Temple, but their prominence in a sect which had severed itself from the Temple is a reminder of the fact that the priests had other functions also. Hos. 4.6 implies that the Torah (instruction about God, at this stage not to be identified with the as yet non-existent Pentateuch) is deposited with the priests. The reform, deuteronomic in character even if not to be identified with the core of the present book of Deuteronomy, promoted by Josiah, was initiated by a priest and a scribe (II Kings 22.8 ff.); the expert, one might almost say scholarly character of the Priestly Code, found largely in Leviticus and Numbers, but influencing Exodus and the whole Pentateuch, implies the activity of priestly scribes in exile at Babylon before the code finally reached its present form. Encrusted with later legends as is the figure of Ezra, his image as reformer, scribe and priest is yet significant in itself as the image in the tradition of a man who laid the foundations of the theocratic Second Commonwealth, an image with significance whether it corresponds exactly to historical fact or not. CD 13.2–4 enjoins that a priest must be present in a *minyan* (to use a modern term) of ten—'a priest instructed in the book of study'.[3] The evidence from the *Rule* on this point is admittedly not striking: at 8.1 there are to be twelve men and three priests who are to be expert in Law study and interpretation; no impression is given that only priests are such experts, but it is clear that any such expert body must include some of them.

The connexion of the Levites with the task of scholarship in the Law is just as clear, especially if we follow the lucid exposition of Gertner in *Vetus Testamentum*.[4] His task included that of distinguishing two separate verbal roots which lead to the formation of almost

[1] See p. 91.
[2] See pp. 92–95.
[3] The book of *Hagi*; whether this is equivalent to the sacred Scriptures or not, the implication clearly is that the priest is an instructed person.
[4] M. Gertner, 'The Masorah and the Levites' in *Vetus Testamentum* 10, 1960, pp. 241–72.

identical abstract nouns and a consequent confusion of meaning. One root *srr* gives us a noun which was originally spelled *mesorah* and signified among other things taking the command or lead in reading or in singing the Scriptures. The other root *msr* gives us *masorah* or *masoreth*, is concerned with transmission, and so provides the late noun for tradition.[1] The Levites were concerned with *mesorah*, with a clear enunciation of the text. Such an activity was artistic and entirely consistent with the Levites as singers; musical Levites in I Chron. 25.6 include Asaphites after whom one of the collections of the psalms afterwards incorporated into the biblical Psalter as Pss. 50, 73–83, is named. Again, the Levites are included among those able to interpret and 'give the sense' in Neh. 8.7–9; and I Chron. 25.7 shows that those who were musicians were trained in their work and not mere mechanical performers. These artistically and intellectually instructed craftsmen are credited with being men of understanding—*mebinim*—and instructed men—*maśkilim*. They could obey the celebrated exhortation, 'Sing ye praises with understanding' of Ps. 47.7.

The ability to read or sing correctly is not far from the other ability with which the Levites are credited in Neh. 8.7–9, the ability to expound. The two go well and naturally together. The Chronicler therefore triumphantly sets the seal on the raised status of the Levites[2] in II Chron. 35.3 by representing Josiah as saying to 'the Levites that taught all Israel' that 'there shall no more be a burden upon your shoulders', that is, they are relieved from menial tasks and become servants of the Lord in more honorific ways.

The situation at Qumran illustrates a further point made by Gertner: the treatment of the Scriptures as poetry went hand in hand with their interpretation. Hence *midrash* and *mesorah* were allies. But this attitude was not allowed to last. The rabbis disapproved of regarding the Torah as poetry and song, a point well illustrated by their interpretation of David's 'cunning in playing' (I Sam. 16.18) as ability to ask questions in learned disputes (*b. Sanh.* 93b). At Qumran both activities—poetry and exact scholarship—flourish. A hymn of much beauty is incorporated in the *Rule*; and the *Thanksgiving Psalms*, even if sometimes reminiscent of *pastiche*, often compel acknowledgment of real feeling effectively expressed; at the same time *halakah* was a constant preoccupation and if Amos believed that

---

[1] In 1QS 10.5 the noun which is apparently connected with one or other of these roots is in reality derived from yet another, *swr. Mesorah* does not occur in the *Rule*.
[2] Cf. p. 91.

the prophets (absorbed according to I Chron. 25.1 ff. into the Levites) were the natural recipients of divine revelation,[1] the men of Qumran believed that God's final secrets went beyond those known to the prophets[2] who had uttered things which were mysteries, though now understood by the Teacher of Righteousness. Indeed, God's secrets are now revealed not only to the poetic author of the *Thanksgiving Psalms*[3] but also to interpreters of the Law who fulfil his command to make 'a highway for our God' (1QS 8.15 f.).

A picture of the community at Qumran begins to emerge: they were equipped to receive the original revelation and to find in it new secrets which they could interpret, and this ability exactly fitted their organization as a miniature Israel in which priests and Levites were prominent; side by side with this literary and scholarly ability there seems to have dwelt an imaginative capacity which enabled them to absorb new ideas within the stream of a well-respected tradition, and to claim new revelations without violence to the old.

Reference was made above to the term *maskilim*. The *Rule* mentions the *maskil* or instructor at 3.13; 9.12; 9.21 and if a conjectural emendation is correct also at 1.1. Vermès[4] puts forward a theory as to the meaning of the term in the *Rule* which is consistent with the facts and arguments presented above. He refers to the *maskilim* in Dan. 11.33; 12.3 as specially endowed men who instruct others, and cites among other passages Neh. 8.7 f., where the Levites appear to act as *maskilim* although not there so called, as they are, however, in II Chron. 30.22. The association of Levites with *maskilim* appears also in the titles of Pss. 42, 44, 45, 88 (Korah), 74, 78 (Asaph) and 89 (Ethan) and at Ps. 47.7 (see above, p. 71). Vermès concludes that in post-exilic Judaism Levites acted as instructors of the people. It seems that the men of Qumran reflect the practice: CD 13.1–4 shows a Levite as a possible adviser in the Law, should the priest need one, and he may be identifiable with the Guardian (*mebaqqer*). On this basis Vermès suggests a solution to the involved problem set by the technical terms for officials in the sect: '(1) At the head of the whole sect, and at the head of each dependent community, stood two distinct figures, the Priest and the Guardian (2) The Guardian was a Levite. (3) As the teacher of his congregation, this Levite-Guardian was also known by the title *Maskil*, Master.' For a modification of this

---

[1] Amos 3.7.
[2] 1Q pHab. 2.2–10; 7.4–14.
[3] See esp. 1QH 4.
[4] *The Dead Sea Scrolls in English*, pp. 23 ff.

view as it affects understanding of the officials of the sect see the commentary on 9.12.

The sect at Qumran were no doubt only a few of the men of their time who were learned in the Scriptures and able to interpret them so as to support existing customs or make new regulations with the authority of the Law. The Mishnah bears upon its face evidence of its composition from different and often competing decisions, recorded without attempt to adjudicate between them, reflecting many schools contemporary with Qumran. The process in which so many scholars shared was varied and multiform, but its main principles can be indicated. It will be seen that they were followed at Qumran no less than elsewhere.

Interpretation of the Law normally proceeds by bringing scripture to bear upon scripture. The interpreter's activity is expressed in the root *drsh* (enquire) and his creation is a *midrash*. Much of such *midrash* is halakic, that is, it is concerned with the application of the Law to practical instances; but Judaistic literature abounds in *midrash haggadah*, a very comprehensive term embracing all *midrash* which is not halakic, and often found in the form of story. A form of haggadic *midrash* which is characteristic of the scrolls is the *midrash pesher* which valiantly announces after quoting a scripture 'Its meaning is . . .' and proceeds with what to modern readers must appear a most arbitrary application of a text (often already perfectly intelligible in its original historical context) to the time in which the author of the *midrash* is interested, usually his own. The *Habakkuk Commentary* is an excellent example of such *midrash pesher*.

Perhaps most interesting of all is that type of *midrash haggadah* which is really a rewriting of Scripture. Vermès has made this clear in his fascinating book, *Scripture and Tradition in Judaism*. One example is found in the *Genesis Apocryphon* from Cave 1. Here the story of Abraham is manifestly rewritten, though many of the new features are known elsewhere, for example in the Targums. The *Genesis Apocryphon* may be a source for the *Book of Jubilees* which has always been understood for what it is, Genesis rewritten. For many readers Vermès's most intriguing point will be that the priestly recension of the Pentateuch can be understood as nothing else than haggadic *midrash* in this its most developed form, that of rewriting Scripture. In his ch. VI, 'The Story of Balaam',[1] this claim becomes so clear as to be incontestable. The ordinary Bible reader will find in

[1] *Op. cit.*, pp. 127 ff.

Num. 22–24 a presentation of Balaam as a blameless character, certainly no worse than Jonah, and in some ways more amenable. To such a reader it may come as a surprise to learn that from some time in the first two centuries BC there has flourished a tradition within Judaism which makes Balaam the arch-enemy, appearing not only in the original story but in different guises at different times, of Israel, her calling and her mission. This tradition was sufficiently early to influence, through P, the composition of the Bible itself. To prove this we have but to refer to the hostile passages in Num. 31.8, 16 and Josh. 13.22 in material inserted by P and then to find the full explanation in the Targums, Philo and Josephus.[1] It is this later (though very old) tradition of Balaam the Villain to which reference is made in all the New Testament passages which mention him (II Peter 2.15; Jude 11; Rev. 2.14).

Midrash was therefore a creative activity. Although the sect were not the only men of their time to be occupied with it, there seem to be grounds for believing them to have had close relations with the circle of scholars who were responsible for that great midrashic creation, the priestly recension of the Pentateuch and Joshua. These grounds include the attitude to priests and Levites—so much honoured at Qumran—of P and Chronicles (a *midrash* of rewritten Kings)[2] and the calendar used by the sect, which appears to be that which P has imposed upon the sacred history.[3]

The sect at Qumran claimed to be the true Israel and organized itself to reflect what it believed to be the structure of Israel as God had intended her to be. In their many-sided activity, at least, the men of Qumran certainly made good this claim to be Israel. Priestly and scholarly, showing affinities with both Wisdom and Apocalyptic, earnest and ascetic, they were no more devoid of poetry than they were incapable of almost fanatic devotion; their manifold character can best be expressed in some words from a hymn-like prayer which occurs in the *War Scroll*, words there describing 'thy people Israel, which thou hast chosen for thyself from all the nations of the lands, a people of men holy through the covenant, taught the statutes, enlightened in understanding, hearing the glorious voice, seeing the holy angels, open of ear and hearing deep things . . . the expanse of the skies, the host of luminaries, the domain of spirits and

[1] The evidence is set out with admirable clarity by Vermès in the chapter already indicated.
[2] See p. 92.
[3] See p. 90.

the dominion of holy ones . . .'[1] Here in poetic form is an expression of the relation of Qumran to the revelation of God: they kept the statutes and expounded them with understanding and appeared to be formidably conservative. But they were also 'open of ear'.

5. THE SUN

A. THE TEMPLE AND THE SUN

U. Simon writes:[2] 'The Israelite was exhorted not to serve other gods, "the sun, moon, or any of the host of Heaven" (Deut. 17.2 ff.) because he was obviously inclined to do so . . . In the early days of the settlement the Hebrews had their Beth-Shemesh (Josh. 15.10; 19.22; I Sam. 6.9, 12), a house-of-the-sun or cultic place of worship. Most commentators agree that the legislation in Num. 19.1–10 for the offering of a red heifer recalls the ancient practice of a solar sacrifice. The Jebusite rock, which David captured, had also known the cultus of the sun for centuries before . . .' This is a summary of some of the evidence for the site upon which the Temple at Jerusalem was built being a place of sun-worship. Some evidence can be brought to show that Solomon's Temple to some extent perpetuated this tradition, much of the evidence centring upon the traditions surrounding the Golden Gate at Jerusalem and collected together by Morgenstern.[3] A curious aura surrounds this walled-up gate, there being, for example, a Muslim tradition that it would be opened only to admit the conquering Christian.

The Christian tradition which gave rise to this superstition may be discernible in Josephus *BJ* 6.5.3, repeated by Eusebius in *HE* 3.8: an event occurred which was regarded as important at the time of Passover just before the destruction of Jerusalem in AD 70. This was that 'at midnight . . . the East Gate of the Inner Sanctuary had opened of its own accord'. The date was 8 Nisan, which would be significant in a Christian calendar as Palm Sunday, falling as it does a week before Passover.

Much of the evidence collected by Morgenstern is of this weak or dubious character, but there is substance in some of it. Thus a tradition in the Talmud narrates the refusal and subsequent compliance of the 'Gates of Righteousness' to open at the request of

[1] DSW 10.9–12. The translation is taken from Yadin, pp. 304–6.
[2] *Heaven in the Christian Tradition*, p. 249.
[3] J. Morgenstern, 'The Gates of Righteousness', *HUCA* 6, 1929, pp. 1–37.

Solomon, when he wished to carry the ark into the holy of holies. Solomon chanted Pss. 1–24 (cf. Ps. 24.7) and was 'answered' when he quoted II Chron. 6.42. Morgenstern holds that 'Gates of Righteousness' is probably an ancient name of a gate or gates connected with an important religious ceremony, referring to Pss. 24.3 ff.; 118.19. The Talmud Jerushalmi has a particularly interesting passage: in *'Erubin* 5.22c, R. Jose defines points of the compass and says that east is from where the sun rises on the solstice of Tammuz to where it rises on the solstice of Ṭebet; west is from where it sets on the solstice of Ṭebet to where it sets on the solstice of Tammuz. This makes 'east' and 'west' very extensive. The 'early prophets' are said to have had great difficulty in fashioning the eastern gate so that the sun would 'press upon it' on the day of the solstice of Ṭebet and on the day of the solstice of Tammuz.

In fact, it would be impossible for this to happen on both dates if 'press upon it' is, with Morgenstern, to be interpreted as 'shine directly through', since at the summer solstice the sun would be at its extreme northern, at the winter solstice at its extreme southern point of rising. Morgenstern concludes that the rabbis of the Talmud confused the solstices with the vernal and autumnal equinoxes. This seems hardly necessary: if we take 'press upon it' to mean no more than 'strike it', the difficulty of the original constructors will have been to build the gate so that even at the two extreme points of the sun's rising it would strike some part of the gate. (Were they double doors set at an angle to one another?) Whatever confusion lies behind this passage, it seems part of the tradition associating the gate or gates on the east side of the Temple with the sun.

The Talmud goes on to give seven different names for the gate. One, 'Sun Gate', may be the original reading at Jer. 19.2.

Most striking reference of all is in the Mishnah, at *Sukkah* 5.4, where we read in a most interesting description of the ancient ceremonies in connexion with *Sukkoth* that 'Two priests stood at the upper gate which leads down from the Court of the Israelites to the Court of the Women, with two trumpets in their hands.' At certain points they blew on the trumpets. Then, 'when they reached the gate that leads out to the east, they turned their faces to the west and said, "Our fathers when they were in this place turned with their backs toward the Temple of the Lord and their faces toward the east, and they worshipped the sun toward the east; but as for us, our eyes are turned toward the Lord." ' The recital by the priests quotes Ezek.

8.16 and might be dismissed as based upon that passage alone (but cf. Ezek. 11.1). On the other hand, the whole ceremony seems to demand the sun-worship; and the action of turning to the west for the recital seems to be a deliberate reversal of an ancient custom, the procedure down the steps out of the Temple suggesting a meeting with the sun which is at its climax suddenly and dramatically rejected.[1] It would be reasonable to suppose that Ezekiel and the Mishnah are both based on a custom connected with sun-worship. Such a conclusion makes more natural the presence of the 'horses' dedicated to the sun by kings of Judah in the Temple precinct and destroyed by Josiah (II Kings 23.11). These were no mere *objets d'art* but part of a cult which for centuries had been regarded as natural in a shrine which is usually but mistakenly regarded as sacrosanct to the monotheistic worship of Yahweh with only occasional lapses.

We need not follow Morgenstern in his ingenious attempt to recapture the history of a sun-worshipping ceremony which he believes to have taken place at each equinox. It is enough to profit by his interesting collection of evidence to establish that there was a connexion between the Temple and sun-worship at least until the time of the Exile, and in all probability after the Return, although there appear in the Scriptures only traces of it, amounting to no more than veneration for a place rather than to actual worship of the sun at that place. See, for example, I Esdras 5.47 (Ezra 3.1, otherwise parallel, suppressed the reference to the east) and Josephus, *Ant.* 11.5.5; and note the site of the scene in Neh. 8.1 ff.: 8.3 speaks of a 'broad place in front of the water gate', this gate being identified as an eastern gate by Neh. 3.26 and 12.37, and presumably to be connected with the Temple.

B. THE ESSENES AND THE SUN

Josephus tells us in *BJ* 2.8.5 of a striking feature of the Essene manner of life; this is their respectful attitude to the sun. He says that 'in their piety towards the divine they show a peculiar trait; for before the sun has risen they utter no profane word, but certain traditional prayers towards him, as though beseeching him to rise'. Again, when evacuating, they dig a hole and 'cover themselves with a cloak, to avoid offending the rays of God'.[2] The later evidence of Epiphanius

---

[1] For other passages in which the religious importance of the east gate seems to be half preserved, half forgotten, see Mishnah, *Soṭah* 1.5; *Midd.* 1.3; Talmud, *Pes.* 82a; *RH* 27a.

[2] *Ibid.*, 9.

(*c.* 315–403) is usually mentioned in connexion with this veneration for the sun (it does not amount to sun-worship), but then rejected. There is no reason why it should not at least be seriously considered: for Epiphanius heard while he was in Palestine (he left in 367) of a sect called the Sampsaeans, who included some Essene remnants and who lived in the Dead Sea area. Epiphanius may have been wrong in concluding from their name that they were sun-worshippers, but the word connects them in some way with the sun.[1] That the passage in Josephus means that the Essenes worshipped the sun is very unlikely. Josephus would hardly attribute special piety to Jews who practised such idolatry. Philo in the *De vita contemplativa* (27) describes the Therapeutae, an ascetic sect with Essene affinities, as praying at sunrise for a good day, the real 'good day'—the filling of their mind with heavenly light. The matter is discussed in detail by Abbott,[2] who argues that in Josephus the meaning is that the Essenes (no less than the Therapeutae according to Philo) pray *to God* as though beseeching him to dawn on them. This is good interpretation if not accurate translation. Abbott rightly draws attention to Deut. 23.12–14 as the authority for Essene scruples about covering their excrement, but in Deuteronomy the reason is the presence of the LORD in the camp, and nothing is said about offending his rays. It is clear that the Essenes associated the sun with God and we have seen something of the long and manifold strands of thought which associated God with the sun as an example of light.[3] The scraps of evidence mentioned in the previous section may suggest that the worship of Yahweh at Jerusalem contained elements (originally syncretistic) associated with the sun; it is possible that the Essenes and among them the men of Qumran, voluntary exiles from the Temple whose worship they believed to be corrupt, practised in their desert withdrawal those elements which associated God with light and which they deemed necessary and proper for the continuance of the essentials of that worship.

The association of God with the sun is clearly not idolatrous if it is an association simply with the customary times of prayer. In Mishnah *Ber.* 1.2 we see reflected the notion that the morning recital of the *Shema* should be begun as soon as light permits any vision and should 'be finished until the sun shine forth', which seems to mean

---

[1] *ERE* V, 267b–68a. Not all scholars doubt the accuracy of Epiphanius on historical matters. See Black, *The Scrolls and Christian Origins*, pp. 66 ff.

[2] E. A. Abbott, *Notes on New Testament Criticism*, pp. 188–92. See also pp. 239 f.

[3] See p. 40.

that the end should coincide with the appearance of the sun's rays. The Talmud affords passages of similar import. In later Judaism therefore there is no sense of embarrassment at the association of God and sun. The latter is the most splendid example of God's creation, indeed of his creation of light, although the Genesis story distinguishes the creation of light in general from that of the luminaries. It is not fanciful to suggest that the Essenes worshipped God before sunrise as a recalling of his creation: each day repeats the creative act which began the orderly sequence of the ages. Moreover, with the sun God created the determiner of the times and seasons, the divisions of the calendar by which conduct and worship were to be regulated on the annual as well as on the daily scale. See 1QS 10.1 ff. for the sun's regulation of daily liturgical practice in a manner like that of the rest of Judaism.

There is yet another feature of the sect which, especially if they were Essenes, may be connected with the order's marked respect for the sun: this is their self-designation as 'sons of light'.

C. 'SONS OF LIGHT'

In the Priestly account of creation the first creature is light. In previous accounts, as in the pre-philosophical thinking of ancient Babylon and in the proto-philosophical thought of Miletus, all creation derives from a previous existent, chaos, water, the 'undifferentiated' (the ἄπειρον of Anaximander). To say that in Hesiod 'the chaotic darkness vanished before the bright light of day'[1] is misleading, for in Hesiod the thought is still entirely mythical: day is born along with Aither from night who conceives by intercourse with Erebus.[2] The creation of light in Gen. 1 is not only by divine word but significantly separate from the 'evolutionary' order in the chapter, an order which may be expressed as follows:

1. Primeval waters divided by firmament into upper and lower (6–8).
2. Lower waters 'gathered' to allow dry land to appear (9–13).
3. Water and air creatures (20–23).
4. Earth creatures (24–25).

Light is created first of all (4–5) and the creation of the heavenly bodies interupts the above 'evolutionary' scheme. They are evidently

[1] C. F. Whitley in *The Listener*, 15 March 1962.
[2] Hesiod, *Theogony*, 116 (Kirk and Raven, *The Presocratic Philosophers*, no. 24, p 24).

connected with the light already created, and this explains why they are called the 'greater light' and the 'lesser light' instead of sun and moon,[1] which would have brought them into a scheme like that of Anaximander of Miletus, according to whom the earth, air, planets, sun, moon and stars are all differentiated out of the original ἄπειρον. The sun is therefore according to the Priestly school a special creation, the 'greater light'.

It hardly needs mention that the creation of man (26 ff.) is a special act of God, and also lies outside the 'evolutionary' scheme. Man is made in the image of God: the 'greater' and 'lesser' lights may be said to be images of Light. The inspired author of Gen. 1 entertained two parallel lines of thought which he interwove when he wrote about creation: God—Light (from which are derived the 'lights' or 'luminaries')—Man; and, Chaos—Heaven and Earth—Creatures. There is no evidence that God was identified with the sun: rather, the key to the relation of God, sun and man is to be found by way of the interpretation given by the Second Isaiah to a creation doctrine evidently similar to that ultimately expressed in Gen. 1. The passage is Isa. 42.5–43.10, since about the first century the *Haphtarah* of Gen. 1.1–6.8. In it Israel is addressed in a manner which the Qumran sect took deeply to heart, communing as they did so devoutly with the text of Isaiah. In 42.6 the writer causes Yahweh to say, 'I am Yahweh. I have called thee in righteousness and taken thee by thy hand, and I have kept thee; and I have given thee to be a covenant of the people and a light for the nations.' The sun was a light for the earth, Israel for mankind. Yahweh created both. It was therefore natural that those who believed themselves chosen to renew the Israel specially called by God should regard entrance upon membership of their sect as entrance into the covenant, should venerate the 'greater light' and should designate themselves 'sons of light'. (For references see commentary on 1.9.)

6. THE QUMRAN CALENDAR

A. THE SOLAR CALENDAR

The manifest importance of the sun in regulating the seasons, as well as more particularly the agricultural festivals which take their

---

[1] 'The stars also' at the end of Gen. 1.16 is a very obvious afterthought and may be the addition of a subsequent editor. It will be noticed how it breaks the logical sequence and contributes nothing to the thought of vv. 14–19.

character from the seasons, was acknowledged by the Egyptians in their acceptance of a solar calendar. This seems natural to us who regulate our year by the sun and whose months are constructed to make up 365 days and do not correspond at all with the lunar months. We should not be surprised therefore to find evidence that in ancient Israel a solar calendar at one time threatened to rival the lunar. The primary evidence for this solar calendar is not in the Bible but in *Jubilees*, and in part of *I Enoch*; to this evidence we must now turn.

It is widely recognized that *I Enoch* is composite, R. H. Charles having divided it and assigned dates to it as follows:

Chapters	Date
1–5	?
6–11	From a lost *Book of Noah*, to which also belong 54–55.2, 60, 65–69.25, 106–7
12–36	Pre-Maccabaean
37–71	105–64 BC
72–82	Before 110 BC
83–90	165–161 BC
93.1–10 91.12–17 }	Pre-Maccabaean
91–104	105–64 BC

Some of Charles's dates may need radical alteration in view of evidence from Qumran; but his belief that the book is composite seems as reasonable as ever. In any case, it is unnecessary to discuss the book in detail. Reference may be made to the bibliography. Our concern is with chs. 72–82, which Charles calls the 'Book of the Heavenly Luminaries'. It is, in fact, an astronomical treatise in which the behaviour of the sun and of the moon is carefully described. There are six portals in the east and six in the west, replacing the heathen signs of the zodiac. The sun 'rises in the first month in the great portal, which is the fourth' (72.6). As the description proceeds it becomes clear that this is at the spring equinox. The sun enters the sixth portal at the summer solstice and returns to the fourth for the autumnal equinox. Entry into the first portal marks the winter solstice. The author declares the number of days during which the sun rises from a numbered portal and sets in the portal which corresponds in the west. These are clearly his months, and as clearly determined by the sun rather than by the moon. The year thus marked out by the sun as described in *I Enoch* 72 can be set out thus:

Month	Portal	Number of Days
1	4	30
2	5	30
3	6	31
		('on account of its sign', i.e. an extra day for the summer solstice)
4	6	30
5	5	30
6	4	31
		('on account of its sign', i.e. an extra day for the autumnal equinox)
7	3	30
8	2	30
9	1	31
		(winter solstice)
10	1	30
11	2	30
12	3	31
		(spring equinox)

'The book of the Heavenly Luminaries' (*I Enoch* 72–82) then goes on to describe the behaviour of the moon, but great care is taken to show clearly the superiority of the sun and stars as a foundation for the calendar; in five years 'the moon falls behind the sun and stars to the number of thirty days. And the sun and the stars bring in all the years exactly, so that they do not advance or delay their position by a single day unto eternity; but complete the years with perfect justice in 364 days' (*I Enoch* 74.11 f.).

Whether *I Enoch* 72–82 was known to the author of *Jubilees* or not, its astronomy formed the basis of the calendar which *Jubilees* is concerned vigorously to commend. This book was written in the late Hasmonaean period, about the year 110 BC, and is in effect a rewriting of Genesis under the influence of the conviction that the pattern not only of each year but of cycles of years—jubilee cycles of forty-nine years—is of divine ordination and that the events within these spans of time are divinely caused, and made to conform to a time schedule which God has revealed to his chosen. The book is therefore concerned with history and chronology, and its teaching on the calendar is a subordinate part of the latter; but we are concerned here with the calendar, and with the emphatic reference to it in *Jub.* 6.32–38, especially v. 32: there Moses, after being told of God's covenant with Noah, which enjoins keeping the festivals known to later generations, is ordered, 'Command thou the children of Israel that they observe the years according to this reckoning—three hundred and sixty-four days, and these will constitute a complete year, and they will not disturb its time from its days and from its feasts; for everything will fall out in them according to their testimony, and they will not leave out any day nor disturb any feasts.' This verse and the rest of the passage (vv. 33–38) show very clearly both the connexion in the author's mind between calendar and history and also his deep concern that divinely ordained festivals should be kept exactly on the days which God decreed for them. The specific mention of 364 days is sufficient evidence that the calendar is solar, a fact for which *Jub.* 2.9 could indeed have prepared us: 'And God appointed the sun to be a great sign on the earth for days and for sabbaths and for months and for feasts and for years and for sabbaths of years and for jubilees and for all seasons of the years.' This is a very significant rewriting of Gen. 1.14–18: the moon has been quietly dropped. That this is controversial the author knows well. At 6.36 he writes, 'For there will be those who will assuredly make observations of the moon—now it disturbs the seasons and comes in from year to year ten days too soon.'[1]

The author, then, insists upon a solar year of 364 days as superior to the lunar year of 354 days. The interest in liturgy and indeed in chronology is consciously served by a year of 364 days which divides exactly into fifty-two weeks so that each feast falls every year on the same day of the week. Each month consists of thirty days, and bears no name but only a number. In order to co-ordinate the months with the days, every three months a day is intercalated, the result being the calendar already found in *I Enoch* 72–82; ninety-one days or thirteen

[1] The translation is that of R. H. Charles, *The Book of Jubilees*, p. 58. (In *AP* II, p. 23, 'how' takes the place of 'now'.) Charles's note in *Jubilees* makes clear that 'Our author is decidedly opposed to the use of the moon in determining the seasons and feasts.' Jaubert translates, 'ceux qui fondent leurs observations sur la lune—laquelle dérange les saisons et arrive d'année en année dix jours trop tôt' (A. Jaubert, *La date de la Cène*, p. 156).

weeks make a quarter or season and the months can be set out thus:

Months:															
		I, IV, VII, X				II, V, VIII, XI					III, VI, IX, XII			
Wednesday	1	8	15	22	29		6	13	20	27		4	11	18	25
Thursday	2	9	16	23	30		7	14	21	28		5	12	19	26
Friday	3	10	17	24		1	8	15	22	29		6	13	20	27
Saturday	4	11	18	25		2	9	16	23	30		7	14	21	28
Sunday	5	12	19	26		3	10	17	24		1	8	15	22	29
Monday	6	13	20	27		4	11	18	25		2	9	16	23	30
Tuesday	7	14	21	28		5	12	19	26		3	10	17	24	31

The intercalary days are called days of the seasons (*Jub.* 6.23–28; cf. *I Enoch* 72.13–32; 82.10–18). The seasons are named at *Jub.* 2.2 winter, spring and autumn, summer (the order is accidental), but at 29.16 an interesting reference to the calendar occurs when the seasons are named. Jacob is said to have sent presents 'to his mother Rebecca also four times a year, between the times of the months, between ploughing and reaping, and between autumn and the rain, and between winter and spring' (29.15 f.). Charles refers approvingly to Rönsch's conjecture that here we have four dates, the first of the fourth month, the first of the seventh, the first of the tenth, and the first of the first. This seems correct, as also the further conjecture that the dates are minor festivals attributed to Noah's inauguration at *Jub.* 6.23: 'And on the new moon of the first month, and on the new moon of the fourth month, and on the new moon of the seventh month, and on the new moon of the tenth month are the days of remembrance, and the days of the seasons in the four divisions of the year.'

This apparent—and unexpected—respect for the moon can be easily explained: 'new moon' means no more than 'first day', a curious verbal influence from the very lunar calendar which is being rejected; and the phrase 'the days of the seasons in the four divisions of the year' obviously refers to the intercalary days. A further licence must then be allowed the author to that which enables him to describe the first of a month in a solar year as a 'new moon': this is his treatment of these intercalary days—which have been numbered in the table above as 31 in the third, sixth, ninth and twelfth months—as the first days of the following months. Neither enumeration is correct: they do not belong to any months but only to the weeks and to the seasons; the phrase 'the days of the seasons in the four divisions of the year' is, on the other hand, quite accurate, and 'between the times of the months' may well mean 'on the days between the months'—technically put, on the intercalary days.

It must be admitted that the calendar of *I Enoch* 72–82 and of *Jubilees* which we have been describing, though based with such fervour upon the sun, did not wholly consist with the sun's year. The respect for equinoxes and solstices suggests that the author of *Jubilees* or at any rate any who actually used the calendar must have noticed in due course the failure of these milestones in the year to coincide with the intercalary days which are supposed to accommodate them. At the end of a jubilee (forty-nine years) the deficiency between the calendrical and the astronomical year would amount to 49 times $1\frac{1}{4}$ days, that is $61\frac{1}{4}$ days. By this time the correlation of festivals with seasons would be completely upset. How this deficiency was repaired—or forestalled—is not known for certain and *Jub.* 6.31 ff. suggests a deliberate intransigence over this problem. Testuz discusses this difficulty,[1] his more probable suggestion being that a means of correction was based on the fact that after four lots of seven years, that is after twenty-eight years, the discrepancy would amount to thirty-five days. Seven days would be added after each seven years in any case to mark the sabbatical year of 'release' (Deut. 15.1, 9; Lev. 25.1–4). These may well have been regarded as no infringement of *Jub.* 6.31 ff.'s urgent commandment not to change the calendar in any particular, since they occur between and not in the years. Now, after each twenty-eight years the addition of another seven days (that is, at this point fourteen days in all) would mean the addition of the necessary thirty-five days over the entire period of twenty-eight years.

As Testuz is aware, *Jub.* 7.37 appears to contradict this theory with its unexpected injunction to carry out the 'release' in the fifth year; but Charles's argument that at 7.37 there is a lacuna in the text is very persuasive: the author appears to be following from v. 36 the text of Lev. 19.23 ff., and in the fifth year we should have expected the fruit—left ungathered for three years and offered as firstfruits on the fourth—to be announced as free to be eaten. There will then be no need to suppose that *Jubilees* made the fifth year its sabbatical year, an arrangement in any case most inappropriate for a book with such great respect for the sabbath and jubilee concepts.

---

[1] M. Testuz, *Les Idées religieuses du livre des jubilés*, pp. 126 ff.

B. THE ORIGIN OF THE CALENDAR

Jub. 4.17 credits Enoch with being 'the first among men that are born on earth who learnt writing and knowledge and wisdom and who wrote down the signs of heaven according to the order of their months in a book, that men might know the seasons of the years according to the order of their separate months'. According to 4.21 he was taught by angels everything including 'the rule of the sun'.[1] The angels are closely related to the stars and are sometimes identified with them (cf. Job. 38.7). Enoch revealed this secret knowledge to his son Methuselah and from him the tradition passed to his son Lamech and from Lamech to Noah. So much we can learn from *Jub.* 7.38, but this passage raises the question of the authorities used by the author.

At 7.26 *Jubilees* suddenly introduces a passage in the first person. Noah is clearly the speaker, and his direct speech continues to the end of v. 39. It is reasonable to suppose that the author culled the passage from a lost *Book of Noah*, to which Charles would assign also 10.1–15. Charles further maintained that the author knew certain parts of *I Enoch*. We have seen that this book is composite;[2] and it is probable that careful study would reveal that the parts known to the author of *Jubilees* were known to him as separate works, being not yet combined into *Enoch* as we know it today. Testuz, who holds this view, lists the passages which refer to other works: Enoch's writings, 4.16 f.; Noah's writings, 10.13; at 21.10 the 'words of Enoch' and the 'words of Noah' are referred to along with 'books of my ancestors' by Abraham, in a passage (ch. 21) whose close affinity to *Test. Levi* 9 Charles demonstrates; again, in 45.16 the dying Israel (Jacob) gives all his books and those of his fathers to his son Levi.

The tradition therefore concerning the calendar and related matters is consistent with the sense of its resting upon divine authority; for it belongs to the ancient divinely bestowed wisdom of the patriarchs. Behind these positive views lies the strong negative attitude of rejecting the pagan Hellenistic world.

Charles ascribed *I Enoch* 6–11 to the *Book of Noah*. This section contains a passage (6–8) which describes the activity on earth of the fallen angels more briefly narrated in Gen. 6.1–4 and *Jub.* 5.1 ff. In *I Enoch* 8 some of these wicked angels teach men astrology, the constellations, the knowledge of the clouds, the signs of the earth, the signs of the sun (all these probably connected with divination and

---

[1] For the importance of Enoch see pp. 20, 66 ff.
[2] See p. 81 above.

augury) and 'the course of the moon', suggesting a more sober instruction on which a calendar could be based. *Jub.* 6.34 ff. ascribed the lunar calendar to Gentile influence, and we may suspect that the hostility both in the *Book of Noah* (i.e. *I Enoch* 6–8) and in *Jubilees* is due to its introduction by the Seleucid rulers, for in Dan. 7.25 Antiochus Epiphanes 'shall think to change the times'. Thus in the literature which we have been considering good angels teach Enoch the solar calendar while the lunar calendar (which prevailed in rabbinic Judaism) is ascribed to the evil influence of fallen angels and its introduction into Palestine to pagan influence.

Although the lunar calendar was open to objection on account of the variability of the moon (a point emphasized by *Jubilees* and *I Enoch*), it may well be that its introduction by the Seleucids was also a main cause of its rejection, even though the date of its introduction appears, on the authority of Al-Biruni, an Arab scholar of the tenth century, to be no earlier than 112–111 BC. The high priests kept the method of calculation secret. Inherited from the Hellenic world, this method of calculation probably derived ultimately from Babylon, from the Chaldaeans as the Greeks called them; for the Babylonian priest Berosus had written his Βαβυλωνιακά at the beginning of the third century BC.[1] Again, a Babylonian named Kidinnu is quoted by Hipparchus of Nicaea (180–125 BC). The Greeks themselves were as astronomers more interested in the sun; the Pythagorean school and others had calculated the solar year already by the fourth century BC. Thus, in fact, it is probable that the solar calendar of *Jubilees*, *I Enoch* and Qumran derived from Greek sources no less than that the rejected lunar calendar was transmitted by them.

These are more likely to be the historical facts, but the scholars who reasserted the solar calendar in the period with which we are concerned clearly claimed to be not reasserting but preserving a calendar which was not only more ancient but which had been positively laid down by divine ordinance from the beginning of time.

Possibly there was a primitive solar calendar known to the Hebrews which regulated the liturgical year by the observance of equinoxes and solstices, a calendar in part superimposed upon an even older lunar calendar. When a school of thought within the Judaism of a more sophisticated age wished to reassert the solar calendar, it did

---

[1] Vitruvius tells us that Berosus, a priest of Bel (or Marduk; cf. Isa. 46.1: Jer. 50.2; 51.44) migrated to Cos at that time and lectured on Babylonian science. See S. Toulmin and J. Goodfield, *The Fabric of the Heavens*, p. 45.

so in a far more elaborate and thorough fashion than by insisting on the mere observance of equinoxes and solstices; it borrowed from the Greek world for its necessary scientific knowledge, but at the same time contrived to absorb this knowledge within the scheme of divine revelation and represented it as part of the Law delivered to Moses. This school of thought went further: the new knowledge was even older than Moses. Thus taught, for example, the author of *Jubilees*, while the author of *I Enoch* curiously identifies himself with the patriarch and so assumes for his astronomy an unassailable authority.

Passages in *Jubilees* and passages in the Scrolls, including the *Rule* (10, 5 ff.) are so emphatic against alteration of the calendar in any particular that one is more and more confirmed in the belief that the authors of all these passages saw in the calendar which they were recommending a transcript of the fabric and mechanics of the universe, a *logos* according to which God commanded all to walk who undertook to 'do the truth' (see 1QS 1.5). It was not only even that the Torah enjoined it, but that the very secrets of the universe were involved in it. Testuz argues[1] that a Pythagorean view of the construction of the universe lies at the heart of the whole system of worship in which the calendar finds its place and which it regulates. It is well known that Pythagoras and his school in Sicily (sixth to fifth century BC) were so impressed by the relation of quantity to quality, illustrated by that between the length of a string and the sound emitted when it was vibrated, that they believed that the relations between numbers would alone provide the key to the nature of things. Thus the philosopher could attain to perfect knowledge through mathematics. How much this view of the universe influenced Plato can be seen in the *Republic* and in the concept in the *Timaeus* which held that the λόγος (the ground of being) and the δημιουργία (the principle of manufacture) of the elements were triangular (*Timaeus* 53 c ff.). In an earlier passage in the *Timaeus* (47 a ff.) Plato expresses from a philosophical point of view what the author of *Jubilees* felt with religious passion: 'Sight in my opinion has been the cause of the greatest advantage to us, for not one of the words now being spoken about the universe would ever have been uttered without men having seen either stars or sun or heaven. But as it is, day and night by being seen, and with them months and cycles of years and equinoxes and solstices, have not only both wrought the system of the conception of time, but also given an impulse to the quest for the nature of the universe' (*Timaeus* 47 a).

[1] *Op. cit.*, pp. 134 ff.

Even the numbers dear to the author of *Jubilees* seem to have a Pythagorean origin, if we may trust the evidence of Philo (*De specialibus legibus* 2.177). The right-angled triangle, whose sides a, b and c (c being the hypotenuse) are related to one another by the formula $a^2 + b^2 = c^2$, was taken to illustrate the relation of 3, 4 and 5, for $3^2 + 4^2 = 5^2$. $3 + 4 + 5 = 12$, the number of the zodiacal signs; but $3^2 + 4^2 + 5^2 = 50$, a number which Philo regards as particularly holy (*De vita contemplativa* 65), because of its being made up by the potentiality of the right-angled triangle, which is the principle of the generation of the universe.

The part played by the numbers 3 (months in a quarter), 4 (the quarters or seasons), 12 (the months in the year, the product of 3×4), 7 (days in each week, years in a 'week' of years, the sum of $3 + 4$) and 49 (7×7), a jubilee period of years, is manifest.

The date of the final composition of *Jubilees* is put by Schürer, Charles and Testuz at near 110 BC (by Charles at 109–105), a period when hatred of the Gentiles was embittered by the knowledge of unpatriotic and irreligious assimilation by many Judaeans to the Hellenism of the Seleucids, a tendency which had been temporarily checked by early Maccabaean successes, but which the later kings of their line themselves exhibited. There can be little doubt that the patriotic and rigidly orthodox author of *Jubilees* demanded the supersession of the lunar calendar learnt from the hated Seleucid Hellenism by a calendar which he claimed was in accordance with divine revelation through the creation. No doubt quite unaware that this calendar also was tainted with Greek origins, he gave the story of its origin a typically Judaean character: the secret had been imparted by an angel to a patriarch (Enoch) and was now revealed again by an angel to Moses. His calendar's correspondence with the fabric of the universe is secondary in importance to its authority as divinely revealed; but this correspondence is very important: to alter it in any particular would throw the entire pattern of the devout and worshipping life into disharmony with the Creator.

An account of the *I Enoch* and *Jubilees* calendar has already been given[1] and the tradition associated with it has been described. The following sections will suggest that the solar calendar was connected with the priestly tradition in Judaism, and that when the men of Qumran took over and sought to preserve this tradition they took with them the idea of a solar calendar, since the contemporary priests

[1] See p. 80 above.

of Jerusalem, no longer like the sect entitled to call themselves 'sons of Zadok', had been in the sect's eyes corrupted by (among other causes) the acceptance of the lunar calendar of the Seleucid kings.

C.   THE CALENDAR AND THE PENTATEUCH

Students of the Old Testament are familiar with the study of the strata of different dates which attentive reading of the Pentateuch provokes. Whatever modifications may be urged of the original Graf-Wellhausen theory which divided the Pentateuch into four main strata (J, E, D and P), P, the priestly recension which seems finally to have constituted the Pentateuch as we know it, seems a reality. Jaubert[1] shows that the dates of the Hexateuch which are expressed in numbers of days and of months, as well as agreeing with the *Jubilees* calendar for liturgical days, and in a preference for the first day of a month and a respect for the sabbath rest, show a remarkable preference for Friday as the end of a journey (preparatory for the sabbath) and for Wednesday for the beginnings of important periods or enterprises. Wednesday is the first day of the *Jubilees* calendar; it begins the year and therefore not only the first month but also the important fourth, seventh and tenth months.[2] Similar affinities can be shown with Chronicles, Ezra-Nehemiah and Ezekiel. The Chronicler is a faithful disciple of the priestly school, Ezekiel can be claimed as one of their chief inspirers. All these thinkers have a Babylonian background in common; a case therefore appears for regarding Babylon in the time of the Exile as the origin for Judaism of the solar calendar. Such a conclusion would be surprising, since we have already seen that the orthodox Jewish calendar appears to have derived from Babylon, also at the time of the Exile.

It would indeed be a superficial judgment to conclude that the tradition represented by Ezekiel and the priestly recension of the Pentateuch (and other associated literature) derived from Babylon. The names of the months with which the lunar calendar is associated are known to have arisen from that source, but the rival solar system comes from elements deliberately preserving ancient customs with religious zeal, probably in opposition to Babylonian influence. Ezekiel's imagery was no doubt largely that of his Babylonian environment, but in some important matters he was ultra-conservative, and may well have preserved his native traditions against those of the country of his exile.

[1] *La date de la Cène*, pp. 32 ff.   [2] Cf. p. 84.

D. THE TEMPLE AND THE PRIESTHOOD

Ezekiel's conservatism could not be better illustrated than by his attitude to the Temple and to its priesthood. In chs. 40–48 he describes the ideal Temple as it is to be restored in the future; and an essential part of its restored character is a priesthood with high status.

Ezekiel's conception of the priesthood is important for our understanding of the Qumran covenanters' idea of their own sect, and it is necessary to sketch the history behind it. Solomon appointed Zadok as his priest immediately after his accession, and the family thus began its very long history as custodians of the royal sanctuary, ended in 171 BC by the murder of Onias III (II Macc. 4.34). Until then the family succeeded in surviving many vagaries of history, but were sometimes threatened with rivals in the administration of the sanctuary. Thus in 621 BC Josiah's reforms resulted in the unemployment of many priests of local high places. Deuteronomy, identifying priests with Levites, envisages the re-employment of these local priests at Jerusalem (Deut. 18.6–8), but II Kings 23.9 tells us that this was not put into practice. The local priests therefore found themselves in an economic plight, and no doubt some managed by begging eventually to obtain a place at Jerusalem (cf. I Sam. 2.36). In any case, the assistants of the Zadokite family no less than the Zadokites themselves are regarded by D as Levites. Ezekiel is opposed to this assimilation: the plight of the country priests is a divine punishment for their 'going astray' from the central sanctuary (whose character as the only place where the LORD might be worshipped he unhistorically assumes to antedate the local high places) and the Levites must 'bear' the punishment of 'their iniquity'; the sons of Zadok, alone worthy to be called 'the priests of the Levites', who kept charge of the sanctuary when the mere Levites went astray, are the only men qualified to officiate at Jerusalem, while the Levites are to perform menial tasks (Ezek. 44.9–16; 48.11).

The Priestly Code is less drastic. It opens the priesthood not merely to the sons of Zadok but to Aaron and his sons (Ex. 28.1, etc.). This is a wider category, but authors in the same tradition allotted the office of the chief priest (later called 'high priest') to first-born sons of Zadok. Writing as late as *c.* 180 BC the author of Ecclesiasticus shows special respect for the sons of Zadok. For him, after Moses and Aaron, Phinehas son of Eleazar 'is the third in glory' (Ecclus. 45.23 f.)—a position won by his zeal in the incident described in

Num. 25.6–13—and to his line is granted the priesthood for ever.
The Hebrew of Ecclus. 45.24 says 'high priesthood', and at 50.24
the divine promise to Simon is called 'the covenant of Phinehas', a
reference to 'the covenant of an everlasting priesthood' of Num. 25.13.
Phinehas is a son of Eleazar and grandson of Aaron, and from the
Eleazar line Zadok is descended (Num. 25.7 and I Chron. 24.3).
P knows of another branch of Aaron's descendants, through Aaron's
son Ithamar. The Chronicler is apparently aware of the lesser
importance of this branch.

No doubt the historical Zadok was a priest of an ancient Jerusalem
shrine adopted by David when he conquered the city; the genealogies
of P and the Chronicler are pious inventions and neither their rami-
fications nor the motives which inspired them need detain us. More
important are the beliefs of the priestly editors and the Chronicler,
for these had an important influence on the sect whose ideas we are
seeking to understand.

The Chronicler raised immensely the status of the Levites, giving
them important parts in his idealized history by inventing stories
about them and compiling lists of their names. His work belongs to
the period about 200 BC and his importance for our purpose is the
evidence he affords for the high regard in which the priesthood and
the Levites were held in some quarters in the years immediately
before those which saw the rise of those forms of Judaism which
include the sect of Qumran.

The *Rule* provides evidence for believing that the sect thought of
itself as representing the sons of Zadok[1] and containing within itself
priests and Levites with liturgical functions to perform.[2] These
functions are connected with the duties assigned to Levites in
Deuteronomy, where 'the priests the Levites' are to prescribe the Law
(17.9–13), evidently to preserve a copy of it in its new (Deuteronomic)
form (17.18; cf. 31.25 f.), and to read it before a solemn assembly
every seventh year at the Feast of Tabernacles (31.9–13).[3] Again,
the Levites pronounce the ceremonial curses on Mount Ebal
(27.14 ff.).[4]

A fragment found in Cave 4 which has been entitled *The Book of
the Priestly Courses* furnishes further evidence that the men of Qumran
followed the calendar of *I Enoch* 72–82 and *Jubilees*. This fragment is

---

[1] 5.2, 9; cf. CD 4.2–4; IQ Sa 1.2, 24; 2.3.
[2] E.g. IQS 1.21; 2.2, 5, 11, 20.
[3] Cf. IQS 1.21 f.
[4] Cf. IQS 2.5–18.

evidence also for the priestly interests of the sect: it shows that they organized a rota of priests like the list of those who officiated at the Temple in Jerusalem. I Chron. 24.1–19 gives the list of twenty-four 'courses' or divisions (διαιρέσεις) who supplied priests from their numbers to perform the daily duties of worship in the Temple. Each course served for a week (Mishnah, *Sukkah* 5.8; *Tamid* 5.1) so that in a normal year of twelve lunar months or forty-eight weeks each course would be on duty twice. Zacharias, the father of John the Baptist, being a name found often among Levites in I Chronicles and a member of the course of Abijah (I Chron. 24.10), learnt from Gabriel of the coming birth of his son when he was on such service (Luke 1.5 ff.).

The sect appointed twenty-six courses instead of twenty-four; this is known from the *War Scroll* 2.1 f. From this passage and from the *Book of the Priestly Courses* the calendar of the sect has been worked out by Talmon,[1] and his results agree with Mlle Jaubert's presentation of the solar calendar already described.

Talmon's argument may be summarized as follows. DSW 2.1 f. makes quite clear that the sect divided the cycle of priestly duty into twenty-six courses. Thus each course served one week in each half-year of a year containing fifty-two weeks, entering upon a week of duty twice in a year.

The table of the *Book of the Priestly Courses* is headed, 'The First Year, its appointed days', implying that the time-table was different for at least some of the years. Indeed, the courses both in the Temple and at Qumran may have been changed by progressive rotation.

The list of courses in the fragment is parallel to that given in I Chron. 24.7–18, and no name occurs in the *Book of the Priestly Courses* which does not appear also in I Chronicles; but Maaziah, the twenty-fourth in I Chronicles, is the first, Jehoiarib, first in I Chronicles, is the second in the *Book*. Maaziah and Jedaiah enter on their second spell of duty twenty-three weeks after their first. We may presume this to be the case for all. In a twenty-six-week cycle we should have expected it would have been after twenty-five weeks. The sect evidently accepted the list in I Chronicles and added two courses which served between them four periods in a year. They thus adapted the traditional list to their calendar as it is implied in the *War Scroll*.

[1] S. Talmon, 'The Calendar Reckoning of the Sect from the Judaean Desert' in *SH* IV, pp. 162 ff.

The order of the courses can be restored partly by the fragmentary evidence of the *Book of the Priestly Courses* and partly by comparison with the list in I Chron. 24.7–18; but it is possible also to allot the place of each course in the calendar year, for the *Book of the Priestly Courses* gives us hints connected with important days in the calendar; for example, the Passover (I.14) is the third day of Maaziah, the last day of Passover (I.21) is the third day of Jehoiarib, and the waving of the Omer (I.26)[1] is the first day of Jedaiah.

A calendar constructed to include these assignments leaves no names to allot to the four weeks XII.29–I.4, I.5–11, XII.15–21, XII.22–28, when no festivals occurred, and the *Book of the Priestly Courses* is too fragmentary to supply them; the calendar has to be reconstructed with two anonymous courses opening the year (beginning for this purpose XII.29) and closing it.

Talmon draws the following conclusions: the sect were like the Sadducees, Boethusians and Samaritans in regarding 'the morrow after the sabbath' of Lev. 23.15 as the first day of the week,[2] but unlike them in that they began counting on the first Sunday after Unleavened Bread; further, since the waving of the Omer fell on a Sunday and on the first day of Jedaiah, we may conclude that each course's week began on a Sunday. Again, the Feast of Weeks (or Pentecost),[3] fifty days later (III.15), also falls on the first day of the week. The *Book of the Priestly Courses* has a clear statement, 'On the first in Jeshua, the Feast of Weeks.' The number of courses between this point and the first of Jedaiah (when, as we saw, the counting began) gives us exactly the fifty days required.

We may conclude from all these pieces of evidence that a calendar constructed to incorporate all the regulations implied by the *Book of the Priestly Courses* is identical with that of *I Enoch* 72–82 and of *Jubilees*, the solar calendar set out fully by Jaubert and explained on pp. 80–85; that the sect at Qumran not only preserved the functions of priests and Levites but also regulated them and their liturgy by this solar calendar; that, while the form of the calendar which they used was more modern than they would have admitted, by their use of *a* solar calendar they may well have been preserving a very ancient tradition connected with the Temple and the Zadokite priesthood.

The connexion of the sect with the Temple and its priesthood is

[1] For I.26 as the sect's date of the waving of the Omer and the beginning of the counting of the Omer see p. 97.

[2] See p. 96.

[3] See p. 95.

twofold: the sect arises historically from a desire to replace both the defiled Temple and the defiled priesthood, and the conception of its organization[1] derives directly from that of the priests organized for Temple duty. Maier stresses at several points that the 'union' (*Einung*, translating *yachad*) which is one of the self-designations of the sect and its priestly organization reflect the current form of association of the priests serving the sanctuary of the Temple. If the whole sect represents the Temple, the laity represent the sanctuary and the priests of the sect the holy of holies. Further, the priests believed themselves to serve among the angels; and this fellowship with the heavenly company helped to explain the divine character of the knowledge of cosmos and calendar which they held and which ruled their practice, a practice shared with the angels (see esp. 1QH 3.22; 11.11). The association of angels with priests arises from the conviction that the priests are like the angels of the presence in serving 'before God'.[2] Maier does not quote the instance of Gabriel and Zacharias in Luke 1.8–20: both serve 'before God', Zacharias (v. 8) ἔναντι τοῦ θεοῦ and Gabriel (v. 19) ἐνώπιον τοῦ θεοῦ.

E. THE FEAST OF WEEKS

The *Rule* as we now possess it opens with a passage giving the substance of the promises made by those who entered the covenant, that is, those assuming membership of the sect, and follows it with liturgical directions for the ceremony at which these promises are made. In order to understand this we must briefly review the history of the practice of the renewal of the covenant in Israel at a solemn festival.

If we are right to see embedded in the book of Exodus at 22.29b–30; 23.12, 15–19 a primitive decalogue, one of the earliest injunctions accepted by the Israelites was that to keep three feasts in the year (Ex. 23.14) of which one was to be 'the feast of harvest, the first fruits of thy labours' (23.16). In a later form of this still primitive decalogue this feast is called 'the feast of weeks' (Ex. 34.22). Deuteronomy, after the injunctions concerning the Passover (16.1–8), orders 'Seven weeks shalt thou number unto thee: from the time thou beginnest to put the sickle to the standing corn shalt thou begin to number seven weeks. And thou shalt keep the feast of weeks . . .' (16.9 f.).

The later code of Leviticus (see 23.10–21) introduces the ceremony of waving the first sheaf cut on the day which marks the

---

[1] See p. 69.   [2] Maier, I, p. 16, and II, pp. 10–11.

beginning of the 'numbering' mentioned by Deuteronomy. The RSV of Lev. 23.15 f. will give clearly a passage which gave rise to much controversy: 'And you shall count from the morrow after the sabbath, from the day that you brought the sheaf of the wave offering; seven full weeks shall they be, counting fifty days to the morrow after the seventh sabbath.'

That the feast fell on the fiftieth day was clear: indeed, it came later to be called the day of the fiftieth (the Greek for fiftieth is Pentecost) as in Tobit 2.1; II Macc. 12.32; Acts 2.1, 20.16; I Cor. 16.8. Disagreement arose when the question was asked: Fiftieth day from when? Certainly, 'from the morrow after the sabbath' according to Lev. 23.15, but a long and bitter dispute raged between the Sadducees and Pharisees as to which day was meant by this phrase. The Mishnah tractate *Menachoth* 10.3 reflects this dispute, eventually won by the Pharisees. In that passage the Boethusians are the Sadducees.

The counting began from a day connected with the Feast of Passover and Unleavened Bread. The Pharisees interpreted sabbath to mean the first day of Unleavened Bread, i.e. 15 Nisan by the normal lunar calendar. The counting therefore began on 16 Nisan and Weeks, or Pentecost, fell on 6 Sivan. The LXX at Lev. 23.11 supports this method of calculation by calling the day at which counting started 'the morrow of the first'. The Targums Jerushalmi and Onkelos, as well as Philo and Josephus, testify to the ultimate victory of this Pharisaic conception before it was recorded in the Mishnah.

An alternative way of counting was that of the Sadducees (or Boethusians), the Samaritans and the later Qaraites. This took the 'sabbath' in the sense of the seventh day of the week and as that which fell within the seven days of Unleavened Bread. Counting would thus start from the day after the sabbath after Passover. The LXX of Lev. 23.15 might be taken to support this with its phrase 'the morrow of the sabbath', inconsistently with the rendering at v. 11. Pentecost would thus fall on a different day each year.

A curious variant by which the sabbath was taken as the seventh day of Unleavened Bread, i.e. 21 Nisan, and counting began on 22 Nisan has been preserved by the Ethiopian Falashas.

We are more concerned with yet a fourth method of counting, found in *Jubilees* and based upon the solar calendar of that book. *Jub.* 6.16 f. most interestingly sees the original covenant as that between God and Noah, whose sign was the rainbow, and continues, 'For this reason it is ordained and written on the heavenly tables, that they should celebrate the feast of weeks in this month once a year, to renew the covenant every year.' The following passage says that the festival was celebrated in heaven from the creation and observed on earth until Noah's death, but neglected after this until Abraham. After Jacob and his children in the days of Moses (who is addressed in this passage) it was neglected until 'ye celebrated it anew on this mountain'. We shall return to this important conception of a festival for renewal of the covenant. For the present our subject is its annual date; the month is the third month, and later we find Abraham celebrating the feast 'in the third month, in the middle of the month' (15.1). We have already seen that the months contained thirty days according to this calendar (the thirty-first not strictly belonging to any month), so that the date seems to be III.15, and *Jub.* 44.4 f. supports this deduction. Further support is readily forthcoming from the fact that in this calendar Unleavened Bread week is from Wednesday I.15 to Tuesday I.21, so that the day after the sabbath after this is I.26 (in this calendar this is true for every year). Counting the fifty days—or seven weeks—from I.26 brings us to III.15.

The festival, then, with which the *Rule* is concerned in its opening passage is most probably identical with this Feast of Weeks, observed according to the solar calendar; they celebrated it as a Feast of the Renewal of the Covenant. How had Weeks, or Pentecost, acquired this character? This question cannot be answered with certainty, but a possible clue lies in the paramount importance attached to the Scriptures, and in the live and active tradition of interpretation and reinterpretation by which *haggadah* and *halakah* were formed. A glimpse of this is given in the section on Qumran and Tradition.[1] It appears that from a date about two centuries before Christ, when the Old Testament was reaching its present form, the exegetical practice which had so strongly influenced that form was itself strongly affected by the synagogue lectionary, which assigned to sabbaths a passage of the Law (*seder*) and a passage from the prophets (*haphtarah*). The character of festivals seems to have been influenced by the scriptures read on those occasions, or on the sabbaths near to the days on which they occurred. For example, Snaith has persuasively argued that Büchler is right in his judgment

---

[1] P. 72 above.

that the tradition of remembering Rachel on Tishri 1 arose from the *seder* read on that day appointed by the lectionary, which allotted readings for festivals and sabbaths on the basis of a triennal cycle.[1] The Feast of Weeks had originally its own distinct agricultural character. It acquired the character of celebration of the giving of the Law of Mount Sinai; some explanation must be found for this pronounced change and nothing is more likely than that the Scriptures effected it, and it is natural to look for the possibility that they effected it by way of the lectionary. Ex. 19–20 was read on the first two sabbaths of *Sivan* (or month III), but the Talmud (*b. Meg.* 31a) says that Ex. 19 was read on the Feast of Weeks. It is reasonable to suppose that the striking *seder* Ex. 19 was quite early transferred from a nearby sabbath to the festival and so gave it its new character of commemorating the covenant made at the giving of the Law on Mount Sinai.[2]

In the New Testament Pentecost clearly bears the character of a covenant renewal, recalling the great event on Sinai. The feast is mentioned three times, receiving a full exposition in story form (*haggadah*) in Acts 2, an exposition implying the final, eschatological fulfilment of the festival. The passage is clearly typological, v. 1–4 describing a new Sinai when the Holy Spirit speaks again to all the nations of the world. This may well reflect a rabbinic haggadic addition to the lore of Sinai to the effect that all the nations of the world had heard in their own languages the voice from Sinai, but that Israel alone had undertaken to obey. Now the nations are given an opportunity to hear the word of God again (5–11), and the curse of Babel is reversed.

Van Goudoever[3] rightly observes that 'the Passover season and that of the fifty days formed an important liturgical period for Luke', but he is unable to find a satisfactory solution of the forty days between the Resurrection and Ascension. We may suggest that the original understanding of the early Church counting for this Pentecost began from the paschal self-offering of Jesus, who on the *third* day rose from the dead, on the *tenth* appeared to his disciples for the second time (John 20.26: the appearance to them with Thomas is a week after the appearance on the third day in v. 19), had *forty* days' inter-

---

[1] N. H. Snaith, *The Jewish New Year Festival*, p. 168.

[2] It is probable that the Sinai lesson was read on Pentecost originally in the Second Year of the triennial cycle.

[3] J. Van Goudoever, *Biblical Calendars*, p. 281. See also pp. 201, 259 f. and index *s.v.* Ascension.

course with them, and so made up the fifty days. Luke has partially revealed this scheme with his otherwise unexplained forty days, partly obliterated it by implying an unspecified number of days between the Ascension and the pouring forth of the Spirit.[1] The covenant ceremony theme is again prominent, Peter being the agent of admission and his converts being required to repent and be baptized (Acts 2.37–39) in a manner analogous to, though certainly not identical with, that of the Qumran ceremony.

The arrangement of Scripture according to a lectionary may then provide a clue to the origin of the association of the Law and the Covenant with the Feast of Weeks as dating from before New Testament times. Such a solution is not mentioned by Bent Noack in his essay, 'The Day of Pentecost'.[2] The careful arguments by which he arrives at a date for this association deserve review and discussion: the Bible employs the term Weeks for the feast (Ex. 34.22; Num. 28.26; Deut. 16.10, 16) which succeeded the old Ingathering (Ex. 23.16, etc.: see the explanation above, p. 95), and it is not until the literature of the Hellenistic era that the word Pentecost, i.e. Fiftieth, appears. In Tobit 2.1 the manner of its use suggests that it is a comparatively new expression. The same impression is given by II Macc. 12.31 f. Rabbinic sources do not speak of 'Fiftieth' but of the Feast of Fifty Days, although Josephus uses πεντηκοστή e.g. Ant. 3.10.6, where he mistakenly says that it translates the Heb. 'aṣereth, which was indeed used as a title of the feast, but meant a solemn assembly. The other references in Josephus are Ant. 13.8.4; 14.13.4; 17.10.2; BJ 1.13.3; 2.3.1; 6.5.3. In all but the first he feels it necessary to explain that this is the name of a feast. This is assuredly not an apology for using the term, but an explanation for his non-Jewish readers. Philo also uses the term for the feast (De decalogo 160; De specialibus legibus 2.176). It would seem that by NT times it was usual, as Paul's unselfconscious use of it (I Cor. 16.8) would suggest. Noack thinks it would be well understood in the Diaspora and therefore used without explanation by Paul, and he adduces an inscription from Hierapolis which uses it for the feast as further proof of its use in the Diaspora. Noack does not in any case connect the name Pentecost with the association of the feast with the ideas of Law and Covenant, but thinks that this association arose between Philo and Josephus on the

---

[1] The New Testament outside the Lucan writings knows nothing of an interval between the Ascension and the gift of the Holy Spirit.

[2] In the *Annual of the Swedish Theological Institute* I, 1963, pp. 73 ff.

one hand and Rabbi Jose ben Halaphta on the other, Rabbi Jose saying that the Ten Commandments were given on 6 Sivan (the Pharisaic and rabbinic date for Weeks). R. Jose's date is between 130 and 165.

It may well be true that the rabbis, whether of NT times or of the early Tannaitic period, attached no significance to the term 'of fifty days' or 'fiftieth'; but it helped to transfer attention from the old agricultural character of the feast to an event which took place fifty days after Passover. Concurrently with the passing away of the agricultural character of Weeks, the Scriptures read in the synagogue could not fail to suggest an historical character for it. Noack makes no reference to the synagogue lectionary, but argues rather that the rabbinic evidence will not take us back earlier than AD 100 for the association with Law and Covenant. In the course of this argument he mentions *Yoma* 4b as showing that in the time of the two rabbis mentioned there (R. Jose, and R. Akiba, who was martyred AD 135) the reinterpretation of Weeks was not yet an established fact; but *Yoma* 4b does not imply this in the least, but rather the contrary; for it explains a point on which R. Jose (here called the Galilaean; he was from Sepphoris) and R. Akiba differed from the Tannaim, namely the exact date of Sivan on which the Torah was given to Moses. R. Jose says that the Ten Commandments were given on the sixth and the rest of the Torah on the seventh. R. Akiba is said to agree that the Torah was given on the seventh. The passage remarks at the outset that 'we have been taught: On the sixth day of the month was the Torah given to Israel', referring to *Shab*. 86b, where we read: 'Our rabbis taught: On the sixth day of the month were the ten commandments given to Israel. R. Jose maintained: On the seventh thereof.' It is, then, an error on the part of Noack to suppose that R. Akiba and R. Jose 'discuss the question whether or not the Law was proclaimed on the day of the Feast of Weeks'. Their argument is about a detail, the exact date, whether 6 Sivan or 7 Sivan. The former is indeed the Pharisaic and final rabbinic date for the Feast of Weeks, but those who held that the Law was given on the latter date are merely giving time for the cloud to cover Moses first (Ex. 24.15 f.). The association with the Feast of Weeks is not questioned, but forms the basis of the debate.

We have in any case seen that the *Book of Jubilees* regards the feast as that of the Renewal of the Covenant and candidly draws attention to its double nature (6.21). This period, when *Jubilees* was written, perhaps as early as 133 BC, seems therefore to show conclusively the association of covenant with the feast much earlier than New Testament times. Noack's concern is to find rabbinic evidence for this, and he draws attention to the fact that there is no tractate in Mishnah or Talmud on the subject of the feast. After our review of the evidence it may be possible to form a theory which will account for all the facts, including this remarkable absence of a tractate on *Shebu'oth*.

The synagogue lectionary provided the original association of the scene on Sinai with the Feast of Weeks. With such a hypothesis the form of Acts 2 agrees perfectly. We find that round about the date 140 this association is accepted in rabbinic circles. In the meantime it is neglected in rabbinic texts and no tractate on the feast is ever composed. The explanation offered here is based on the facts that *Jub.* 6 is clearly written in a controversial situation, and that the rabbinic emphasis falls upon association of the feast with the giving of the Law, but the emphasis in *Jubilees* and Qumran falls upon association with the renewal of the covenant; and that the author of *Jubilees* disagreed with the Pharisees, precursors of rabbinic Judaism, as to the right way of calculating the date, or to put it less mildly and more truly, as to their calendar altogether.

Jubilees regards neglect of the Feast of Weeks as very grave; this is perfectly logical, since its observance was a renewal of the covenant. Pharisees adhered rather to the covenant without regarding a renewal of it as necessary. To accept the necessity for renewal was to admit oneself unclean: the Pharisee believed that he could attain and maintain his purity without such a ceremony so long as he adhered to the Torah. The Jews who produced *Jubilees*, pursuing the same ideals as the men of Qumran if not themselves identical with them, were opponents of the Pharisees, not least on this very issue. For them purification and renewal were necessary to save Israel. It was Pharisaic Judaism which prevailed in the Mishnah and Talmud, and it was therefore natural that it should exclude a tractate on a feast which their opponents had monopolized and to which they had given what was to them a false significance. No doubt the men of Qumran would have supplied such a tractate, but it would have been unacceptable indeed to the men of Jamnia.

The Feast of Weeks is part of the annual calendar, upon which the lectionary is based. The lectionary has influenced the Jewish conception of how history happened and for the men of Qumran, too, their calendar gives character to each year as a means of recapitulating the nation's history under the guidance and according to the will of God. Just as the calendar divided up the year in significant ways, another scheme divided up all the years of history into significant epochs, no doubt originally connected no less than the calendar with an astrological view of the universe. This conception of history reduced it to a scheme of Jubilee cycles.[1] The first cycle begins with the first year of the world's history, its events are said to occur Anno Mundi 1, and the last year in any particular Jubilee cycle (the Jubilee Year) is also the first year in the next Jubilee cycle. Thus, for example, the first Jubilee Year is AM 50, which also begins the second Jubilee cycle. To obtain the next and subsequent Jubilee years we add for each cycle seven times seven or forty-nine.[2] This mathematical fact in itself shows the fundamental affinity of the calendar with the Jubilee cycle: from Passover to Pentecost is also a matter of counting seven weeks, or seven times seven.[3]

The fiftieth Jubilee cycle, the Jubilee of Jubilees, the great period for the author of *Jubilees* begins with Anno Mundi 2402 (i.e. year 2402 from the creation). The great event of that year was the deliverance from Egypt followed by the giving of the Law on Sinai, whose association with Weeks or Pentecost raised the importance of that feast in the regard of the author and his colleagues. This began a new era, that of the Law; the fiftieth Jubilee Year (AM 2451) sees the entry into Canaan corresponding roughly to the Talmudic dating of the era of the Exodus from AM 2449 (*Jub.* 50.4). At the opening of the book it appears that the revelation to Moses will include all that is to happen until God descends to dwell with his people (1.26), but history is traced from the creation only as far as the giving of the Law, with an immediate anticipation of the entry into Canaan. Whatever the explanation of this fact—which seems to imply the promise of further historical writing in the same manner—it seems probable that in the eyes of the author the era of the Law could end only with the divine appearance on earth and the inauguration thereby of a new age, an age so new and so catastrophically begun that it would mean the beginning of a new world.

---

[1] See E. Wiesenberg, 'The Jubilee of Jubilees' in *RQ* 3, 1961, pp. 3 ff.

[2] This is the method in *Jubilees*. Lev. 25.10 suggests that the Jubilee period is fifty years. See Testuz, *Les idées religieuses du livre des jubilés*, p. 138.

[3] The custom of counting the 'Omer' (the word meant originally a measure of barley offered on the second day of Passover (Lev. 23.11)), continues to this day, although the destruction of the Temple stopped the bringing of the offering on the first day. The Omer period (*sephirah*) from Passover to Pentecost has now sad associations, for many tragedies have befallen the Jews within these dates.

This conception of a new age (αἰών or *tequphah*) is an essential part of the beliefs both of the Qumran sect and of the early Church. Both believed that they were living at the time of its inauguration, Paul being convinced that the era of the Law was being closed before the eyes of himself and his contemporaries (II Cor. 5.17; Rom. 10.4). The men of Qumran held tenaciously to the view that they lived in the era of the Law, but in expectation of its imminent end; they therefore went into the desert to cast up a highway for their God (1QS 8.12–18, which quotes Isa. 40.3; cf. Mark 1.3; Luke 3.4 ff.; Matt. 3.3; John 1.23), interpreting the exhortation both literally and metaphorically, saying that it meant the study of the Law.

For Paul, 'Christ is the end of the Law, giving justification to every believer' (Rom. 10.4), a conclusion to which his personal experience and consequent doctrinal thinking led him. Now the covenant was to be entered by baptism into Christ, not by undertaking the works of the Law. He would have been impatient with any attempt to base such a conclusion on a reckoning of years and epochs; and even elsewhere in the New Testament such thinking may be not so much recalled as transcended. Yet it is interesting to conjecture what was the original concept which was thus transcended. Already in *Jub.* 40.9 and 46.2 the reason for the temporary absence of Satan from Egypt is not that the period is connected with the Jubilee Year but that God was with Joseph. Similarly, when the devil leaves Jesus 'for a time' it is because Jesus has vanquished him by the power of the Holy Spirit (Luke 4.1 f. and 13 f.) and when he returns (Luke 22.3) it is because this is permitted by God (Luke 22.53). But Jesus according to Luke inaugurates a new era (4.16 ff.) and in doing so claims to fulfil the scripture which consists mainly of Isa. 61.1 f., a prophetic transcending of Lev. 25.8 ff. In this Leviticus passage, the Law proclaims liberty to slaves at a fixed time which will recur, in Deutero-Isaiah the Spirit proclaims liberty in a new era without end, for all who are oppressed. This concentration upon the Jubilee period and upon transcending it contrasts sharply with contemporary custom which observed the *shemiṭṭah* (or allowing land to lie fallow on the seventh or sabbath year),[1] but did not apparently pay any attention to the Jubilee cycles, a neglect which the author or authors of *Jubilees* and the sect at Qumran were probably united in seeking to reverse. The end of the present Jubilee period would see the liberation

---

[1] Lev. 25.1–7; Josephus, *Ant.* 11.8.6; 13.8.1; 14.10.6; 14.16.2; 15.1.2; I Macc. 6.49, 53; Tacitus, *Hist.* 5.4.

of the true Israel and the restoration of God's worship by God's people.

In the New Testament, as we have seen, the new era is brought about by the exodus of the Lord in Jerusalem (Luke 9.31), inaugurated by a Passover, consummated by Pentecost when those days have 'fully come' (Acts 2.1), and entered by means of the covenant of baptism.[1]

F.   THE RENEWAL OF THE COVENANT

To return to Qumran: the giving of the Law in the covenant from Sinai inaugurated a great era, and its giving was annually commemorated in the Feast of Weeks, or Pentecost. This feast was used by the sect as a time of solemn renewal of the covenant, and the form which this ceremony took was determined by a long tradition of such ceremonies recorded in the Scriptures. The liturgy at Qumran is described in 1.16–2.18 and clearly recalls the liturgy of Deut. 27–30, but to appreciate its character it is necessary to recall some of the other covenants made between the LORD and the Israelites according to the Old Testament.

The covenant which usually springs to mind is indeed that made through Moses on Mount Sinai, but the LORD's original covenant was made with Abraham when he had called him out of a pagan environment and promised to make him the father of a great nation. The priestly account of the matter is given at Gen. 17.1–14, and the editors candidly reveal their knowledge that this had not been, in fact, a covenant with Yahweh (or the LORD) by their retention of the divine name El Shaddai in v. 1. Their representation of it as nevertheless a covenant with Yahweh is justified by the theological explanation which P puts into the mouth of God ('*Elohim*) in Ex. 6.2 f. The first covenant with Yahweh *in his own name* is, in fact, that made through Moses on Mount Sinai. The various codes of the covenant incorporated by P into this event reveal once again that characteristic

---

[1] The quotation of Isa. 61.1 f. at Luke 4.18 f. may be part of a sermon based on the scriptures read at the beginning of Tishri: Isa. 61.2 ff. is the *haphtarah* for the sabbath after *R'osh Hashshanah* (New Year) and *Shemiṭṭah* was proclaimed on Tishri 10 (Day of Atonement). The ideas of release and renewal and of the return of God's favour were abroad at such a season and the Lord's words are extremely apt for it, although his claim goes beyond the immediate time. I am indebted for this information to the Rev. C. H. Cave, who in an unpublished paper shows that all the scriptures recalled by Luke 4.16 ff. are drawn from readings for the last half of Tishri and the first of Marcheshvan, i.e. the weeks following *R'osh Hashshanah* and *Yom Kippur*. Cf. A Guilding, *The Fourth Gospel and Jewish Worship*, Clarendon Press, 1960, p. 125.

—and paradoxical—combination of rigid loyalty to tradition with variety of interpretation which enabled the discovery of new revelation to continue through history in company with the preservation of a fixed content revealed in the past.[1] Which laws did Yahweh enjoin upon the people through Moses? To supply the answer, the editors might have chosen the ritual decalogue of Ex. 22.29b–30; 23.12, 15–19 or that of 34.14–26, with some or all of the *midrashim* which now accompany them, or they might have chosen exclusively what we call the Ten Commandments (Ex. 20.2–17) with or without the *midrashim* which follow them and which are mingled with the earlier of the two primitive decalogues mentioned above and with their own *midrashim*. In fact, all were strung together so that the early decalogue became part of the commentary upon Ex. 20.2–17, the decalogue which was specially chosen to follow on the great theophany of Ex. 19.

The code of the covenant with Moses, then, showed already manifold stratification in the P tradition, and this live and continuing collection of *halakoth* did not become fixed by being incorporated into the Scriptures. Interpretation and application continued; and while we are familiar with such features of its course as history has left us, and know that the Mishnah, early compendium of rabbinic *halakah*, represents the triumph of the Pharisees, we had little knowledge of the systems of other schools until the documents of Qumran were discovered.

If the sect could be encouraged by history to create and to impose on its members its own version of the Law's application and its own version of the interpretation of that history, it could be similarly encouraged by the story of the covenants. If no one code could be said to be that demanded at Sinai, the covenant there ratified (Ex. 24.1–8) was also but one of the covenants in history: through Nathan the LORD had made a covenant with David and his house, connected indeed with his covenant with Israel (II Sam. 7; I Chron. 17); and P, whose attitude to the rival Ithamar branch of the priestly family of Aaron is liberal (Lev. 10.6), nevertheless includes the story of the LORD's rewarding Phinehas, son of Eleazar, by making 'the covenant of an everlasting priesthood' with the Eleazar branch in Num. 25.10–13. This covenant was a reward for zeal, like that shown by the sons of Levi in Ex. 32.26–29 for which they are praised in Moses' Blessing at Deut. 33.8–11.

[1] See p. 69.

In addition to these covenants with special elements of the people there are instances of other covenants between the LORD and his whole people than that made at Sinai: thus Joshua according to the deuteronomic redactor reads the Law, together with blessings and curses, in Josh. 8.30–35, and Deut. 27.1–26 gives us the Shechem liturgy supposedly used on this occasion. One element in this liturgy appears more clearly in the shorter form found at Deut. 11.26–32 in which a blessing is set upon Mount Gerizim and a curse upon Mount Ebal, these places becoming at Deut. 27.12 f. the places on which to stand for blessing and cursing respectively. 27.14 gives the curses to the Levites as a liturgical task and vv. 14–26 seem to carry unmistakable signs of great antiquity. Even without further detailed argument it seems clear that Deut. 27–30 describes a covenant ceremony with its liturgy, a body of material which has assimilated a number of ancient liturgical patterns to a scene which Moses commands shall take place when the people eventually pass over Jordan (27.2).

It is clear that the covenant ceremony was very ancient in Israel, and that it was indissolubly linked with the Law. The famous passage in Jer. 31.31–34, whatever its date, is eloquent witness to the hope for a consummation of the process by which the LORD was linked to the hearts of his people by his Law.[1] To us it reads like the expression of the hope of eschatological fulfilment when the Law as a literal system of statutes, which could be known as dates and scientific facts are known, would be replaced by a knowing of the LORD as a man 'knows' his friend. But it could be so regarded that its fulfilment would be brought about by diligent learning, so that no man would need any longer to bid his neighbour to know the LORD: he could be confident that all his neighbours had fulfilled their legal duty towards him. Such a confidence could be entertained in his fellows by any member of a Pharisaic *chaburah*, and equally certainly by any member of the sect. Their conception of a new covenant was indeed one which must be entered with real conviction (1QS 2.11–18) and which could be described as 'engraved for ever' apparently in the mind of a man[2] (10.6, 8), but it was the old covenant renewed, still linked to the Law as a body of precepts to be carefully observed. The passage from Jeremiah could therefore give warrant for new forms of the old covenant ceremony, new forms still preserving the essence of the past.

It was the form given to the ceremony by the scholars who pro-

[1] In Hebrew Jer. 31.30–33.
[2] Cf. Jer. 31.33 (32).

duced Deuteronomy in Deut. 27–30 on which the ceremony in 1QS 1.16–2.18 is based. The Qumran ceremony was adapted to their own time and circumstances, but examination of the text shows points at which its language owes a debt not only to Deuteronomy but to developments in the more recent past. Thus, for example, in 1QS 1.20 'all who are entering' recalls 'all the people' at Neh. 8.6, where also there is a double 'Amen'. The covenant here, whose agents are represented—intelligibly if unhistorically—as Nehemiah and Ezra together, is associated with *Sukkoth* and not with Weeks, but the reminiscence of Moses and of 'the curse' at Neh. 10.29 shows the continuity of the covenant ceremonial tradition as it appears in the *Rule*. Neh. 9.38 (10.1 in Heb.) makes clear that the ceremony was that of a covenant for Nehemiah and his contemporaries, and the whole passage is instructive by the evidence which it supplies of what was undertaken in the covenant and of the prominence in it of priests and Levites as at Qumran. For further material on the covenant ceremony see the commentary on 1.16 and 1.18.

THE RULE OF QUMRAN

INTRODUCTORY

1. THE TEXT

THE *Rule of Qumran* is one of the non-biblical scrolls from the original discovery in 1947. It is published in M. Burrows, J. C. Trever and W. H. Brownlee, *The Dead Sea Scrolls of St Mark's Monastery*, Vol. II, Fasc. 2: *Plates and Transcription of the Manual of Discipline*, New Haven, 1951. A. M. Habermann published a pointed text (along with that of the other main scrolls) in Jerusalem in 1952. A much-enlarged edition of this pointed text of the scrolls appeared in 1959, and it is the pointed text of the *Rule* in this second edition which has been used as a basis for the present book, although the text adopted, the translation and the interpretation depart from it at several points.

The *Rule* was clearly a very important book for the Qumran community. Parts of eleven other manuscripts have been found in Caves 4 and 5. In a review of Wernberg-Møller's edition, in *RB* 67, 1960, pp. 410 ff., Milik reports that in Cave 4 he identified fragments of the manuscripts of the *Rule*, for which the designations 4QSa, b, c, d, e, f, g, h, i, j have been given; and that a twelfth, 5Q 11, containing a part of the *Rule* 2.4–7 and 12–14 was found in Cave 5, which yielded also another manuscript 5Q 13 which quotes 1QS 3.4–5 (5Q 13.4.2–3). In the same review Milik gives a number of variants, some of which have strong claims to be regarded as the correct reading. Where these are adopted they are noted in the commentary.

2. ANALYSIS

Any analysis of a literary composition must reflect the interpretation which the analyst wishes to place upon the work as a whole and is to that extent subjective; but the scheme of divisions used in this book attempts to give due weight to indications from the text and from its arrangement in the main manuscript.

The text itself supplies some 'headings' in formulae such as 'For the master to instruct . . .' (3.13): besides indications like this, spaces left by the scribe in the manuscript may be significant and at least invite consideration whether they are intentional pointers to a change of subject. Again, marks in the margin and indentation of certain lines may indicate where at any rate one scribe thought that there was a natural break. Guilbert[1] has made a full assessment of these aids, discussed the indications in the text itself, and finally used all this evidence to set out a most workmanlike analysis of the scroll. The present edition has made considerable use of this analysis, but adapted it slightly; further, it offers a different interpretation of some passages from that which Guilbert implies by his headings.

1.1–15   General introduction: duty of authorities and requirements for entrants.

1.16–3.12   Entry into the community.
> 1.16–2.18   Rite for entry into the covenant.
> 2.19–25a   Ceremony for assembly of members.
> 2.25b–3.12   Denunication of those who refuse to enter the covenant.

3.13–4.26   Doctrine of the community.
> 3.13–4.1   The two spirits.
> 4.2–14   The work of the spirits in the lives of men.
> 4.15–26   God's final plan for the two spirits.

5.1–6.23   Purpose and way of life of the community.
> 5.1–7a   General statement of purpose and way.
> 5.7b–9   The way of the community alone to be followed.
> 5.10–20a   Members not to associate with other Israelites.
> 5.20b–6.8a   Rules for life within the community.
> 6.8b–13a   Rules for a session of members.
> 6.13b–23   Steps by which a new member enters the community.

6.24–7.25   Penitential code of the community.

8.1–9.26   Model of a pioneer community to pave the way for the main community.
> 8.1–9.11   Constitution of the pioneer community.
> 9.12–26   Guidance for the instructor of the pioneer community.

[1] P. Guilbert, 'Le plan de la Règle de la Communauté' in *RQ* 1, 1958–9, pp.323 ff.

10.1–11.22   Closing hymn.
   10.1–8   Calendar of worship.
   10.9–11.15a   Hymn.
   11.15b–22   Benediction.

3. COMPOSITION AND DATE

Even before reading the *Rule* analysis of it will prompt consideration of the question whether it must not be regarded as composite. We do not yet perhaps possess enough evidence to follow the hint of Milik[1] that the discovery especially in Cave 4 of fragments of the *Rule* and of CD, sometimes combining passages which in these longer mss. belong to separate works, is evidence for a 'hybrid type of life', that is celibate and married sections of the Essene order living in the same place. Our task is limited to examining the internal evidence of the *Rule*. Some parts of it immediately invite consideration as originally separate items, and it is hardly necessary to do more than draw together arguments which arise naturally in the commentary.

In the commentary on 1.18 Rabin's argument that the *War Scroll* is composite is recalled. This scroll includes the *Book of the Order of his Time*, one of whose parts is a Blessing and Curse, to be uttered, after the defeat of the men of Belial, by priests, Levites and elders; this liturgy is apparently used at the opening of the *Rule*, although owing to the fragmentary nature of the passage in the *War Scroll* it cannot be said with certainty that the two passages are identical. Again, the formula of confession at 1.24 appears also in CD 20.28–30. 1.18–2.18 may therefore be regarded as a passage of liturgy used but not composed by the compiler of the *Rule*.

No parallel can be found for the introduction 1.1–17 and this seems to be peculiar to the *Rule*. The author is then apparently drawing up a description of the way in which the sect conducted itself, beginning logically enough with the ceremony by which members were initiated; the occasion does not demand original writing, but rather a compilation of important elements in the life of the sect.

2.19–3.12 reads like authoritative comment and judgment on what has preceded it: the writer describes briefly regulations for after the

---

[1] J. T. Milik, *Ten Years of Discovery in the Wilderness of Judaea*, p. 96.

ceremony and pronounces his *mishpaṭ* on circumstances arising from any probationer refusing to enter the sect. This passage also may therefore be ascribed to the compiler, unless indeed he was drawing on already existent regulations.

In the present discussion emphasis naturally falls on the teaching on the Two Spirits, 3.13–4.26. On pp. 46 ff. some of the evidence is given for the conclusion that this passage is one form of an older work which enjoyed a circulation well beyond Qumran and influenced later theological treatises. The teaching is striking and individual, concentrated in but not confined to this passage alone, showing kinship with a wide range of thinkers, both religious and philosophical. This important doctrinal work was clearly essential to the compiler's purpose.

The *halakah* of 5.1–7.25 was equally germane. At 5.1 we meet a definite heading, and the commentary at this point gives the reasons for regarding a passage beginning here as originally independent, see also on 5.7 'transgress', especially since mss. have been discovered which give some of the same material—at least that of col. 5—in simpler form. Difficulty attends any attempt to determine the length of this section; yet 5.7b ff. may be said to repeat 5.1–7a, and while it may be a little hazardous to attempt to subdivide any of the relatively long halakic section 5.1–7.25, some further indication for such a division may properly be suggested. 5.13b–20a repeats some of the teaching in 2.25–3.12, and since this latter falls within a passage ascribed above to the compiler, it is possible either that he is the author of the regulations here or that 5.13b–20a illustrates the fact that already existent *halakah* guided him in the earlier comment which he made on the ceremony of initiation. This latter view receives support from the argument in the commentary on 5.14 'in his work and in his property' that the whole of 5.1–6.23 (though composite) may date from the time before the desert withdrawal (cf. 8.1–9.26).

6.1 again betrays an originally separate heading and 6.1–7 clearly legislates for the life of the sect during this early period. 6.13b–23, regulating the steps by which a new member enters the community, is a highly characteristic passage; presumably part of regulations drawn up early, it is likely to have been incorporated rather than created by the compiler.

6.24–7.25 is the sect's penitential code; while appropriate to the foundation of the community it seems by its miscellaneous character and because of other facts pointed out in the commentary to be itself composite. We seem compelled by such evidence to regard this like other halakic sections as consisting of regulations whose origin and chronological relations with one another can never now be determined; but the note at 6.24 on the interesting phrase 'the words' argues that this may be a title of an actual book on whose authority these regulations are set out.

Imprecise as this discussion of 5.1–7.25 must appear, it seems more in accordance with the evidence to make these comments than to attempt to draw up a definite scheme illustrating the composition of this section.

Whatever the origin of any of the foregoing sections, their character is such that their inclusion demands no explanation. 8.1–9.26 is different: if Sutcliffe, whom we have followed in the commentary, is right, this section on the pioneer community might appear to be an awkward insertion, and this consideration lends some weight to Vermès's contention that the passage concerns an inner council. On the other hand, a clue may be sought in the scriptures from the book of Isaiah, 8.16–18, 28.16 and above all 40.3. If this last passage was, as so many commentators (in our view rightly) maintain, fundamental and decisive in begetting the community (as distinct from the order which comprised a number of branches) in the brain of its founder, the passage 8.1–9.26 which was built upon it might well have become invested with sanctity. Its inclusion would therefore be a natural act of piety even though from a later literary point of view it seems to be out of place. That 8.1–9.26 was, in fact, originally separate, whatever its character and intention, is a theory powerfully supported by the ms. evidence mentioned in the commentary on 'the anointed ones of Aaron and Israel' (9.11).

The final section 10.1–11.22 is manifestly composite, very skilfully blending elements of a liturgical calendar with eloquent praise, and utterances of deep personal devotion with credal assertions of warm conviction. It is a most reasonable conjecture that the author is the same as the author of the *Psalms of Thanksgiving*. He may be the founder of the community, more probably the figure known as the Teacher of Righteousness who was not the founder but a re-founder twenty years after its beginning.

Much remains obscure, and only a very tentative account can be given of the author: the work has undergone a number of changes, earlier forms being represented by mss. from Cave 4. Even its earliest form was an amalgam of different elements brought together by an unknown compiler who used the work of the founder, of the Teacher of Righteousness and of unknown scholars who worked out the *halakah* obeyed by the sect.

If the movement began its life some time in the early Maccabaean period, the manifesto 8.1–9.26, together with other halakic elements not easy to disengage from the rest, may represent the earliest stratum of material and belong to the period about 130 BC. The concluding hymn, if it really came from the Teacher of Righteousness, would accordingly be dated about 110 BC onwards. Other elements fall some time before, between or after these dates, the compilation of the whole having been a process producing the exemplar of 1QS about 100 BC. 1QS itself may therefore be dated some time in the first century BC, a result agreeing with the palaeographical conclusions of F. M. Cross,[1] who puts it in the first quarter of that century.

[1] F. M. Cross, *The Ancient Library of Qumran*, p. 89.

IV

TRANSLATION AND COMMENTARY

Note: In the commentary a number of passages relevant to that under review are often listed before the comment is made. These are given in the following order: passages from elsewhere in the *Rule* (without reference letters), passages from other scrolls, scriptural references, and finally passages from other works. These lists will themselves suggest affinities and interpretations which will not always require further explanations such as the notes are designed to give in other cases.

GENERAL INTRODUCTION
I.1–15

1 For [the Instructor and for the me]n his brothers, [the book of the orde]r of the community.

To seek 2God [with all the heart and all the soul, to] do what is good and right before him according to 3the command which he gave through Moses and through all his servants the prophets; and to love all 4that he has chosen and to hate all that he has rejected; to keep away from all evil 5and to hold fast to all good deeds; and to practise truth and righteousness and justice 6on the earth; and to follow no more the way of the stubbornness of a guilty heart and of lustful eyes, 7to do every evil.

To admit all who promise to practise the precepts of God 8into the covenant of grace, so that they may be united with the counsel of God and walk before him perfectly according to all 9that has been revealed at the times set for making them known; and so that they may love all the sons of light, each 10according to his part in the counsel of God, and hate all the sons of darkness each according to his guilt 11in the vengeance of God.

And all who devote themselves to his truth shall bring all their knowledge and their powers 12and their wealth into the community of God, to purify their knowledge by the truth of the precepts of God and to order their powers 13according to the perfection of his ways and all their wealth by the counsel of his righteousness.

They shall not depart from any one [14]of all the commandments of God about their seasons nor advance their times nor retard any one [15]of their festivals; and they shall not stray from the precepts of his truth to walk to right or left.

1.1–10 appears to lay down general regulations for a person or persons in authority, 11–15 regulations (again only general) for candidates, both in connexion with admission to membership of the community. The whole passage therefore forms a general introduction to the main work.

1.1. For [the Instructor and the me]n his brothers 3.13; 9.12, 21; 1QSb 1.1; 3.22; 5.20; CD 12.21; 13.22; Dan. 11.33, 35; 12.3, 10. Carmignac (*RQ* 2, 1959–60, p. 85) restores and emends the text thus, a departure from Habermann. The Instructor represents the *maśkil*, the one who is himself instructed and can therefore instruct others. In Daniel it suggests one who has been initiated into a secret by revelation. See p. 67.

[the book of the orde]r of the community The restoration well justified by 4QSa and provides a title for the work, which is in is the main an order or *Rule*. 1.16; 2.20, 21; 5.1, 23; 6.8, 22; DSW 3.3, 13; 4.6, etc; 1QSa 1.1, 6, 21, 23; CD 7.6; 10.4; 12.19, etc. Yadin, pp. 148 ff., has a useful summary of the uses of the word for order (*serek*). See on 1.16.

1.2. [with all the heart . . .] This restoration is authorized by 4QSa, c.

1.3. through Moses 5.8; 8.15, 22; CD 5.21; DSW 10.6; 1QH 17.12; Josh. 20.2; 21.2; 22.9; 23.6; I Kings 2.3; I Chron. 6.49; 15.15; II Chron. 8.13; 23.18; 33.8; Neh. 9.14; Dan. 9.11, 13, etc; Mark 1.44; 10.3; Luke 2.22; 5.14; 16.29 ff.; John 1.17 etc. However much the sect respected other servants of God who were entrusted with revelation, the Law given to Moses remained the basis of their belief and their covenant.

his servants the prophets 8.16; 1QpHab 2.9; 7.5; 4QpHosb 2.5; Amos 3.7 is the origin of the phrase here and in the other passages. The senses in which Amos believed a prophet to be the recipient of revelation are discussed on pp. 63–65. By some time in the second century BC the process was complete by which the prophets had ceased to be historical persons and had become books, books which were held by the sect to contain a number of secrets (*razim*) which the Teacher of Righteousness was specially gifted in interpreting (1QpHab 2.2–14; 7.1–10). This interpretation consisted in applying passages to contemporary situations without regard to their origin or context. See p. 68 and F. F. Bruce, *Biblical Exegesis in the Qumran Texts*, pp. 8 ff., 67, who well says that the 'principle, that the divine purpose cannot properly be understood until the *pesher* has been revealed as well as the *raz*, underlies the biblical exegesis in the Qumran commentaries' (p. 9). The *raz* is the mystery, the *pesher* is the interpretation which it awaits. A still later form of this doctrine is represented by the passage at the beginning of the *Pirqe 'Aboth*, where the stages of tradition are Moses, Joshua, elders, prophets, men of the Great Synagogue.

1.3–4. to love . . . and to hate . . . CD 2.15; 1Q22 1.5 f.; Isa. 7.15 f.; Amos 5.15; Philo, *Quod omnis probus liber* 83. The objects of the verbs here are clearly impersonal. Contrast 1.9 f. below.

1.5. to practise truth 1.19; 5.3; 6.15; 8.2; 10.17; DSW 13.1 f., 9; 14.12; 1QH 1.30; 6.9; 13.4; 1Q22 1.11; 4Q Ma 10; Ezek. 18.9; Tobit 4.6; 13.6; John 3.21; I John 1.6. *Test. Reub.* 6.9; *Test. Benj.* 10.3. The phrase can be understood simply to mean 'to practise the true law', but it carries with it the further meanings of dealing sincerely with one's neighbour and of acting rightly according to one's own real feelings, and not by mere outward show. In 1QpHab 7.10 ff. the members of the sect are called 'the men of truth'. See 2.11–18 and p. 46.

1.6. the stubbornness of a guilty heart CD 2.17 f.; Jer. 11.8; 13.10; 23.17.

1.7. to admit all who promise Or 'all who volunteer'. The men of the sect, though God's chosen, must each make his own decision to practise the Law of Moses as interpreted in their community. The Master has the twofold duty of constituting a sect and practising its laws on the one hand, and on the other of admitting all who volunteer to follow him in this.

1.8. the covenant of grace The term covenant is found very often in the Qumran literature, and the sense of belonging to God through it is strong in the *Rule*, CD, DSW, 1QH. Cf. I Sam. 20.8; II Chron. 15.12; and esp. Deut. 7.9, 12; I Kings 8.23; II Chron. 6.14; Neh. 1.5; 9.32, in which God is invoked as he who maintains the covenant and the grace towards Israel. **covenant of grace** does not seem to occur until this scroll. It means the covenant entered on initiation into membership of the sect who believed themselves to be constituted by the grace or mercy of God. For covenant in general see on 1.16.

counsel of God 1.10; 3.6 (bis); 11.18; 1QH 4.13; 6.10, 11, 13; 1QSa 1.3; 1QSb 4.24; 4QpNah 5; 4QpPs37b 4; Isa. 19.17; Jer. 49.20; 50.45; Ps. 33.11; Prov. 19.21; Ezra 10.3; Luke 7.30; Acts 2.23; 4.28; 5.38; 13.36; 20.27; Eph. 1.11; Heb. 6.17. In all the biblical references the word means 'counsel', but very often in the scrolls it means 'council' and a common phrase is 'council of the community', which means the community in full assembly (see 3.2). This council is believed to owe its existence to the counsel (or plan) of God and to make decisions which are according to his counsel; thus the council of the community, when it makes a pronouncement after deliberating according to what it holds to be the divinely ordered procedure, can almost identify itself with the counsel of God. The idea is not alien to the New Testament: Acts 1.24–26 makes an excellent commentary on this fusion of council with counsel, and Acts 15.28 ('it seemed good to the Holy Spirit and to us') may reflect the practice of regarding corporate decision after prayer as that of the Holy Spirit (the counsellor) as well as of the Church (the council).

1.9 all that has been revealed at the times set for making them known (Cf. 3.10.) It is part of the doctrine of the sect that important interpretations of the Scriptures are revealed at certain divinely appointed times, providing explanation of the meaning of contemporary events (as in the commentaries on books of the Scriptures found in the caves) and also injunctions as to the right conduct at particular times. This is the interpretation of Betz, Wernberg-Møller and Foerster (NTS 8, 1961–2, p. 124) who refers to 9.12 f. and 20 f., and believes 8.11 f. to be decisive. Betz, *Offenbarung*, p. 45, refers to DSW 14.13; 1QH frgt. 5.11. A similar interpretation is an important part of the argument of M. Weise, *Kultzeiten und Kultischer Bundesschluss in der 'Ordensregel' vom Toten Meer*, p. 65. The translation 'concerning the feasts' rather than 'at the times fixed for making them known' strains the Hebrew, especially in the use of the preposition *l-*. It is no doubt true that one who entered the sect thereby avowed his belief in the authenticity of their calendar, but that does not appear to be the subject here. For the whole subject of revelation in Qumran see pp. 63 ff.

to love all the sons of light . . . and hate all the sons of darkness See on 1.4. For the commandment to love Lev. 19.18 will suffice to represent the whole Bible. For hatred see Gen. 29.30; Matt. 10.37; Luke 14.26, where to hate means to love less, and Lev. 19.17; II Chron. 19.2; Pss. 5.5; 45.7; 139.21; Prov. 6.16; 8.13;

John 3.20; I John 2.9, 11; 3.15; 4.20; Jude 23; Rev. 2.6; *Test. Gad* 4.1; 5.2; 6.2. From these and similar passages it is clear that the Bible nowhere commends that hatred in the heart which is like murder (I John 3.15); but Sutcliffe is right to say that the men of Qumran derived from the Bible this principle: 'God hates sin and sinners too, precisely in so far as they are attached to sin' ('Hatred at Qumran' in *RQ* 2, 1959–60, pp. 345 ff.). To hate in this sense is therefore to abhor, to shrink from contamination by the evil object hated. This is the way in which the sect are to hate all the sons of darkness, because they are God's enemies, rather than because they are their own personal enemies. It is therefore wrong to claim that the tradition referred to in Matt. 5.43 is here identified. On the other hand, the extension of the concept neighbour to all mankind and the bidding to love enemies (Matt. 5.44; Luke 6.27) is widely admitted to be original to Jesus. In his day a neighbour was normally a fellow Jew (cf. Luke 10.29 ff.) and was extended to include all men only in AD 110, in the time of ben Azzai. Josephus (*BJ* 2.8.7) tells us that the Essene swore 'to hate the wicked always and to fight together with the good'.

sons of light 2.16; 3.13, 24 f.; DSW 1.1, 3, 9, 11, 13; Luke 16.8; John 12.36; Eph. 5.8; I Thess. 5.5. See Chapter II 5 c, pp. 79 f. above.

1.11. vengeance of God 2.9; 4.12; DSW 3.6; 4.12; CD 1.17; 8.12; 19.24; Num. 31.3; Jer. 50.15, 28; 51.11. These passages use the same form of the Hebrew word used here, but the masculine form with the same meaning is found in other passages both in the OT and in the scrolls. The passages cited use the phrase **vengeance of God,** an idea based on Deut. 32.35, used by Paul at Rom. 12.19 and used also at Heb. 10.30. It is a thoroughly eschatological notion: God will vindicate and indeed avenge his elect in the final judgment. This is the notion found here and in the NT at Luke 18.8 and II Thess. 1.8. **In the vengeance** means then 'in the day of vengeance' (so Wernberg-Møller). See also note on 9.23.

Knowledge E.g. 2.3; 3.1 f., 15; 4.4, 26; 8.9; 9.17; 10.9; 1QpHab 11.1; 1QH 2.13, 18; 3.23; 10.29; 12.13, etc; CD 2.3; Gen. 2.9, 17; Num. 24.16; Ps. 94.10; Prov. 1.7, etc; Isa. 5.13; 11.2; 53.11; Hos. 6.6; Luke 11.52; Rom. 11.33; I Cor. 12.8; 14.6; II Cor. 11.6; Phil. 3.8; Col. 2.3. This list includes some of the biblical references which illustrate that knowledge often means knowledge of God (which man usually is shown to lack) or God's knowledge of man (cf. I Cor. 13.12)

—knowledge which either is or includes knowledge connected with our knowing a person, rather than knowing facts. Thus the word used absolutely carries a religious overtone. In this scroll its particular meaning is to be defined by the context. Bo Reicke (NTS 1, 1954–5, p. 138) suggests here 'mind' or 'interest', but the three forms of contribution mentioned in this passage can be related to specific duties incumbent upon all members. Their physical powers must be daily at the community's disposal, and so must their wealth. This is just as true of the knowledge of the law or the prophets which they possess or which they may acquire in the daily study incumbent upon them as members of the sect. See 4 passim.

1.12. **wealth** 5.2; CD 13.11; Acts 2.44 ff.; 4.34 ff.; Pliny, *HN* 5.15.4; Philo, *Quod omnis probus liber* 76; Josephus, *Ant.* 18.1.5; *BJ* 2.8.3. Black (*The Scrolls and Christian Origins*, p. 123) suggests plausibly that the *Shema* is the background of this passage, and that the community adhered to its own interpretation of Deut. 6.4 ff., probably connected with the Targumic version, which took 'with all thy strength' as 'with all thy possessions'. Such was often the birth of an important *halakah*. Josephus in *BJ* says 'it was the regulation (Gk. *nomos*) for those who were to enter the sect to place their property at the disposal of the order'. Whiston here translates with proper caution, '. . . let what they have be common to the whole order.' It is not certain that Josephus meant 'surrender their property to the order'. The point is important, since it appears that the communizing of wealth took much the same form in the early Church according to the passages in Acts, although their practice was not in every respect identical with that at Qumran. Thus we should probably translate Acts 2.45 as in NEB, recognizing the frequentative use of the verbs. Acts 4.32–35 appears indeed to suggest that all who had property sold it without waiting for need to be shown and that the apostles administered the common fund thus formed, but 5.4 makes clear that this was emphatically not a condition of membership of the Church, for Peter asks Ananias, 'When it was turned into money, was it not still at your own disposal?' Early Christians in Jerusalem practised voluntary charity to the extent of distributing their capital, no doubt in expectation of an early return of the Lord which would mean the end of the age. This has little affinity with communism, whether with modern communism which is a communism of production, or with that of the Essenes (whom the men of Qumran are taken to be) which was a communism of production and of consumption. It is indeed misleading to speak of the 'communism of the early Church', but at Qumran communism was practised, although the form which it took there did not involve an outright common ownership of capital. It must be emphasized that the motive is altogether religious: all the members' knowledge and powers are to be contributed as well as their wealth, and their knowledge and powers will be purified within the community of God just as their wealth will be purified by being administered by the counsel of his righteousness, that is by the counsel obtained in this assembly of righteous ones.

1.14. their seasons   See on 1.9 above.

ENTRY INTO THE COMMUNITY
1.16–3.12
RITE FOR ENTRY INTO THE COVENANT: 1.16–2.18

16 All who enter the order of the community shall enter into a covenant in the presence of God to act [17]according to all that he has commanded and not to withdraw from following him through any fear or terror or trial [18]which take place during the dominion of Belial.

When they enter into the covenant the priests [19]and the Levites shall bless the God of salvation and all the deeds of his faithfulness; and all [20]who are entering into the covenant say after them 'Amen, amen'.

21 The priests recount the righteous acts of God in the deeds of his power [22]and recite all the gracious acts of mercy towards Israel; and the Levites recount [23]the iniquities of the children of Israel and all their guilty transgressions and their sins under the dominion [24]of Belial. And all who are entering into the covenant confess after them, saying:

> 'We have committed iniquity,
> [25][We have transgressed],
> We [have sinned],
> We have done evil,

we and our fathers before us in conducting our lives [26][against the covenant of] truth and righteousness [and God has passed] his judgment upon us and upon our fathers,

COLUMN TWO

[1]but he has bestowed upon us mercies in his gracious acts from everlasting to everlasting.'

The priests bless all [2]the men of the lot of God who walk perfectly in all his ways and say:

'May he bless thee with all ³good and guard thee from all evil, and enlighten thy heart with the understanding of life and bestow on thee knowledge of eternity; ⁴and may he lift up the face of his graciousness upon thee for eternal peace.'

The Levites curse all the men ⁵of the lot of Belial and respond and say:

'Cursed be thou for all the evil deeds of thy guilty wickedness! May ⁶God deliver thee to the terror at the hand of all who wreak revenge! May he dog thee with destruction at the hand of all who exact ⁷vengeance! Cursed be thou without mercy for the darkness of thy deeds and damned be thou ⁸in the mist of everlasting fire! May God not be gracious when thou callest nor forgive by covering thine iniquities! ⁹May he lift up the face of his wrath to wreak vengeance upon thee and mayest thou have no peace at the mouth of any intercessors!'

10 And all those entering into the covenant say after the blessing and the cursing 'Amen, amen'.

11 The priests and Levites continue and say:

'Cursed in the idols of his heart be he who comes ¹²to enter into this covenant but sets before his face his iniquitous stumbling-block to draw back by means of it, and when ¹³he hears the words of this covenant blesses himself in his own heart with the words "It will be well with me ¹⁴even though I go on in the stubbornness of my heart." Utterly destroyed shall be his spirit, thirsty with all his surfeit, without ¹⁵pardon; and may God's wrath and his zeal for his precepts flare up against him for everlasting destruction! May there cling to him all ¹⁶the curses of this covenant and may God set him apart for evil! Let him be cut off from among the sons of light in his drawing back ¹⁷from God through his idols! And let his iniquitous stumbling-block apportion his lot among those accursed for ever!'

18 And all those entering the covenant shall respond and say after them 'Amen, amen'.

1.16. order   1.1; 2.20, 21; 5.1, 23; 6.8, 22; DSW 3.3, 13; 4.6 ff.; 5.3, 4; 6.10 ff.; 7.1, 17; 8.14; 9.10; 13.1; 15.4, 5; 16.3; 18.6; 1QSa 1.1, 6, 21, 23; CD 7.6, 8; 10.4; 12.19, 22; 13.7; 14.3, 12; 19.2, 4. Not biblical, but occurs in Aramaic fragment of *Test. Levi* from Cave 4. The corresponding Greek word is usually τάξις and the following NT passages may be compared, relatively few though they are: Luke 1.8; I Cor. 14.40; Col. 2.5; Heb. 5.6, 10; 6.20; 7.11, 17, 21. The use of the word (in Hebrew *serek*) in DSW (where it occurs frequently) is instructive. According to Yadin it is used there for disciplinary rule, for custom, or order, and sometimes for the whole body thought of as in battle formation or as carrying out a prescribed order. This

military usage is illustrated by DSW 13.1, where the word appears
to denote the whole congregation conceived as a military unit. Yadin
therefore concludes that since according to DSW the members called
their sect *serek*, the meaning here is 'approximately "the sect of the
community" '. But Yadin's own explanation of the uses of the word
entitles us to claim that **order of the community** means the community constituted according to a certain order or rational structure.
This suggests that *serek* has something in common with the Greek
κόσμος, in the New Testament almost always 'world'; but this sense
is developed from the radical meaning of κόσμος as order, then world-
order or universe. See pp. 28–30.

a covenant in the presence of God   The term covenant is so
frequent in the scrolls that it would be tedious to give all the references. In the *Rule* it occurs here and in cols. 2 and 5 frequently, in the
latter part of DSW, and throughout both 1QH and CD. The biblical
references given in the note at 1.8 on **the covenant of grace** are
only to passages where the two terms occur together. The sections
on the covenant ceremony connected with the Festival of Weeks
discuss many passages relevant to the present section of the *Rule* (pp.
95–107), which describes the ceremony by which members enter the
sect, that is enter into covenant with God. In CD 2.1 the members are
addressed as those that are in the covenant.

1.17. all that he has commanded   Black (*op. cit.*, p. 122)
comments most aptly on the 'element of "perfectionism" in this
secretly revealed legalism of Qumran' and their description of it as
'the perfect way'. 'The sectarians are to be obedient and perfect in
all that is revealed to them (cf. 1QS 1.8–9; 5.9; 8.1, 15; 9.13, 19), in
"everything which He has commanded" (1.17; 5.1, 8; 9.24), to keep
"*all* the words of God" (1.14; 3.11), to "depart from *all* evil" (1.4, 7;
2.3; 5.1), "every perversity" (6.15; 8.18; 9.21).' This ideal of legal
perfection must not be confused with the inner qualitative perfection
which is the ideal of the Christian ethic. Job is perfect (Job 1.1)
because he neglected none of his prescribed duties (1.5 f.), and the
righteous man in Judaism does not claim to be superior to this. Thus
Luke can describe Zacharias and Elizabeth as 'righteous before God'
and 'blameless' because of their adherence to 'all the commandments
and ordinances of the Lord' (Luke 1.6) obviously without intending
an inner moral sinless state. Indeed, even Jesus' own counsel as
represented by Matt. 5.48 must be interpreted in the light of the Old
Testament vocabulary in which—in this gospel—it is expressed:

'perfection' means leaving out no one who may be the object of your kindness, and does not here raise the question of the possibility of inner purity. That question is raised and answered in Luke 18.9–14.

trial . . . during the dominion of Belial   1.23; 2.19; 3.23; CD 1.5; cf. 1QH 3.28. The dominion of Belial (see below) is the time during which the prince of the demons holds sway over the world and which leads up to the age of the Messiah. In it the righteous must endure suffering at the hands of the devil and his servants until their deliverance by the coming of the Messiah. Cf. 1QpHab 5.7 f.; CD 6.10, 14; 1QSa 1.3. The kingdom of the devil is called 'the kingdom of the enemy' in *Test. Dan* 6.2, 4 and the very word by which the devil is so often known, Satan, means the adversary or enemy. In Luke 4.6 the devil specifically claims authority over the whole world and in II Cor. 4.4 is even called 'the God of this world (or age)': his kingdom is indeed coterminous with this world, but is limited to a certain season.

The word here translated **trial** (*maṣreph*) means a furnace or refiner's fire, as Prov. 17.3 and 27.21 make quite clear. Flusser, 'The Baptism of John and the Dead Sea Sect' (in *Essays on the Dead Sea Scrolls*, pp. 227 ff.), gives these references and points out that the metaphor is constant in the scrolls, occurring, for example, at CD 20.27 and in the *Rule* again in the passage about the Two Spirits (3.13–4.26), where fire is to destroy the wicked (4.18 ff.), which itself recalls Mal. 3.2 f. where the fire is again a refiner's fire and is also to purify the righteous. The other occurrence of the word in the *Rule* (8.4) clearly envisages this latter meaning. Flusser finds the same conception in *Or. Sib.* 3.71–74, 84–87, but these references seem to be to destruction of the wicked; but he may be right in regarding I Cor. 3.12–15 as a reflection of the same apocalyptic tradition of trial of the righteous as is found here and with striking clarity in DSW 17.1, 9, the latter passage being translated in Yadin's edition 'be ye strong in God's crucible'. The NT equivalent is πειρασμός, and the conception appears there more often as the testing of the faithful than as the destruction of the wicked. The word carries this eschatological sense at Matt. 6.13; Mark 14.38 pars.; Luke 8.13; 11.4; Heb. 3.8 (citing Ps. 95.8); James 1.2, 12; I Peter 1.6; 4.12; II Peter 2.9; Rev. 3.10. James 1.12 combines two key words—πειρασμός and ὑπομένειν—to express the Christian's action of endurance. In Rom. 5.3 f. Paul says that persecution creates ὑπομονή which in turn creates δοκιμή, the condition of having been tried in the furnace and found true and steadfast. I Peter 4.12 speaks of 'the firing which has come about to test you'.

Belial occurs several times in the books of Samuel and also in Deut., Judges, I Kings and II Chron. in the phrase 'sons of Belial', where, even if the derivation is uncertain, it evidently means 'worthlessness'. It is a proper name for the chief of the demons only in the Qumran literature; but the form Beliar appears once in the NT in a passage almost certainly out of place and of doubtful Pauline origin (II Cor. 6.15); but it is common in *Test. XII Patr; Or. Sib.* and *Jubilees.*

In the scrolls the dominion of Belial is, like the existence of evil, a secret of God (3.22 f.; 4.18 f. and 1QH 15.19 f.). A time has been set for the existence of unrighteousness: Belial wields **dominion** (*memsheleth*), but it is God who will **reign**; as the Jewish Service for *R'osh Hashshanah* (New Year) puts it, '. . . for thou shalt make the dominion of arrogance to pass away from the earth and thou shalt reign, O Lord, alone over all thy works . . .' (Singer, pp. 239a–240; see S. Aalen, *NTS* 8, 1961–2, p. 229).

1.18. the priests and the Levites shall bless   Instruction for the actual ceremony and rite begins here; the blessings followed by curses are founded on Deut. 27–30 (p. 107). Yadin (pp. 223 ff.) points out the interesting parallel between the present passage and DSW 12.1 ff. The references of parallel passages are:

1QS	DSW
1.18 ff.	12.1 ff.
1.1 ff.	13.2–3
2.4 ff.	13.1–2
	and
	13.4

In DSW the formulae occur in a passage which has been only partially preserved, but they appear to constitute the Blessing and Curse, in a ceremony conducted by the chief priest with the co-operation of priests, Levites and elders, uttered after the defeat of the men of Belial's lot. The passage falls within the portion B (2) of Yadin's division of the *War Scroll* into A: War Series; B (1): Battle Serek; B (2): Ritual Serek; C: Kittim Series. Rabin allots A and B (1) to the *Book of the War* and B (2) to the *Book Serek 'Itto* (*The Order of His Time*), finding the titles in DSW 15.4–6. This is part of his very persuasive thesis that the *War Scroll* is composite.[1] We can easily imagine the covenant liturgy as a well-known formula woven by different authors (or perhaps the same author) into different documents, including the *Rule* and DSW. See the discussion on pp. 113 ff. on the composite nature of the *Rule*.

1.21. priests . . . Levites   The ceremonial necessity for this division seems to be based on ancient practice. See pp. 69 ff. Cf. 2.1, 4; DSW, 7.9, 13; 13.1; 15.4; 18.5; CD 10.5; 13.2–6; 14.3–7; Num. 3–5.

the righteous acts of God are contrasted with **the iniquities of the children of Israel**, implying the ingratitude of the latter. Cf. 10.24; 1QH 9.9; 17.20 (and elsewhere also in the *Psalms of Thanksgiving* for the contrast of God's righteousness and man's powerlessness to do right); in CD 4.9 and 8.14–18 the biblical doctrine that God made his covenant with his people and gave them their land because of his righteousness, not theirs, receives clear expression. The actual recital of these acts of God and of the iniquities of Israel also follows biblical models, e.g. Pss. 78; 105; 106; Neh. 9.6 ff. The last is an excellent instance, occurring as it does as part of a covenant ceremony no less than this passage. The famous speech of Stephen in Acts 7.2–53 uses this type of literature as a model.

1.24. confess   The formula of confession has been incorporated into the narrative section of CD (20.28–30) and the description there of those who make this confession and fulfil other conditions seems to be borrowed from fixed ritual and ethical features of the life of the members of the sect. This is another indication of the manner in which the Qumran works were composed. The confession formula appears at its simplest in I Kings 8.47 (II Chron. 6.37 repeats in a virtually identical form), consisting of three verbs. In Ps. 106.6 it recurs with the theme of 'we and our fathers' interwoven, not kept separately to the end, as here in the *Rule*. Dan. 9.5 preserves the formula faithfully and adds two verbs. Other relevant passages are Neh. 9.33; Ezek. 2.3; *Jub.* 1.22. In the last the 'we and our fathers' theme is again found. The text translated is of Habermann, who has the warrant of three letters remaining at the end of the verb for **we have sinned**, but has supplied **we have transgressed** to fill a gap in the ms., in agreement with Millar Burrows and Brownlee. Wernberg-Møller is surely wrong to say that I Kings 8.47; Ps. 106.6; Dan. 9.5 support the

---

[1] C. Rabin, 'The Literary Structure of the War Scroll' in *Essays on the Dead Sea Scrolls*, pp. 31–48.

restoration, for these passages agree in a three-verb formula, using the same verbs (in slightly differing forms) in the same order; the standard translation is 'We have sinned, we have committed iniquity, we have done evil.' The *Rule* has changed the order of the first and second verbs and apparently—so the gap suggests—introduced a further verb—**we have transgressed**—which it places second. There seems to be a reminiscence of the formula at 11.9, where three nouns appear in the order, iniquities, transgressions, sins, and this perhaps supports Habermann in his restoration here. Thus the *Rule* in this passage will have presented a four-verb instead of the usual three-verb formula. It is probably significant that the formula in the relatively late Lev. 16.21 and in the Mishnah, *Yoma* 3.8; 4.2; 6.2 is 'iniquities, transgressions, sins' always in that order—which has indeed been the traditional order ever since; this traditional form is found in scripture only at Lev. 16.21. The usual scriptural form is 'sins, iniquities, evil'. The two formulae overlap as to two of the expressions and therefore, to combine the usual scriptural with the traditional formula, the *Rule* has here invented a four-verb version.

2.1. mercies in his gracious acts The contrast between the action of God and that of Israel throughout history is repeated. See above on 1.21.

2.2. lot of God means the portion of mankind allotted to God, a curiously anthropomorphic metaphor used for the 'portion' of God or of light also in DSW 13.9, 12; 15.1; 17.6, 7; CD 13.12. **Lot of Belial** occurs below at 2.5; cf. 4.24; DSW 1.1, 5, 11; 4.2; 13.2, 4 and 13.5, where both **lot of God** and **lot of Belial** occur. Deut. 32.9; Ecclus. 17.17 illustrate the idea well, but do not use the word *goral*, which is found here and in the other scrolls passages given, and also at Lev. 16.8, 10, where it is used in such a way as perhaps to foreshadow the conception in the *Rule* of two 'lots' of men, one for God, the other for Belial. The corresponding Greek word is κλῆρος and the metaphor continues in the NT, as at Col. 1.12; cf. I Peter 5.3; for associated words and conceptions cf. Rom. 8.17; Gal. 3.29; Eph. 1.11. For the whole subject of the two divisions of mankind see on 'The Two Spirits' (pp. 37–56 and below 3.13–4.26).

May he bless thee The blessing which follows is an expansion of Num. 6.24–26 (the Blessing of the Priests) like that in *Jub.* 12.29. See also 1QSb, esp. 3.5, 25; 4.27 f. (called 'A Formulary of Blessings' in Gaster, pp. 97 ff.); DSW 13.1–6. The expansion prays for virtues like those given special attention at 4.2–8; 11.3–8. The language is reflected in the fourth *berakah* of the *Shemoneh 'Eśreh* or Prayer of *Eighteen Benedictions* (Mishnah, *Ber.* 4.3; 5.2; *Ta'an.* 2.2).

2.3. enlighten thy heart   4.2; 1QH 3.3; 4.5, 27; 1QSb 4.27. Num. 6.25 uses the same verb with the LORD's 'face' as object followed by 'upon thee'. In the *Psalms of Thanksgiving* passages it is the face of the singer or of men which God has 'illuminated'; thus a very similar image avoids the anthropomorphism still observable in Num. 6.25. The psalmist prays that God will enlighten his eyes so that he sleep not in death (13.3 [Hebrew 13.4]; cf. Prov. 29.13), and less poetically but more spiritually another psalm speaks of the LORD's commandment enlightening the eyes (19.8; Hebrew 19.9). While it is not the eyes which know God but the heart, as in Jer. 24.7, and it may be hardened so as not to acknowledge him (e.g. Ex. 10.1; I Sam. 6.6; Ps. 95.8), and a new heart of flesh is then needed (Ezek. 11.19; 36.26), yet the heart which 'knows' and the eyes which 'see' God are closely connected, as the phrase here neatly shows. The NT uses the same unexpected conjunction: the pure in heart will see God (Matt. 5.8), hardening of the heart is equivalent to spiritual blindness (Mark 6.52; and esp. 8.17 f.) and a veil covers the unbelieving heart (II Cor. 3.15). In II Cor. 4.6 Paul has the striking phrase (which he attributes to God): '*Light* shall *shine* out of darkness, which has *shined* in your *hearts* for the *enlightenment* of the *knowledge* of the glory of God in the *face* of Christ.' Italics mark the words which betray the inheritance of this verse. Enlightenment in the NT is closely connected with the initial experience of baptism upon conversion, as in Heb. 6.4; 10.32, and those who 'know' the full riches of the Christian revelation are described in Eph. 1.18 as having the eyes of the heart enlightened, a conception in which the two images have finally coalesced.

2.4. the Levites curse—as in Deut. 27.14. See p. 106, and for the substance of the blessings and curses see Deut. 28.3 ff. and 16 ff. As with the blessings so with the curses the emphasis in the *Rule* falls on general moral or immoral action (**evil deeds of thy guilty wickedness** is indeed comprehensive); and the form which the curse will take is punishment at the hand of human persecutors and torturers, reflecting the context in which the *Rule* was written and the men of Qumran were living. This seems to be the natural explanation of the first two curses, and it is supported by the fact that in Deuteronomy also the curses are followed by a grim prophecy that they will fall upon a disobedient Israel in the future (28.20 ff.) at the hand of her enemies (28.25 ff.). The **terror** is, in fact, that of RV mg. at Deut. 28.25, where the meaning is 'you shall become a terror', i.e. a people stricken with terror, as also at Ezek. 23.46. This is a conception readily intelligible to those Jews and others of the twentieth century who have lived 'under the terror' or in a period aptly called 'the Terror'. Wernberg-Møller believes the agents of punishment envisaged here are angels and refers to *Test. Levi* 3.2 f.; *Targ. in Lev.* 26.25 and *I Enoch* 62.11. The last passage certainly has phrases reminiscent of the *Rule* here, but there the angels punish those very persecutors of the elect who are here thought of as the agents of God's punishment for faithless Israelites, just as in the same way these human torturers provide the testing furnace for the righteous (see on **trial** 1.17 above).

2.8. mist of everlasting fire   4.13; 1QpHab 10.5, 13; 1QH 6.18; CD 2.5; Ezek. 21.32; 30.15 f. (the last recalled by DSW 14.1); *Test. Judah* 25.3 (Beliar will be destroyed by fire for ever); *Test. Zebulun* 10.3 (a similar fate for the wicked). Fire is the means by which the LORD will destroy the wicked in his final judgment, the event at the end of history, following the woes so far considered, the event to which the thought of the passage has now moved. It seems that the fire destroys for ever; again, it is here literally 'fire of the ages', which suggests that it, too, lasts for ever, throughout all ages which may succeed one another. That the punishment is everlasting does not follow, since the fire's victims are immediately destroyed, for ever. So may Mark 9.43 be understood, and in the parallel Matt. 18.8 the different phrase τὸ πῦρ τὸ αἰώνιον means the 'fire of the age (to come)' rather than everlasting fire, still less fire which punishes for ever. Matt. 25.31–46, in which the Son of Man and angels appear, reflecting *I Enoch* 62.5 ff., is the only passage in the NT speaking of punishment as αἰώνιος (Matt. 25.46) and probably means 'of the new age' just as the righteous are to enjoy the life of the new age (*ibid.*). Fire is associated with darkness at 1QS 4.13 and *I Enoch* 103.8. This may seem strange, but in fact proceeds from one conception of the being of God, who is a pillar of cloud by day and of fire by night (Ex. 13.21 f.) and speaks from the midst of fire and yet from thick darkness (Deut. 5.22). Later thought associates sometimes the darkness, sometimes the fire, sometimes both with the divine punishment or with hell itself (Matt. 8.12; 22.13; Jude 6 f.; II Peter 2.4).

forgive by covering thine iniquities   3.6, 8; 5.6; 8.6, 10; 9.4; 11.14; 1QH 4.37; 17.12; frgt. 2.13; DSW 2.5; CD 2.5; 3.18; 4.6, 9, 10; 14.19; 20.34; Lev. 4.20, 26, 31, etc. Abel's blood cried from the ground which had received it (Gen. 4.10 f.) and so Cain's sin could not be hidden or covered. The grim words of Job 16.18, 'O earth, cover not thou my blood', thus mean 'Let the sin committed against me cry out loud', while Ps. 32.1 is used by Paul at Rom. 4.7 to express the blessedness of one whose sin is covered, i.e. forgiven. In Gen. 4.10; Job 16.18 and Ps. 32.1 the verb is the common *kasah*. An alternative word is that whose root is *kpr* and whose use in the OT justifies the EVV rendering of 'make atonement for' although its original meaning is 'cover'. The list of references at the beginning of this note are all to uses of this latter verb, those from Leviticus being examples of combination of 'covering' and 'forgiving', as here in the *Rule*. The essential point is a paramount theme of the *Psalms of Thanksgiving*. In his commentary Licht (p. 41) explains the author's thought on this matter: sin is part of the constitution of man and he requires purification from it. This is impossible for him to achieve (though fulfilment of ritual requirements may purify him from the concomitant physical contamination) except as a gift from God, who purifies by the spirit of holiness (1QH 16.12; for the phrase cf. Rom. 1.4). The men of Qumran were as convinced as Paul of the fact that God alone can cleanse, and so work atonement for man by his grace. Mansoor, in his edition of the *Psalms of Thanksgiving*, commenting on 1QH 4.37 claims that the idea expressed in the root *kpr* has a double reference. If it refers to God it means that he forgives, if to man, that he offers repentance, and so has a share in God's gracious action towards him. He believes that the mutual relation of these two aspects 'seems to have been the distinctive element of the Qumran sect'. The action of a member of the sect which is his response or approach to the divine action contained in 'covering' his iniquity is to enter the sect and keep faithfully its way of life. Lines 11–18 below show clearly that this involves inner sincerity behind the prescribed actions which constitute obedience to that way. The men of Qumran would have understood well the plight of Lady Macbeth, whose hand seemed permanently stained with blood, which has become a powerful psychic embodiment of her spiritual guilt.

4QSb reads here the singular 'iniquity', suggesting that the author or the scribe of that ms. was thinking of the doctrine held by the author of 1QH: it is not only, perhaps not chiefly particular sins but the radical sinful element in his nature for which the sinner must seek atonement or 'covering' from God.

2.9. intercessors   The translation is in doubt. The Hebrew suggests literally 'those who hold fast to the fathers' (i.e. perhaps to the covenant of the fathers, as Dupont-Sommer) or 'the steadfast ones of the fathers' (so Guilbert: '*adeptes des pères*', understanding the phrase of the faithful members of the sect). Habermann suggests 'inheritors of the fathers'; and Brownlee 'all who hold enmity' on the ground that the word translated 'fathers' ('*aboth*) is also the plural of a word meaning 'enmity'. The translation adopted follows Wernberg-Møller, who connects with a Syriac expression based upon the older Accadian *ṣābitat abūtu* and believes that the phrase may have existed in Aramaic for centuries, Aramaic influence on the language of the scrolls being certain. See Wernberg-Møller *ad loc*. He notes that the **intercessors** are angels in *Test. Dan* 6.2; *Test. Levi* 3.5; 5.6 f., and often in *I Enoch* (9.3; 15.2; 39.5; 47.2 etc), and refers to Charles's note on *I Enoch* 9.10. This last passage must be taken closely with *I Enoch* 9.3, which shows that the cries of those who have died (9.10) are addressed to the Most High by way of the angels. Charles gives reason for his conclusion that the intercession of angels for the living as well as for the dead was a popular doctrine based on the OT, referring to Job 5.1; 33.23; Zech. 1.12; Tobit 12.12, 15; cf. Rev. 8.3. O. Betz, in his book *Der Paraklet*, makes this even clearer by giving ample evidence for the prevalence in late Judaism of the conception of a cosmic law court in which God is judge and where the procedure reflects that described in the Mishnah and Talmud tractates *Sanhedrin*; the advocate on either side is also chief witness, and he presents his case in a set form consisting of praise, recollection of facts, and prayer for protection of his client and the condemnation of the adversary. Michael appears regularly as the witness for Israel as in Dan. 10.13, 21; 12.1; Jude 9. The present passage makes good sense against this general background and perhaps implies that for inexpiable sins no advocacy will avail. Betz (*op. cit.*, p. 58) refers to II Peter 2.6: Sodom and Gomorrha are examples of the final judgment. In *Jub.* 16.6, 9 Abraham's intercession for Sodom (Gen. 18.20–33) is omitted. Charles rightly contrasts Acts 10.4, which robustly believes that no intermediaries are needed to convey a righteous man's prayers to God; but the way in which this is expressed suggests a certain formality in the way prayers are to ascend, and in his gospel Luke has a picture very like that at *I Enoch* 9.3–10 in 18.7, with which cf. Rev. 6.10. Nevertheless, in these passages and in the main NT teaching prayers ascend to God directly; although Christ is a perpetual intercessor (Rom. 8.34; Heb. 7.25; 9.24), it is not suggested that he conveys our prayers for us to God, who would not otherwise hear them; the Holy Spirit indeed intercedes by making inarticulate prayers articulate (Rom. 8.26 f.), but while the Christian prays, explicitly or implicitly, *in* and *through* Christ, like his Jewish brother he may pray directly to God (Rom. 5.1 f.).

2.10. Amen, amen   For the double assent see 1.20 and Num. 5.22; Neh. 8.6 (referred to on p. 107). Cf. Matt. 5.37; James 5.12; John 1.51; 5.19, etc.

2.11. Cursed in the idols of his heart   Deut. 29.18 f., also envisages the Israelite who may assent with the lips, but resolve in his heart not to change his ways because of the oath which he is taking. There the particular mental reservation envisaged is concerning actual idols. The present passage owes its vocabulary to Deut. 29.18 f., but enlarges and deepens the sense. In order to do so the author has here (11–15) also drawn upon Deut. 27.15, 17, 18 (cf. Lev. 19.14 for prohibition of putting a stumbling-block before the blind), perhaps allegorizing a little. Here the hypocritical candidate is himself the blind man, setting a **stumbling-block** (2.17; 1QH 4.15; Ezek. 14.3–7) before himself, and the **idols** he has set up on his heart, as Ezekiel puts it (14.4). Habermann in his note interprets differently by paraphrasing the Hebrew text to mean that that man is accursed who causes to err one who comes from the covenant of the sect and sets before him a stumbling-block, etc. This makes good sense and it may be claimed that 'causes to err one who comes' is a more natural translation than 'comes to enter', but the text continues with 'in or into', not 'from'. Habermann refers to Ps. 35.4 and Zeph. 1.6, but in neither case is the wording close to this passage.

2.14. destroyed shall be his spirit   See 4.19 and pp. 156–58.

thirsty with all his surfeit   The vocabulary is taken from Deut. 29.19 and the meaning is uncertain. RV (and RSV more specifically) are supported by *BDB* in assuming a proverbial phrase, but it does not seem to have been used very aptly in the context. Wernberg-Møller translates 'thirst as well as saturation', claiming the support of 1QpHab 11.13 f., but admitting that the application here is not clear.

2.15. everlasting destruction   5.13; DSW 1.5; 9.5. The idea, and some of the vocabulary of the words preceding this phrase, are found in Deut. 29.19 f. The exact phrase does not occur in the Bible. DSW 1.5 prophesies everlasting destruction for all the lot of Belial.

2.16. set him apart for evil   Deut. 29.21.

sons of light   See 3.13 and pp. 79 ff.

2.17. lot See on 2.1; but here the use of the word is slightly different: rather than 'portion' it means 'destiny' or 'fate'. Yet another meaning of the word appears at 5.3.

accursed for ever *I Enoch* 5.5; *Jub.* 36.10. As these passages show, the final judgment by God is expressed as his eternal curse upon the wicked.

CEREMONY FOR ASSEMBLY OF MEMBERS: 2.19–25a

19 This shall be their practice year by year all the days of the dominion of Belial: the priests shall enter ²⁰first, in order, according to their spiritual status one after the other. And the Levites shall enter after them. ²¹And all the people shall enter third in order, one after the other, by thousands and hundreds ²²and fifties and tens, so that every man of Israel may know each the place of his standing in the community of God ²³according to the eternal plan. No one shall move down from the place of his standing and no one shall move up from the place of his lot, ²⁴for all shall be in a community of truth, humble goodness, love of grace and kindly consideration ²⁵ᵃone towards another in a community of holiness, and they shall be members of an eternal assembly.

2.19. year by year As the section on the Feast of Weeks and the Renewal of the Covenant shows (pp. 95 ff.), the event took place annually on this feast. Cf. 5.8, 23.

all the days of the dominion of Belial See on 1.17. The sect and all its practice were dependent upon the assumption that this dominion was due to end within a foreseeable time and be replaced by the reign of God.

the priests shall enter first . . . The organization of the sect is like that in CD 14.3 ff., except that there a fourth class, the proselytes, follows the children of Israel, who in our passage are expressed as **all the people**. The most probable explanation is that CD contains instructions for the sect in various settlements, in some of which at least Gentile proselytes were admitted and whose life involved some contact with Gentiles (which may indeed be implied by CD 11.2). Such a class was not envisaged in the strict and eremitic community at Qumran.

2.21. by thousands and hundreds . . . The organization of the people in these divisions is clearly explained by Yadin (pp. 59 ff.). It corresponds to that recommended by Jethro in Ex. 18.21 and is found again in the Bible at Deut. 1.15; Num. 31.14, 48, 52; I Sam. 8.12; II Sam. 18.1, 4. That this was a method still used at the time of the writing of the scrolls is shown by I Macc. 3.55 and Josephus, *BJ* 2.20.7. That it had a solemn significance as divinely ordered is shown by Deut. 1.9 ff. and by the detailed description of the sect organized in divisions each with its banner found in DSW. The same divisions are found in CD 12.23–13.1. That it had the further solemnity of reflecting the structure of the universe is also shown by Yadin (see p. 69).

2.22. the place of his standing   In Hebrew, his *beth ma'amad*. For the *ma'amad* see Yadin, pp. 206 f., and Danby, *Mishnah*, p. 794, who explains thus: 'It is the name given to a group of representatives from outlying districts corresponding to the twenty-four "courses of priests". Part of them went up to the Temple as witnesses of the offering of the sacrifices (*Ta'an.* 4.2), and part came together in their own town, where they held prayers at fixed times during the day coinciding with the fixed times of sacrifice in the Temple.' The term occurs in this technical sense at 6.12; DSW 2.3; 5.4; 6.1, 4; 8.3 etc; 1QH 3.21; 11.13; and elsewhere in the scrolls in senses derived from this use (as CD 20.5); in Scripture it is not found in this meaning, but it looks as if the sect was organized in twenty-six courses of priests (see p. 93) with corresponding *ma'amadoth*.

2.23. the place of his lot   Apparently here an alternative expression for **place of his standing**; **lot** here therefore means the position in the community assigned to a man on entry, in a particular ten within a particular fifty, and belonging to a particular *ma'amad* associated with a particular priestly course. For other meanings of **lot** see on 2.1 and 2.17.

2.25a. eternal assembly   The structure and behaviour of the assembly express the will of God for Israel and the assembly will therefore be the form in which Israel, after the final struggle with evil, will enter the world to come.

community of holiness   For another title of the community, **counsel of God**, interchangeable with **council of God**, see note on 1.8. Here is another title which recurs at 8.21; 1SQa 2.9; DSW 3.4; 1QH 7.10; CD 20.24. For a discussion of titles of the community see the note on 5.13 (**men of holiness**).

DENUNCIATION OF THOSE WHO REFUSE TO ENTER
THE COVENANT: 2.25b–3.12

25b And everyone who refuses to enter ²⁶the [covenant of Go]d, to follow the way of the stubbornness of his heart, shall not enter the community of his truth, for his soul has revolted at

COLUMN THREE

¹the disciplines involved in the knowledge of precepts of righteousness, he has not mastered his backslidings; and with Israel he shall not be counted ²and his knowledge and his power and his wealth shall not come into the counsel of the community; for he ploughs with evil step and defilement clings ³to his drawing back. He will not prevail by following the stubbornness of his heart, and darkness will he see as the ways of light. In the well of the perfect ⁴he will not be counted. He will not be made guiltless by atonement and he will not be purified in waters for purification; he shall not sanctify himself in seas ⁵or rivers nor will he be purified in all the waters of cleansing. Unclean, unclean shall he be all the days of his rejection of the precepts ⁶of God with its refusal to discipline himself in the community of his counsel. For in a spirit of true counsel about the ways of man will all his iniquities find atonement, ⁷that he may look upon the light of life; and in a holy spirit of being united with his truth he will be purified from all ⁸his iniquities, and in a spirit of uprightness and humility his sin will be atoned. In the subjection of his soul to all the ordinances of God his flesh will be purified ⁹in being sprinkled with waters for purification and by sanctification in waters of purity.

But let him order his steps to walk perfectly ¹⁰in all the ways of God according as he commanded at the fixed times of his making them known, and not swerve to right or left and not ¹¹go beyond any one of all his words. Then he will be acceptable through pleasing atonement before God and it will be for him a covenant ¹²of eternal community.

It seems natural to interpret this passage (2.25b–3.12) as a commination against those who, after their probation, refuse to enter the covenant, balancing the part of the scroll so far considered (1.1–2.24) which deals with those who do enter it. (So apparently Brownlee and Guilbert.) Wernberg-Møller (whose exact interpretation is not clear) compares CD 8.19, but there the question of someone refusing to **enter** does not arise. Flusser ('The Baptism of John and the Dead Sea Sect', p. 217) regards the one **who refuses to enter** as 'the member of the sect who refuses to take part in the annual covenant of the sect', but there is nothing in the scroll to suggest that the recusant envisaged is already a member, since until now the scroll has been considering the question of becoming a member and its conditions.

2.26. shall not enter the community   There is no other way of becoming a member except by taking part in the covenant ceremony.

3.1. disciplines   Wernberg-Møller's note shows that he reads the Hebrew word here translated, although his translation 'instructions' fails fully to support his useful comment. J. A. Sanders, in *Suffering in Divine Discipline in the Old Testament and Post-Biblical Judaism*, has shown the significance of the root *ysr*: according to the prophets God has willed to discipline his people both by the obvious ways of his law and of his warnings uttered through them, and by their sufferings as a nation. In the Psalms and elsewhere in later literature the individual may be subjected to disciplinary suffering. The sect believed that it was necessary for them as individuals and as a body to accept voluntarily the disciplines (*yissurim*) which God demanded of those who would cleanse themselves thoroughly so as to be truly his people. Cf. Ps. 94.12. Habermann reads *yissode*, 'foundations' (of knowledge), the two words being admittedly very difficult to distinguish in an ancient manuscript. 'Discipline' is probably the right reading also at 6.26, the word occurring again at 1QH 17.22; CD 7.5, 8; 19.4.

he has not mastered his backslidings   Habermann reads Hebrew words which, as he comments, might be translated 'he has not held fast to him (sc. God) who restores to him his life' (so Brownlee also); but the writing is obscure and Habermann suggests a further alternative, a reading without 'not' which would give 'so as to cling to his apostasies'.

The reading adopted here retains the negative and the verb in a *hiph'il* form having as its object *limeshubothayu* (backslidings or apostasies). Cf. Jer. 2.19. Vermès, reading apparently *liteshubothau* as the object of the verb, translates 'has not confirmed the conversion of his life' which fits admirably the context of a probationer quailing before the final step.

Guilbert and Wernberg-Møller favour the reading *lmshub* found in 4QSc, taking it as an Aramaic infinitive, and the latter translates 'he is unable to repent, so that he might live' for the literal 'he is unable to return (to) his life' and compares Acts 11.8, a misprint for 11.18.

with Israel he shall not be counted   For only members of the sect will in the final judgment of God be reckoned as Israelites.

3.2. knowledge . . . power . . . wealth   See note on **knowledge** and **wealth** at 1.11.

counsel   See on 1.8 **counsel of God**.

he ploughs   Lit. 'his ploughing is'. Guilbert well refers to Hos. 10.13 and translates '*sa machination*'. The expression is indeed a metaphor, but this may properly be retained in translation. Habermann compares Prov. 3.29. See also I Sam. 23.9.

3.3. darkness will he see as the ways of light No doubt because he belongs to the dominion of darkness and is led by that spirit. See, e.g., 3.20 f.

the well of the perfect There is here probably a reference to the sect who form an 'oasis of perfect ones' in the desert. Cf. 'the well of Jacob' as a title for Israel at Deut. 33.28 and allied metaphors at Ps. 68.26 and Isa. 48.1.

3.4. He will not be made guiltless . . . Flusser (*op. cit.*) explains some important principles connected with Jewish ideas of defilement and purification. Ritual acts cleanse from ritual defilement, repentance from moral defects. The sect is the first group within Judaism of whom we know who believed that moral failure (sin in our modern sense) incurred ritual defilement. They taught that to be cleansed from sin demanded *both* repentance *and* ritual purification. Emphasis in this passage of the *Rule* falls upon the fact that ritual uncleanness still clings to a man who has performed the necessary purification rituals, unless he has undergone the necessary inner purification which the **spirit of true counsel** will give him if he submits to the prescribed disciplines.

In the Mishnah, *Yoma* 8.9 expresses a great deal of what is taught here in the *Rule*: 'For transgressions that are between man and God the Day of Atonement effects atonement, but for transgressions that are between a man and his fellow the Day of Atonement effects atonement only if he has appeased his fellow.' The same *mishnah* closes with a passage containing another idea found frequently in the *Rule*, that the spirit which God bestows on the loyal member of the sect is like waters for purification, so that God is even described as sprinkling this spirit upon him (1QS 4.21). At the end of *Yoma* R. Akiba is quoted: 'Blessed are ye, O Israel. Before whom are ye made clean and who makes you clean? Your Father in heaven, as it is written, *And I will sprinkle clean water upon you and ye shall be clean.* And again it says, *O Lord the hope* (miqveh) *of Israel*;—as the *Miqveh* cleanses the unclean so does the Holy One, blessed be he, cleanse Israel.' The first citation is from Ezek. 36.25 and the second from Jer. 17.13, where Akiba has seen a double meaning in *miqveh*—'hope' and 'immersion-pool' (see Danby, *Mishnah*, p. 172 n. 8). In the Mishnah there is a whole tractate (*Miqvaoth*) on Immersion-pools. It is debated whether or not the cisterns at Qumran were used for this purpose. There would be little doubt of this if we could be sure that the amount of water available was such that it could be used so prodigally.

That sin defiles ceremonially is a thought met again at 5.13 f. and 8.16–19. It is interesting to consider whether the notion finds its way into the NT. Flusser refers to I Cor. 1.30; 6.11; Eph. 5.26, where spiritual rather than ceremonial holiness is meant, and it is obvious from these and other passages that a sense of inner defilement by sin and the need and possibility of its removal by inner purification are subjects which Jesus and NT writers express by the natural metaphors connected with water, viz. washing and purification. There is one passage indeed in which it seems as though the author thinks of Christian baptism as bestowing ceremonial as well as inner purification. This is Heb. 10.22 ('having your bodies washed with pure water'), cited by Flusser, who remarks that Heb. 9.9 f. shows that the author did not regard Jewish waters of purification as valid for cleansing at the level of conscience. Whatever the truth about Heb. 10.22, as Flusser goes on to show, I Peter 3.21 opposes the conception that Christian baptism bestows ceremonial washing of the body. Similarly, the Fourth Gospel insists on the necessity for spiritual rebirth, i.e. through baptism which effects an inner purification—see John 3.3 ff. Cf. Mark 1.8 pars.; John 1.33, etc. Jesus in the Fourth Gospel repudiates the idea that a baptized Christian needs fuller purification (13.10), claiming indeed that it is the word which purifies (15.3). Cf. Mark 7.1 ff. (par. Matt. 15.1 ff.); Luke 11.37 ff.; Matt. 23.25 ff.

atonement   See on 2.8, **forgive by covering**, where the belief of the sect is explained. It seems as if atonement rituals in general (such as Lev. 1.4; 4.20, 26, 31, 35) are the subject here, although Wernberg-Møller (*ad loc.*) and Lehmann (who in ' "Yom Kippur" in Qumran', *RQ* 3, 1961–2, pp. 117 ff., groups this passage with the *Scroll of Three Tongues of Fire*, the *Priestly Blessings*, the *Pesher on Jacob's Blessings*, *Yom Kippur Prayers* and the *Scroll of Mysteries*) refer it to the Day of Atonement (Ex. 30.10; Lev. 16; 23.26–32; Num. 29.7–11). Wernberg-Møller regards it as natural that the annual renewal of the covenant should take place on the Day of Atonement, but see pp. 104–7 for the view that the occasion was the Feast of Weeks. Talmon (*SH* IV, p. 165) would connect with the failure of all those outside the sect to keep the correct calendar: this means that none of their rituals would be effective. While it is true that the sect had probably withdrawn from the Temple and its cult partly on these grounds, it seems from the context here that the disabling factor is the rebellious attitude of the individual who has drawn back from entering the sect.

waters for purification   3.9; 4.21; Num. 19.9, 12 f., 20, 21; 31.23. Num. 19 gives full instruction for the preparation of these waters by means of mixing in water the ashes of a red heifer (cf. *HDB* IV, pp. 207 ff.). Regulations governing this practice form the tractate *Parah*, found in the Sixth Division of the Mishnah, whose subject is 'Cleannesses' or *Ṭohoroth*, a word which gives the title to the following tractate, itself followed by *Miqvaoth* (Immersion-pools) and *Niddah* (The Menstruant). *Waters for Purification* translates what may be represented by 'waters of *niddah*'. The phrase occurs frequently in the Mishnah, especially in *Parah*. In his note at the beginning of the tractate *Niddah* Danby explains that the word means literally 'impurity' or 'separation' and acquired the more specialized sense of (*a*) a menstruous woman, (*b*) menstrual impurity; but to translate our phrase by 'waters of impurity' would be misleading, since the specially prepared water is for the removal of impurity. Moreover, as the use of the word in Num. 19 shows, this specialized use does not abrogate the more general use and *niddah* in the scrolls frequently describes moral impurity. Yet the practice of ceremonial lustration even for moral impurity is based on the rules for removal of uncleanness derived from physically caused taboos, as found in Lev. 15. In his comment on *Meg.* 2.4 Rabbinowitz remarks that 'ablution takes a prominent place in the ceremonial of rabbinic Judaism. One of the forms of ablution is the *tebilah*, which is the complete immersion of the whole body under water. The biblical injunction "And he shall bathe his flesh in running water" (Lev. 15.13) was interpreted by the rabbis to require immersion to take place either in a natural spring or stream or else in a ritual bath. This had to contain not less than 40 *Seah* of water (about 120 gallons), which was not poured into the bath but had to be made to enter it in a manner resembling the method by which a natural pool of running water is filled . . . Since the destruction of the Temple the rite of immersion has become imperative only in the case of the menstruous woman, and of converts to Judaism prior to their reception into the faith' (J. Rabbinowitz, *Mishnah Megillah*, p. 79). *Tebilah* is the normal word for baptism and the rite is the ancestor both of that of John the Baptist (who bathed his converts in running water and insisted on repentance as well as partaking in the rite) and of Christian baptism, which like that at Qumran is a baptism of both water and spirit, although each community would interpret 'spirit' differently. Archaeology may be able to tell us whether the cisterns at Qumran would meet the legal requirements derived from Lev. 15.13, but opinion is divided on the question whether they were ritual baths or not (see, for example, R. de Vaux, *L'Archéologie et les manuscrits de la mer morte*, pp. 98 f.). CD 10.12 f. forbids immersion in insufficient water and refers interestingly to 'pools in rocks'. In his note Rabin refers to *Miqvaoth* 2.4. The only *miqveh* so far known to survive from the period and apparently answering to the halakic requirements has been found at Masada (*Illustrated London News*, 31 Oct. 1964, p. 696). There is no evidence that at any time 'running water' was held to be necessary for Christian baptism. The phrase from Lev. 15.13 is literally 'living water', and is normal Hebrew for fresh or running water to this day. John 4.10–14 suggests that the Church claimed that baptism into Jesus was baptism into living water in a profound sense so that literally 'living', i.e. running, water was no longer necessary. The same passage hints the superiority of Jesus to Jacob, and therefore that of the water which he could give to that of the 'well of Jacob', i.e. of Judaism (see above on 3.3, **the well of the perfect**).

3.4–5. seas or rivers . . . all the waters of cleansing No form of running or 'living' water nor any ritually correctly prepared waters will avail where the inner purification is absent. For all the legalism of the sect, their thorough moral demands eloquently express the fundamental self-honesty of the thoughtful Jew. **Waters of cleansing** uses the vocabulary of Lev. 16.4, 24, etc., although not actually a biblical phrase (Wernberg-Møller). The noun is not found in this masculine form (*rachaṣ*) in midrashic or talmudic Hebrew, but the feminine form (*rechiṣah*) occurs in *Num. Rabbah*, sec. 14, where Naaman is said to be cured by 'Jordan washing'. This feminine form is indeed read here by 4QSh.

Parah 8.8 and *Miqvaoth* 5.4 declare all seas valid as immersion-pools; for sea water used for ceremonial hand-washing, see Josephus, *Ant.* 12.2.13, and for running rivers for similar washing of the body, *Or. Sib.* 4.65. Josephus, *Ant.* 14.10.23, and Acts 16.13 associate water (the former the sea; the latter a river) with a place of prayer.

3.5. Unclean, unclean Lev. 13.45 f.

3.6. in a spirit of true counsel See pp. 34–37 on **spirit** and for **true counsel** see above on **counsel of God** (1.8).

the ways of man According to his spiritual constitution these ways are in darkness (3.21; 4.11) or light (3.3), there being spirits of light and of darkness (3.25). Way (*derek*) is used frequently in the scrolls in this type of metaphor. See on the Two Spirits (3.13–4.26), pp. 37–56. The sect evidently thought it essential for every member to understand the psychology of man as they believed it to be constituted by God, and that on this knowledge and its acceptance depended—at least in part—a man's salvation.

find atonement Or 'be covered'. See on 2.8, **covering thine iniquities.**

3.7. the light of life Life-giving enlightenment. See 2.3 and note, and cf. Ps. 56.13 (Hebrew 56.14); Job 33.30 (*Peshitta*); Isa. 53.11 (LXX and 1QIsa (a)); the law and the wisdom derived from it are meant, and it is by associating R. Jochanan ben Zakkai with his work for the law and its preservation that his pupils can address him as 'light of the world' (*'Aboth de R. Nathan* 25). The title is given to Jesus by the Fourth Gospel (John 8.12) because he is the incarnation of the Logos, therefore of that divine wisdom destined to fulfil and for Christians in a great measure to supersede the wisdom of the Law. On light in general and its association with wisdom and the Law see pp. 43–46.

in a holy spirit of being united with his truth See above on 3.4 **he will not be made guiltless . . .** where the ideas in this passage are discussed. To be united with God's truth means to be united with those who practise God's truth by study of and obedience to the Law.

In the subjection of his soul See on 3.1, **disciplines.**

3.10. at the fixed times See on 1.9.

DOCTRINE OF THE COMMUNITY

3.13–4.26
THE TWO SPIRITS: THEIR WORK IN THE LIVES OF MEN: 3.13–4.14

13 For the Instructor to instruct and teach all the sons of light about the history of all the sons of men, 14about their different spirits with their signs, about their deeds in their generations, and about the visitation of their chastisements with 15their final rewards.

From the God of knowledge is all the present and future and before they came to be he prepared all their pattern; 16and when they come to be at the times decreed for them it is as the pattern of his glory that they will fulfil their actions, and they cannot be changed. In his hand 17are precepts for all and he will supply them with all their needs.

He created man for dominion over [18]the earth; and he set in him two spirits for him to set his course by them until the set time of his visitation. They are the spirits [19]of truth and of perversity. In a dwelling of light are the generations of truth and from a well of darkness come the generations of perversity. [20]In the hand of the prince of lights is the dominion of all sons of righteousness: in the ways of light they will walk. In the hand of the angel [21]of darkness is all the dominion of the sons of perversity and in the ways of darkness they will walk.

And by the angel of darkness are the errors of [22]all the sons of righteousness; and all their sins and iniquities and guiltiness and deeds of transgression are in his dominion [23]according to the secrets of God for his appointed time. All their afflictions and the set times of their troubles are under the dominion of his hostility [24]and all the spirits of his portion are set to trip up the sons of light, but the God of Israel and his angel of truth are the help of the [25]sons of light.

It was he who created the spirits of light and darkness and upon them founded every work [26]and upon their ways established every deed. One God loves for all

COLUMN FOUR

[1]eternity and in all its deeds he will rejoice for ever; the other—he loathes its assembly and all its ways he hates everlastingly.

2 These are their ways on earth: to lighten the heart of man and to make straight before him all the ways of righteousness, of truth, and to implant in his heart fear of the precepts [3]of God, a spirit of humility, patience, great compassion, eternal goodness, prudence, understanding, mighty wisdom, which trusts in all [4]the deeds of God and rests upon the abundance of his mercies; a spirit of knowledge in every design for work, zeal for the precepts of righteousness and a holy design [5]with steadfast intent; abundance of mercies upon all the sons of truth but a purity of glory loathing all the idols of uncleanness; humble conduct [6]with wide discernment concealing for the sake of truth the secrets of knowledge—these are the counsels of the spirit for the sons of truth on earth.

The visitation of all who walk by it will be healing [7]and abundance of peace with length of days, fruitfulness of seed with all eternal blessings and joy in eternity with everlasting life, a crown of glory [8]with a garment of majesty in eternal light.

9 But to the spirit of perversity belong a greedy mind and slackness of hands in serving righteousness, evil and lying, pride and a haughty heart, deceit and cruel treachery; [10]hypocrisy in plenty, shortness of temper but full measure of folly and zeal in insolence; deeds abominable in a spirit of lust and ways of uncleanness in the service of impurity; [11]an abusive tongue, blindness of eyes and heaviness of ears, stiffness of

neck and a heart hardened to walk in all the ways of darkness and evil cunning.

The visitation [12]of all who walk in it will be a multitude of blows at the hand of all the angels of destruction to fell them for ever in the furious wrath of God the avenger, everlasting terror and continuous reproach, [13]with the humiliation of annihilation in darkening fires.

All the end-times for their generations are spent in sad mourning and bitter miseries, while it is dark until [14]their annihilation without remnant or rescue for them.

For the whole passage 3.13–4.26 see pp. 37–56, where the doctrine is discussed. A detailed analysis will assist understanding of text and commentary at this point.

3.13–14   Title of the section: instruction about men, the spirits which influence them, their distinguishing marks, associated virtues and final reward or punishment.

3.15–16   God is the author of all that is to be and nothing can be changed (cf. 4.25b–26).

3.17–19   Man has dominion over the earth; he is guided by two spirits, one of truth, the other of perversity.

3.20–21a   The two spirits and the men in their hands.

3.21b–25a   The influence of the spirit of perversity on the sons of light.

3.25b–4.1   God created both spirits; he loves the one and hates the other everlastingly.

4.2–6a   Ways of the sons of light.

4.6b–8   Reward of the sons of light.

4.9–11a   Ways of the sons of darkness.

4.11b–14   Reward of the sons of darkness.

4.15–16a   Mixture of good and evil in each man (cf. 4.24–25a).

4.16b–18a   Strife between the spirits (cf. 4.23c).

4.18b–19a   Final destruction of evil (cf. 4.23b).

4.19b–20a   Final vindication of truth.

4.20b–22a   Final purification of the righteous.

4.22b–23a   Enlightenment of the righteous.

4.23b   Final destruction of evil (cf. 4.18b–19a).

4.23c   Strife between the spirits (cf. 4.16b–18a).

4.24–25a   Mixture of good and evil in each man (cf. 4.15–16a).

4.25b–26   God is the author of all that is to be (cf. 3.15–16).

The style is to a certain extent chiastic, the predestinarian sections opening and closing the discourse (3.15–16 and 4.25b–26) and other similar passages balancing one another by their position in it. This is made very clear in Licht's Table at the end of 'An Analysis of the Treatise of the Two Spirits in DSD' in *SH* IV, p. 100.

3.13. the Instructor See on 1.1 and pp. 67 and 72 ff.

sons of light See pp. 79 ff.

history Lit. 'generations'. 3.19; 4.15; DSW 3.14; 5.1; 10.14; CD 4.5; Gen. 2.4a; 5.1; 6.9; 10.1; 11.10; 25.12; 36.1; Ex. 6.16; Num. 1.20; 3.1; Ruth 4.18; I Chron. 1.29; 5.7. 7.2; 8.28; 9.9; 26.31; Matt. 1.17; Luke 1.48; Eph. 3.5.

To describe the 'generations' of mankind is to write its history. Philo in *Vita Moysis* II.47 calls the historical elements in the Pentateuch (these exclude the creation narratives as well as the legal sections) *genealogic*. This is entirely within the tradition of biblical historical writing. When the priestly editor says 'These are the generations of . . .' he means 'Here is the history of . . .'; but by history he does not mean a chronicle of facts and events, but something more like a description of character by means of such a chronicle. The Jewish account of mankind is almost always historical, not metaphysical. Hence on the rare occasions where metaphysical speculation is given indulgence the vocabulary more appropriate to an historical treatise is bound to be used. To write therefore the 'generations' or history of mankind is to give an account of men's nature. This is reflected by the commentators, who are divided between 'nature' and 'history', but are fundamentally in agreement. Habermann in a note explains 'generations' or *toledoth* as 'what is in the nature of (mankind)'; Dupont-Sommer and Vermès translate 'the nature', Gaster 'the real nature', Wernberg-Møller 'genealogies', explaining in a note that 'origin and history' is meant; Guilbert translates by 'histoire'. The English language preserves in the term 'natural history' the use of the word 'history' to mean an account not necessarily historical in the now usual sense. Indeed, the present phrase might be translated 'the natural history of mankind.' Betz (*Offenbarung*, p. 145 n. 1) is wrong therefore to translate by *Hervorbringung* or *Erschaffung* on the basis of Gen. 2.4, admitting as he does that in 3.19 below it does mean *Geschlechter*—generations, as most commentators take it to be here.

Such an explanation of the way in which history was conceived explains how in the NT the word 'generation' (γενεά) can be used not only to mean 'the men of this age' but 'the men typical of this evil age' as at Matt. 12.39 ff., 45; 16.4; 17.17; 23.36; Mark 8.12, 38;

9.19; Luke 7.31; 9.41; 11.29 ff.; 16.8; 17.25; Acts 2.40; Phil. 2.15. An excellent example of the idea where the term itself is not used is to be found at Acts 17.30 f.

As Maier remarks, in gnostic myths the literal genealogical meaning of the word returns to prominence, and it is against these that I Tim. 1.4 may be directed. In them history plays no part whatever, but genealogies of powers or aeons are offered as an explanation of the character of the universe and man's status within it.

3.14. about their different spirits The spirits of men determine their character, and are themselves apparently the result of admixture of good and evil spirits in different proportions. See the full note below on 4.16, **inheritance of either great or small.**

with their signs Or 'with their distinctive marks'; the part of the treatise which gives this instruction consists of lines 17–24 below. The different spirits are those of light and perversity and the signs which show to which of them, or to what mixture of them, a man belongs include both physical and moral characteristics. See the note on 4.16.

their deeds in their generations The deeds of men serve to classify them into two generations. Here the latter term is used much as γενεά is used in the NT (see the note on **history,** v. 13 above), but the Hebrew word is *doroth*, not *toledoth*, and, as Brownlee argues, 'generations' here means something like 'societies'. This instruction about the deeds typical of the different classes of men is given in 4.2–6a for the sons of light and in 4.9–11 for the sons of darkness.

the visitation of their chastisements The visitation means the time when God acts with regard to men. For the wicked the final outcome is **chastisement** described in 4.11b–14, for the sons of light it will be **rewards**, described in 4.6–8.

3.15. The God of knowledge 1QH 1.26; CD 15.15; 20.4 f.; I Sam. 2.3; Job 36.4; only I Sam. 2.3 and 1QH 1.26 have the same phrase, but the general sense of the passage is well paralleled by *I Enoch* 9.11. There is no suggestion that God is reached by *gnosis*, i.e. special knowledge esoterically imparted and of a quasi-metaphysical character. The knowledge here is not that which the initiate possesses but the knowledge of the future which God alone possesses, as the context sufficiently shows. It does not seem relevant to refer with some to 11.3, where the knowledge is that revealed by God to man in the Law. The doctrine here laid down is discussed pp. 63 ff.

3.17. He created man for dominion 1Q34 3.2.3; Gen. 1.27 f.; Ps. 8.6 (Hebrew 8.7); Ecclus. 10.4; *Jub.* 2.14. The doctrine of the dominion of man over nature is derived from Gen. 1.28 and is explicit in *Jub.* 2.14. In the NT it suffers a radical change: not man as such but the Messiah is to have dominion over a transformed world. The note of Ps. 8.6(7) is heard less than that of Ps. 110.1, for according to the NT it is the evil powers which are to be subjected; here in the *Rule* as in the NT they are seen as influencing men during the time of Belial's sway. This part of NT doctrine is summarized well in I Cor. 15.23–28 (cf. Eph. 1.22) and Heb. 2.6–9, which gives Ps. 8.5–7 (LXX) a Messianic interpretation in a context whose tone is set by Ps. 110.1.

3.18. two spirits   For explanation of this passage and its implications see pp. 37–56. For **the spirits of truth and of perversity**, cf. I John 4.6 and for the spirit of truth, John 14.17; 15.26; 16.13.

3.19. dwelling of light   See p. 47 n. 1. For the association of light and truth cf. Ps. 43.3.

3.20. prince of lights   Only here and CD 5.18 is this precise phrase found in extant Judaeo-Christian literature; but prince is equivalent to angel, and terms derived from the courts of human rulers tend to conceal the fact that the beings meant are of a special order of creation, called 'sons of God' in, e.g., Gen. 6.2 and Job. 2.1 and 'messengers' (*mal'akim*, usually rendered 'angels') in many passages such as Gen. 16.7; 28.12; Ex. 23.20; Judg. 6.11, 20 ff.; Job. 4.18; Pss. 91.11; 104.4. This chief of angels is probably Michael, for he is named as such in DSW 9.15 f.; 17.6 f. Yadin (p. 238) gives an account of the occurrence of the four archangels Michael, Gabriel, Raphael and Uriel (or Phanuel) in *I Enoch* 9.1; 40.9; 54.6; 71.8 f., *Apoc. Moses* 40.3 and midrashic literature (*Num. Rabbah* 2.10; *Pesiqta Rabbathi* 46; *Pirqe R. Eliezer* 4 and the *Seder Gan Eden*). In some lists Uriel's place in the hierarchy of four is taken by Phanuel, and in DSW it is taken by Sariel; but wherever any list of four occurs Michael is mentioned first. He is indisputably the chief angel in the *Books of Adam and Eve* (which include the *Apoc. Moses*) and in *III Bar.* 11.2, etc. In the Bible he appears as the angel champion of Israel in Dan. 10.13, 21 (cf. *Test. Levi* 5.6); 12.1; Jude 9; Rev. 12.7. Guilbert perceptively suggests that the plural *lights* may be due to the fact that this angel controlled the stars whose behaviour in the heavens determined the calendar by which the righteous ones in heaven and on earth regulated their life of worship. In James 1.17 God himself is the controller of the lights, i.e. heavenly bodies. As such he is the Father of lights (Father being used in the sense of maker and controller of the universe as often in Philo and the Fourth Gospel) in whose nature—in contrast to that of the entities which he controls—there is no παραλλαγή (variation of position due to parallax) nor obscuration (ἀποσκίασμα) caused by variability (τροπή—not there solstice, for which it is often the technical term in Greek astronomy).

In the hand Light and darkness (21) are powers or spheres to which men belong as in *II Enoch* 30.15; *Test. Napht.* 2.10; *Test. Levi* 19.1. See pp. 155 ff.

3.21. they will walk That is, conduct themselves. The root is that of the verb *halak* and the ways by which the two generations walk are here designated by a word with a different root. The way of the righteous is often the *halakah* in the sense of a manner of living with certain rules. See 5.1 ff. for an example of a passage of *halakah* or rules of living.

angel of darkness The phrase occurs here twice, and is not known exactly thus in any extant Hebrew literature, although there are many phrases close to it. He is no doubt the same as Beliar (frequently in the *Test. XII Patr.* and in *Jub.* 1.20; 15.33; II Cor. 6.15) or Belial (1QS 1.18, 24; 2.5, 19; CD 4.13, 15; 5.18; 8.2; 12.2; 19.14; DSW 1.1, 5, 13; 4.2; 11.8; 13.2). His other names are the well-known Satan, and Mastema (*Jub.* 10.8; 11.5, 11; 17.16; 18.9, 12; 19.28; 48.2, 9, 12, 15; 49.2; CD 16.5). At 3.23 below **his hostility** translates *mastematho*, the word being there obviously not a proper name, but revealing the function of the power as opposed to man. Like Satan he is the cosmic adversary.

errors of all the sons of righteousness The idea that the righteous possess God's holy spirit yet that spirit may be defiled is discussed on p. 49. See *Test. Napht.* 10.9 (Heb.); CD 5.11; 7.4; Hermas, *Shepherd, Sim.* 5.5.6; *Mand.* 5.2.5. The NT doctrine is that the Holy Spirit is given once for all in baptism, but may be 'grieved' by the conduct of him of whom the spirit is a seal, a mark showing that he belongs to God (Eph. 4.30 f.). Here the doctrine is quite explicit that the evil spirit or spirits can and do afflict those who are in the dominion of the spirit of light. The final cleansing by God is to be by a spirit of holiness (4.20 f.). There are differences between the *Rule* and Paul on the conception of the spirit of holiness or the Holy Spirit (see p. 35), but they have in common the notion that some measure of God's spirit is already given to his own people, although his full gift of the spirit is to come at the final consummation (Rom. 8.23; II Cor. 1.22; 5.5; Eph. 1.14).

3.23. the secrets of God See the note on **trial . . . during**

the dominion of Belial (1.17), and on the secrets of God as concealed in scripture and able to be revealed only to specially gifted persons see pp. 64–75.

4.2. These are their ways on earth   It seems likely that, as Millar Burrows originally suggested (see note in Brownlee), a heading or further introductory phrase such as 'It is the way of the spirit of truth . . .' has been accidentally omitted. It would have been balanced by **But to the spirit of perversity** in 4.9 below.

The concepts of light and darkness are thought of now as being or causing ethical qualities as in *Test. Levi* 17.6 f.; *Test. Benj.* 5.2; 6.4; *Test. Gad* 5.7.

fear of the precepts of God   Romaniuk (*RQ* 4, 1963–4, p. 34) takes as fear of the judgments of God and compares the contemplation of the judgment of evil angels as a source of fear in the author of 1QH (10.33–36). The word here translated **precepts** (the singular is *mishpaṭ*) may indeed mean judgment. The phrase may be a reminiscence of Ps. 119.161, a psalm in which the words of God are pre-eminently his laws, so that fear of God is fear of his Law or laws. The sect, as Romaniuk makes clear, is to substitute fear of God for fear of the persecutor or tempter (1.16–18 and 10.15 f.), and for the deeper fears of being exposed to dangers and difficulties without God's help, such as those felt by Paul (II Cor. 7.5; Gal. 4.11). 'Those who fear God' is almost a title for the sect in 1QH 12.3; CD 10.2; 20.19, 20. The exhortation of the hymn by Tate and Brady, 'Fear him, ye saints, and you will then have nothing else to fear', exactly expresses the doctrine, the hymn being itself founded on Ps. 34 (see esp. v. 9). The idea is found in the context of exhortation to bravery in war in DSW 10.3–4 and in the wider context of the moral life in general in Matt. 10.28; Luke 12.4 f., while the classical passage for trust in God before the admittedly dreadful coming judgment is Rom. 8.31–39.

In Judaism of the NT period 'God-fearers' means something far less exclusive than those who keep the Law of God through fear of him, namely those who while remaining uncircumcised and therefore unclean in the eyes of the devotees of the Law are sufficiently attracted to the synagogue and its worship to witness its divine service and to try to live according to its moral injunctions (Acts 10.2, 22; 13.16, 26, 43, 50; 16.14; 17.4, 17; 18.7).

4.4 spirit of knowledge   See on 1.11 and cf. Hermas, *Shepherd*, *Sim.* 9.15.2.

zeal for the precepts of righteousness Zeal (*qin'ah*) is not always praiseworthy. For example, later generations showed sometimes at least an ambivalent attitude to that of Simeon and Levi in the story of Gen. 34. Elijah, Jehu and Phinehas were all examples of those possessed by zeal for the LORD, but second thoughts with regard to Jehu appear already in Scripture itself (Hos. 1.4), and even Phinehas's drastic action with the spear in Num. 25.7 f. is referred to in non-committal terms in Ps. 106.30, and the impression in the psalm is that Phinehas put an end to the pagan rites associated with Baal-peor rather than that he killed a man and a woman. For the whole matter of **zeal** see O. Betz, 'Die Donnersöhne', in *RQ* 3, 1961–2, pp. 41 ff., and M. Hengel, *Die Zeloten*, especially the section on 'Der Eifer für das Gesetz' (pp. 154 ff.). True zeal for God or for his law was certainly praiseworthy and a mark of the true witness or martyr. I Macc. 2.24 ff. shows that the concept was contemporary with the people of Qumran. Hengel quotes *Rule* 9.21–23 as well as the present passage (*op. cit.*, p. 184). See also 2.15; 4.10, 17; 1QH 1.5; 2.15; 2.31 (where it is clear that 'zeal' can be shown by the enemies of God also); 5.23; 9.3; 12.14; 14.14; frgt. 17.2; Num. 25.13; I Kings 19.10, 14; II Kings 10.16; Ps. 69.9; John 2.17 (quoting Ps. 69.9); Rom. 10.2; Phil. 3.6; Col. 4.13; Acts 21.20; 22.3. The passages from Acts and Rom. 10.2 all show that from a NT point of view 'zeal' even for God may not be a guarantee of doing the will of God. Paul had become convinced of this through his own experience, having begun as one as zealous for the Law as were the men of Qumran. See also on 9.23.

4.5. steadfast intent See on 5.5.

4.6. concealing for the sake of truth the secrets of knowledge This passage and the immediately preceding phrase are the subject of extended notes by Wernberg-Møller. The meaning is by no means clear, but the translation here accords with the pointing and punctuation of Habermann. 6.6 shows that it was an everyday practice in the sect to expound the Law and to seek its secrets, which the specially gifted could discover. 5.3 ff. suggests that the final decision on any interpretation was taken by the full assembly (the Council of the Many), and 9.17 f. shows how such revelation was regarded as demanding a mind fit to receive it. It was to be concealed from those who were not members of the sect. The reason is probably to be found in the sentiment that the practice of a regulation by those who did not belong to 'the truth' (that is, those who practise the truth or Law of God in their everyday lives perfectly, in other words, the sect) would be a defilement of that regulation, something like the association of one ritually unclean with a *chaburah* whose members were meticulous in their observances. His temporary faithfulness to their precepts would not make the presence of the uninitiated any less abhorrent.

4.6–8. the visitation of all who walk by it The blessings promised begin with a list typical of OT ideals as though the keeping of the *Rule* would bring earthly rewards. The idea is a commonplace of the Wisdom literature (cf. Prov. 3.1 ff.). **Healing** is often better translated 'health' in the OT as in Prov. 4.22; 12.18, etc; and is indeed equivalent to **peace** in its sense of prosperity and welfare, not the mere absence of war. For **length of days** see Ex. 23.26; Deut. 4.40; 6.2; Job 5.26; Ps. 55.23. Again, the blessing of literal **fruitfulness of seed** is found in Gen. 49.25; Ex. 23.26; Deut. 7.13; 28.4; 30.9. But there are passages which suggest that these blessings will be given to the righteous in the new age, as at Isa. 49.20; 53.10. This becomes quite definite in the pseudepigraphical literature, e.g. *I Enoch* 5.7–9; 10.16 f.; 11; 25.6; 28.1; 55, 59; *Jub.* 1.29 is very instructive: at the onset of the new age the luminaries will be renewed for healing, peace and blessing. We can therefore understand **the visitation** as the reward which God will bestow at the end of this age to be enjoyed in the new order.

a crown of glory (or very similar phrase) as an expression of some intangible reward from God is found at Ps. 8.5; Prov. 4.9 (cf. 16.31); Isa. 62.3; Ezek. 16.12; I Cor. 9.25; I Thess. 2.19; II Tim. 4.8; Heb. 2.7, 9; James 1.12; I Peter 5.4; Rev. 2.10; 3.11, and outside the Bible in *Test. Benj.* 4.1 and 1QH 9.25.

garment of majesty in eternal light Light, associated so closely with God himself (see p. 40), is reflected upon those who obey him. The idea is adumbrated in Dan. 12.3; Wisd. 3.7; II Cor. 3.18, light being a reward also in *I Enoch* 58.6; 108.12; but the fullest picture, gathering up the ideas of reward shed from the presence of God in the form of light, is to be found in the sublime vision of Rev. 22.3–5.

The impression remains, in view of the phrases **length of days** and **fruitfulness of seed**, that the reward of the righteous is in part this-worldly. We here have a reminder that Jewish eschatological hopes were not centred upon another sphere but on this world, transformed in a new age but still this world. The NT contains plainer indications of this fact in, for example, Mark 10.29 f. (cf.

Matt. 19.28 f. and Luke 18.29 f.); nor is the unexpectedly this-worldly question of Acts 1.6 answered except in terms of this-worldly geography.

4.9. the spirit of perversity is the source of a list of vices such as appears in Rom. 1.18–32; I Cor. 6.9 f.; Gal. 5.19–21; Eph. 5.3. In the first of these abandonment to a life of vice is due to men suppressing the truth by unrighteousness. They are responsible for the first step to degradation, but their evil choice means that God has handed them over to worse depravity (Rom. 1.24, 26, 28 ff.). This could well be a conscious correction by Paul of a doctrine of two spirits, for he uses the interesting term truth in v. 18 and the evidence of *Did.* 5 and *Ep. Barn.* 20 is that such a doctrine persisted into Jewish Christianity (see pp. 48 ff. and the table on p. 51).

The references in the following notes are often due to Wernberg-Møller and Guilbert.

a greedy mind Prov. 28.25; Eph. 4.19.

slackness of hands Eccles. 10.18.

in serving righteousness Isa. 32.17; 1QH 6.19.

haughty heart Jer. 48.29; cf. 1QpHab 8.10.

4.10. hypocrisy For this translation see Wernberg-Møller, who refers to Jastrow I 484 f.

shortness of temper Prov. 14.17, 29; 16.32; *Test. Gad* 4.7; *Pirqe 'Aboth* 4.1; Gal. 5.20, 22; Hermas *Shepherd, Mand.* 5.2.

deeds abominable 1QpHab 12.8.

spirit of lust Hos. 14.12; 5.4. As Seitz points out (*NTS* 6, 1959–60, p. 93 n. 5), *Sukkah* 52b cites the Hosea phrases when dealing with the idea of the *yeṣer haraʿ*, while the midrash *Cant. Rabbah* 7.8 has the phrase *yeṣer zenuth* (inclination to lust). See pp. 42 ff. for a comparison of the rabbinic doctrine of the *yeṣer* with that of the two spirits. Wernberg-Møller gives also the references *Test. Reub.* 3.3; *Test. Jud.* 13.3; 14.2; *Test. Levi* 9.9.

ways of uncleanness CD 3.17 (cf. Ezek. 36.17).

4.11. abusive tongue CD 5.11 f.

blindness of eyes CD 1.9; 16.2 f.

heaviness of ears Isa. 6.10; 59.1.

stiffness of neck 5.5; Ex. 32.9; 33.3, 5; 34.9; Deut. 9.6, 13; Acts 7.51.

a heart hardened Ex. 9.7; 10.1, etc.

ways of darkness Prov. 2.13.

4.12. angels of destruction CD 2.6; *I Enoch* 53.3; 56.1;

62.11; 63.1; 66.1. Cf. 40.7 and Charles's note. They are the agents of Belial (cf. CD 8.2).

God the avenger   Ps. 94.1.

4.13 darkening fires See the note on 2.8 (**mist of everlasting fire**).

while it is dark   Following Habermann, who, however, in a note suggests *behavvoth* for *biheyoth*, the former being transcribed from the plate in *The Dead Sea Scrolls of St Mark's Monastery* II, though the plate itself makes either as likely as the other. Wernberg-Møller acknowledges the possibility of translating *havvoth* as 'disasters', but argues for his own translation of 'abysses', which makes excellent sense. See on 2.8.

4.14. without remnant or rescue   CD 2.6 f.; DSW 1.6; cf. 4.2; 14.5; 1QH 6.32. The phrase is found in Scripture at Ezra 9.14. Cf. *Jub.* 24.30 and *I Enoch* 52.7. The idea of the total annihilation of the wicked (expressed in different terms) is found at Zeph. 1.18.

GOD'S FINAL PLAN FOR THE TWO SPIRITS: 4.15–26

15 These spirits constitute the history of all men; and in their divisions all their hosts receive their heritage for their generations, and in their ways they will walk; and every deed of [16]their activity is according to a man's inheritance of either great or small in their divisions, to times of eternity. For God has established them in equal parts until the last time [17]and has set eternal enmity between their divisions: abhorrent to truth are the works of perversity and abhorrent to perversity are all the ways of truth. Fierce is [18]the struggle between all their principles, for they will not walk together.

But God in the secrets of his prudence and glorious wisdom has granted that there shall be a period to the existence of perversity and at the fixed time [19]of its visitation he will destroy it for ever. Then shall come forth for ever truth upon the earth, for it has been contaminated with the ways of evil during the dominion of perversity until [20]the set time which has been decreed for judgment. Then God in his truth will make manifest all the deeds of man and will purify for himself some from mankind, destroying all spirit of perversity, removing all blemishes of [21]his flesh and purifying him with a spirit of holiness from all deeds of evil. He will sprinkle upon him a spirit of truth like waters for purification from all abominations of falsehood and his contamination [22]with the spirit of uncleanness. Thus will upright ones understand knowledge of the highest and impart the wisdom of the sons of heaven to the perfect of way; for God has chosen them for an eternal covenant [23]and for them is all the glory of Adam, all perversity being gone. All deeds of treachery will be put to shame.

Until now shall the spirits of truth and perversity contend and in the heart of man [24]will walk in wisdom and in folly. According to a man's inheritance of truth and of righteousness will he hate perversity, and according to his heritage in the lot of perversity he will do evil in it and so [25]will loathe truth. For in equal parts God has established them until the time which has been determined which is also for making new; and he knows the activity of their deeds in all the times [26][fixed for them] and allots their inheritance to mankind to know good [or evil. And he bes]towed upon all living beings their lots, to live according to the spirit in them at [the coming day of] visitation.

4.15. the history of all men   See on 3.13.

4.16. inheritance of either great or small   If a man has a preponderance of the spirit of truth, he will belong to that 'host' or army and, if a preponderance of the spirit of perversity, to the 'host' or 'lot' of Belial. 3.21 f. has already shown that the author is aware of the necessity to explain the mixed character of human beings and in particular the admixture of evil in those who belong to the spirit of truth. A remarkable light is thrown on the theory according to which the sect explained this mixed character of man by the publication by J. M. Allegro of 'An Astrological Cryptic Document from Qumran' (in *JSS* 9, 1964, pp. 291–4). If the editor's ingenious and attractive explanation of this rather fragmentary and difficult document is correct, both physical and moral characteristics are explained on astrological principles; for example, it is said in col. II of a certain type of man: '. . . his thighs are long and thin, and his toes are thin and long, and he is of the Second Vault (*'amud*). He has six (parts) spirit in the House of Light, and three in the Pit of Darkness. And this is the time of birth on which he is brought forth—on the festival of Taurus. He will be poor; and this is his beast—Taurus.' For *'amud* ('vault') Allegro compares Job 26.11, where the word occurs in the phrase usually translated 'pillars' rather than 'vaults of heaven'. Cf. also *I Enoch* 18.3.

The author of the tract on the Two Spirits probably refers here to this astrological doctrine which illustrates so clearly the deep cosmological convictions of the sect; but his own particular emphasis falls upon the strong contrast between the two spirits and upon the equal division of the forces of light and darkness in creation as a whole, alongside their unequal division in individuals. He is not apparently concerned with the proportion of light possessed by the wicked. God redeems, indeed, but only those who already possess more light than darkness. The wicked will not be redeemed, but completely destroyed (4.11–14). This outlook corresponds to that of the New Testament in general: Paul believes that the justified have still to face a judgment (e.g. I Cor. 3.12–15; II Cor. 5.21; Rom. 2.6, 16; 8.31–34), but the lot of the wicked is already known: it is to be destroyed, e.g. I Thess. 2.15 f.; II Thess. 2.8–12; cf. Matt. 3.12; 25.41; Luke 19.27; Rev. 19.15–21. For a clear repetition of the doctrine of the two spirits as an explanation of the mixture of good and evil in human nature see 4.23–26 below.

4.18. a period to the existence of perversity   We have already seen that the complete destruction of the wicked was expected (4.11–14). Here is promised the annihilation of the evil principle in the universe itself. Cf. DSW 17.5; *Jub.* 50.5 and *Ass. Moses* 10.1 show this to be part of the doctrine of other writers in Judaism at this period.

4.19. contaminated with the ways of evil   Truth is here oddly personified: it will **come forth** and has apparently until now itself—not only its human adherents—been under the malign influence of perversity. The same sort of personification of evil, righteousness and light appears in the *Fragment of the Book of Secrets* (1Q27 1.6 f.) connected with a final *dénouement* on the stage of the universe. An exactly similar phrase to that used of truth coming forth here is found in 1QH 4.25, probably in both instances derived from Hab. 1.4. In *I Enoch* 10.16 the personification is clearly poetical (the plant of righteousness and truth is to appear). The metaphor of the establishment of unending light is more naturally expected: *I Enoch* 58.6; 92.4 f.; cf. 5.7.

4.20. will make manifest   Editors favour the translation 'purify' or 'select', but see Jastrow I.197 for the translation given here, perhaps more appropriate since it is the *deeds of man* which are the object. The thought here, like that of 1Q27 1.6 f. (see preceding note), is of a final *dénouement*. Until God's final judgment the true nature of men's deeds is not clear. The language here finds a perfect commentary in Ps. 37.6 ff. For the mystery of a just man appearing unjust and *vice versa* one might refer to the whole of the book of Job (see, for example, Job 21), and for the necessity of a final divine revelation in order to show whose deeds are accepted and whose rejected see Matt. 25.31–46.

all the deeds of man   So Brownlee originally, Guilbert, Wernberg-Møller, Dupont-Sommer, Gaster and Vermès in his translation; but in his book *Scripture and Tradition in Judaism*, pp. 56 ff., Vermès had argued at length for a messianic interpretation of this passage, transliterating *geber* and *'ish* (both rendered *man* here) and translating the whole phrase **all the fabric of Geber** rather than **all the deeds of man**, believing *ma'ase* to be an orthographic variant of *ma'aseh*. Similarly **some from mankind** (on which see note below) Vermès translates rather as **the frame of Ish**. *Geber* and *Ish* he takes to be messianic titles on the evidence supplied by 1QH 3.7–10, which certainly uses the same sort of vocabulary and seems to be about the birth of the Messiah, and by the turn given to some passages of Scripture by the LXX and the Targums (particularly Num. 24.17), which use *man* to mean Messiah. Vermès refers for support to an article by Brownlee in *BASOR*, 135, 1954, pp. 36–38. The interpretation given to the whole passage, according to which it is the Messiah who is to be purified and thus enabled to teach the knowledge of the Most High to the righteous (4.22), is strange, and the evidence which Vermès adduces will hardly bear the structure built upon it. The relative dates of publication of his Pelican translation (1962) and the book referred to (1961) suggest that he has not remained satisfied with his own arguments. The more conservative interpretation which implies that a remnant (the sect) will be purified by God is in accordance with all other evidence about the sect's eschatological expectations. For example, 2.25b–3.12 insists on the necessity for all who would be saved to enter the covenant by the proper ceremony and promises purification as by water for those who submit to all the ordinances of God.

will purify for himself   See the note on 3.4 (**He will not be made guiltless**) for a full discussion of the ideas of purification by water and spirit. Flusser ('The Baptism of John . . .', pp. 222 f.) compares the final eschatological purification promised in the present passage with what John the Baptist evidently expected (Mark 1.7 f.; Luke 3.16; Matt. 3.11). The quotations from Joel in Acts 2.16 ff. also suggest that a similar event to that prophesied in the *Rule* here was believed by the early Church to have taken place at Pentecost as narrated in the earlier verses of Acts 2.

some from mankind   Brownlee (originally) and Wernberg-Møller translate the pointing of Habermann, *mibbene 'ish* (lit. 'from the sons of man') but Dupont-Sommer, Guilbert, Gaster and Vermès follow Yadin (*JBL* 74, 1955, pp. 40–43) and Licht (*SH* IV, p. 97) in pointing *mibne* and taking it as a phonetic spelling of *mibneh* (lit.

'building') and translating by some such term as 'body' or 'fabric'.
See also following note.

removing all blemishes of his flesh It must be admitted
that 'removing' represents the mere prefixed preposition 'from' and
that Licht's guess 'tissues' fits this part of the sentence better than
'blemishes' (*ibid.*). The Hebrew word is peculiar to the scrolls and
Licht argues for his translation on the basis of the context in 1QH
5.28; 7.4; 17.25; frgt. 47.5; 1Q36 14.2.

The interpretation of the whole passage if we follow Licht will be
that God will purify the human body, destroying all spirit of evil
from the tissues of his flesh. This is a most attractive suggestion,
because it affords a passage where we see with perfect clarity the
notions that moral or ceremonial defilement (never at this period
sharply distinguished) contaminates the physical body, and that
God's spirit must cleanse the body as well as the spirit of man (the
two being integrated). But, if this interpretation is right, it seems to
imply that God's plan is to redeem or purify all mankind as such, a
doctrine to which the scrolls are everywhere else completely opposed;
although it might be argued that the elect would now represent
mankind, all evil men and evil itself having been destroyed already,
and that what is here being described is a new creation after that
destruction.

Without presuming to make a judgment on this matter, we retain
the older translation, partly because the purification of 'some' seems
consistent with the scrolls' doctrine, partly because this pointing of
the Hebrew seems the more natural.

4.21. with a spirit of holiness See p. 35 for the explanation of
this translation rather than 'holy spirit'. In the essays on Spirit (pp.
34 ff.) and on The Two Spirits (pp. 37 ff.) the inconsistency by
which it is now God, now the spirit of truth, who opposes the spirit
of perversity in man is discussed. The present passage raises a further
question: what is the relation of the *ruach* or *neshamah*, divinely
bestowed source of life in man (cf. Gen. 2.7), and the spirit of truth?
This spirit which is life is to be rendered back to God (Ps. 104.29;
Job 34.14) and it ought then to be pure (IV Ezra 7.78). Evidently it
has moral qualities and we are again reminded that in Eph. 4.30 it
is possible to grieve God's Holy Spirit; but this is the Spirit given in
baptism. In Paul it is by no means always clear whether he is
distinguishable from the spirit which is life (as at I Cor. 2.10 ff. and
5.5). A natural conclusion seems to be that God's originally bestowed

spirit can become as it were absorbed into and contaminated by the flesh, and may therefore need—along with the flesh—purification by the Spirit of God's holiness (or God's Holy Spirit). The usage of the terms and the doctrine in 1QH support this account of the matter. There the spirit which is life—the animating principle of man—is sometimes distinguished from the special divine gift; in 1QH 7.29; 9.16; 15.13 *ruach* means 'soul' in the sense of 'human being', but man *is* flesh (1QH 4.29; 7.17; 15.12, 17; 18.14, 23; frgts. 3.3; 5.10; 6.3; 7.10; 9.9). Consistently he can possess a 'spirit of flesh' (1QH 13.13; 17.25 f.). The holy spirit of God is, as in this passage of the *Rule*, the purifying power (1QH 16.11 f.; cf. 7.6 f.; 17.26; frgt. 2.9, 13).

The action of God in the latter days by his Spirit is then a redemption of what he has already given, here expressed as a purification of what he has already given. Because the spirit given at birth—the gift of life—is from the same divine source as the spirit of holiness, and because no doubt all Jewish thinkers of this period would if pressed have endorsed St Paul's 'there is one spirit' (I Cor. 12.4, 11), the spirit of truth is identifiable with the spirit of holiness. The complete truth revealed by God will sweep away all error and its consequent defilement. The idea is known to the NT: John 14.16 f.; 15.26; 17.17.

The conception of the spirit, indispensable to any thought about the nature of man, can be set forth only in these largely allusive and metaphorical ways (cf. John 20.21 f.), and we ought perhaps to be content with partial statements. Flusser (*op. cit.*, pp. 227 f.) would introduce further imagery into the explanation of this passage, suggesting a connexion between the cleansing power of the spirit and fire: he gives the following references in *Or. Sib.*: 2.196–213, 253–5, 295, 313–16; 3.54, 71–74, 84–87; cf. 7.118–25; 8.243, 411, and believes that this *Rule* passage recalls the words of Mal. 3.2 f. and that I Cor. 3.12–15 should be connected with the same idea. It is certain that the NT compares the power of the spirit to fire as at Matt. 3.10 ff.; Mark 9.49; Luke 3.16 f.; 12.49; Acts 2.3; I Peter 1.7; II Peter 3.7; Jude 7; while Heb. 12.29 which compares God himself to fire suggests that in many other passages in the NT fire is an image of God's judgment wrath, the aspect of his nature which destroys evil. This would make good sense, for example, in Luke 16.24.

all deeds of evil   The laws whose breach means defilement are given in CD 6.15 ff. and 12.1–18 and include both ethical and ceremonial rules, the latter including injunctions against forbidden food based on Lev. 11.43.

4.22. thus will upright ones understand knowledge Flusser (*op. cit.*, p. 224) suggests that the picture in Joel 3.1 f. (EVV 2.28 f.) is paralleled as to substance by this passage. God's people are not only cleansed by God's spirit, but fully instructed by him, for he imparts **knowledge of the highest** and **the wisdom of the sons of heaven.** Acts 2.11 and 2.16–21 show that the ability to proclaim the μεγαλεῖα τοῦ θεοῦ was regarded as an eschatological divine gift (cf. Mark 13.11 pars.; John 16.13–15). But the event in Acts 2 and the event anticipated here are different. In Acts 2 *glossolalia* is explained as a foretold revival of ecstatic prophecy in order to rebut the charge of drunkenness. Luke has inserted 2.5–11 as an alternative explanation of the phenomenon on the entirely inconsistent assumption that the 'other languages' cf. 2.4 are the foreign languages of other nations. Here, on the other hand, the **knowledge** and **wisdom** promised are closely connected with the Law and its special secrets for the initiated and have nothing to do with either ecstatic tongues or foreign languages.

the sons of heaven i.e. angels. 1QSb 3.26 (where 'holy ones' means angels) and 4.25. In 1QS 11.8 the elect are promised an inheritance in the lot of the holy ones and partnership with the sons of heaven. For this sharing the life of angels in the new age cf. Mark 12.25; Luke 20.35; Matt. 22.30.

4.23. the glory of Adam CD 3.20; 1QH 17.15; Ecclus. 49.16 (Heb.). In his note on the last of these passages Segal interprets the glory of Adam, there prophesied as destined to be bestowed on 'all living', as the glory of the being who was created directly by God without the mediation of human generation. This is consistent with taking the present passage as a description of God's new act of creation. Thus Black, *The Scrolls and Christian Origins*, p. 139: 'The glory which Adam lost at the Fall is to be restored to the renewed mankind . . . and a renewed and obedient mankind are to live on for a thousand generations, an expression which in fact practically means "eternal life".' For the last point Black compares CD 7.5 f.

4.23–26.   A summary of the doctrine set out in 3.13–4.22.

4.25. in equal parts Nowhere else so explicitly stated, the idea should not be stressed in its literal meaning. The constant warfare without result until God's own intervention is the main point to be made.

for making new 1QH 13.11 f., where the meaning seems to be, as Licht comments, that the members of the sect are taught what

other men do not know, that it is God's intention to create anew
and to destroy the old order. The idea arises from Isa. 43.19; 65.17
and 66.22. It is taken up in intertestamental literature, *I Enoch* 45.4;
72.1; 91.15 f.; *Jub.* 1.29; *II Bar.* 32.6, and becomes an early expectation in the NT, at II Cor. 5.17, where its christological character is
very clear, II Peter 3.13 and Rev. 21.1.

PURPOSE AND WAY OF LIFE OF THE COMMUNITY
5.1–6.23

GENERAL STATEMENT OF PURPOSE AND WAY: 5.1–7a

1 The Order for all the men of the community who offer themselves
to return from all evil and to hold fast to all that he has commanded
according to his will.

They shall separate from the gathering ²of the men of perversity to
join the community in Law and in property; submit to the authority
of the sons of Zadok, the priests who keep the covenant, according to
the majority of the men ³of the community who hold fast to the covenant (on their authority shall go forth the decisive edict on every
matter of law, property and precept);

practise truth in community with humility, ⁴righteousness and
justice, love of mercy and walking humbly in all their ways. No man
shall walk in the stubbornness of his heart to stray after his own heart
⁵and eyes and the cunning of his own inclination, but he shall in
community circumcise the foreskin of his inclination and his stiff neck;

lay a foundation of truth for Israel to make a community of an
eternal covenant;

6 make atonement for all who offer themselves to holiness in Aaron
or to the house of truth in Israel and those who join them in community;

in dispute and in judgment ⁷ᵃto pronounce guilty all who transgress
the ordinance.

This is the course of their ways, according to all these ordinances,
when they join the community.

5.1. The Order   The heading serves as a self-explanatory introduction; but it should be noted that the Hebrew in Habermann (i.e.
the Cave 1 version, 1QS) reads literally 'And this (is) the order . . .'
making the present passage continuous with the preceding. On the
other hand, Milik in the review-article referred to on p. 111 remarks
that 'dans S^b S^d S^g cette colonne présente une rédaction plus courte
et plus intelligible que dans 1QS' and refers to his original report
on the Cave 4 mss. assigned to him, in *RB* 63, 1956, pp. 60 f. The

Rule is represented in eleven mss. from this cave, if small fragments are
included; most variations are of little importance except in the case
of column 5 (i.e. our present column). Milik directs attention to two
papyrus mss. (presumably two of the three cited in 1960 as S^b S^d S^g),
of which one is written in rather archaic script which F. M. Cross
dates to the beginning of the first century BC. Milik seems justified in
remarking that these two papyrus mss. present in column 5 'une
forme plus brève et sans doute plus primitive que celle de 1QS'.

The beginning of the column in each of these mss. lacks the 'and'
of 1QS and reads: *midrash lamaśkil 'al 'anshe hattorah*. The text of 1QS
suggests that *'anshe hattorah*, the men of the Law, are the men of the
community, those who by joining the sect have become true men of
the Law. The whole phrase will then mean 'Interpretation (of the
Law) for the instructor (to direct) towards the men of the Law' or
'Interpretation for the instructor concerning the men of the Law',
i.e. concerning the community.

If the Cave 4 mss. do indeed represent an older text, this text
seems to be that of an originally independent work and may belong
to the same period to which in our view (following Sutcliffe, see
p. 211) 8.1–9.16 belongs, that is the time when the community was
being founded. Such a time would be appropriate for the issue of
summaries of *halakah* to 'the instructor'—i.e. probably to instructors.
With the growth and full establishment of the community (in period
Ib of de Vaux's reconstruction in *L'Archéologie et les manuscrits de la
mer morte*, pp. 4 ff.), such writings might well have been absorbed
into the composite work which we now call the *Manual of Discipline*
or *Rule of Qumran*, and a document which was originally a handbook
for instructors of members became a part of this rather mixed community brochure.

The first part of the handbook, 5.1–7a, may be described as a
manifesto, since it lists briefly the purpose and method of a community such as is envisaged. It will be formed by separating from the
rest of Israel (men of perversity) and its authority will be the Zadokites
and the great assembly. It will practise truth in a humble fashion,
and thus lay a foundation for a larger community ('Israel'); it will
make atonement for the past sins of those who join, and pass judgment on all rebels.

They shall separate Rabin (*Qumran Studies*, pp. 60 f.) distinguishes between Scribes and Pharisees, mentioned so often
together in the NT. Pharisees formed *chaburoth*, fellowships for keeping

the Law; and a member of any *chaburah* undertook to keep it in the same detailed way as his fellow members. Thus a *chaburah* could always eat and drink together without fear of ceremonial defilement.

The Scribes are understood most clearly when they develop into the slightly later rabbis who 'made an attempt to enforce the validity of the law, as understood in the Pharisee schools, for the whole nation, not only for those who made a vow to keep it' (*ibid.*).

The sect at Qumran may be regarded as analogous to a *chaburah*, the obvious common characteristic being their separation from the rest of Israel for the purpose of keeping the Law as they interpreted it. The conviction that it was necessary to separate from 'the people of the land' arises from history. As Rabin points out, Neh. 10.29–30, describing the manner of adherence to a compact, contains key words almost all of which can be found in the Qumran writings. The compact or covenant made is called an *'amanah*, the word used at CD 20.12.

Morton Smith in *NTS* 7, 1960–1, pp. 347 ff., goes carefully into the historical background of this movement whose members desired to separate themselves from the body of Israel. From the Chronicler's version we understand that Nehemiah's and Ezra's reforms were sectarian, their group being the *bene haggolah* ('sons of exile', or as Morton Smith puts it, 'Organization of returned exiles'). They would receive proselytes from ordinary Judaeans, 'the people of the land' (*'amme ha'areṣ*), and in this were parallel to the sect of Qumran. The Chronicler obscures the situation by representing the *bene haggolah* as the children of Israel and the people of the land as Gentiles (e.g. Ezra 9.1). Thus in Ezra 6.21 (cf. CD 7.3) those who joined the *bene haggolah* are described as 'all such as had separated themselves unto them from the filthiness of the heathen of the land (*goyye ha'areṣ*)'; but the Chronicler makes no attempt to conceal the quite inconsistent fact that neither Nehemiah nor Ezra seemed to desire proselytes at all, but rather desired to exclude from the Judaeans any other Palestinians even if the latter had already been incorporated by marriage. Morton Smith believes 'the Chronicler has misunderstood or misrepresented their problem, and has done so by analogy with his knowledge of the practices of some pietistic sect which therefore must have existed in his time, most likely the sect of which he inserted the covenant in Nehemiah 10' and that 'sectarian movements in Judaism began well before the Maccabaean revolt' (*op. cit.*, p. 358).

5.2. to join the community in Law and in property For the sharing of knowledge of the Law as well as of wealth see the notes on 1.11 and 1.12. The sharing **of property** arises naturally from the act of separating from unreformed Israel. As Hengel (*op. cit.*, pp. 255 ff.) convincingly explains, the motives are both practical and religious: in I Macc. 2.28 Mattathias and his sons have to leave all they possess in order to take to the mountains. Others (v. 29) 'went down into the wilderness to dwell there'—in 'secret places' (i.e. caves). II Macc. 5.27 shows Judas Maccabaeus and nine followers feeding on the poor vegetation of the wilderness to avoid being forced to work on the sabbath by Apollonius; again I Macc. 3.56 gives Judas's venture the character of a holy war (Deut. 20.5–8), implying that all who will follow him must abandon all personal ties with normal life—including both wives and possessions. This note is struck again at II Macc. 8.13 and the following verse reports the sale by pious partisans of all their remaining property as an enacted supplication to God for their rescue from Nicanor's plan to capture and sell them into slavery in order to raise the two thousand talents which Antiochus had to pay to the Romans. Hengel rightly stresses that the renunciation of personal property is bound up with the withdrawal to the wilderness. This is clear in the case of John the Baptist (Mark 1.6; cf. Luke 3.10–14) and indeed in that of Jesus himself, who withdraws to the wilderness when the time has come to act upon his sonship; for he comes from his own town Nazareth (Mark 1.9), where he had lived quite without remark (Mark 6.3) and hears the divine call (1.11). Then the spirit immediately drives him into the wilderness (1.12). According to Matt. 4.3 and Luke 4.3 his first renunciation there, as Son of God, is of bread. He then returns to Galilee convinced that the Kingdom of God is imminent (Mark 1.14 f.) and begins to call disciples, who leave their occupations to follow him (1.18, 20; cf. Matt. 4.20, 22). An isolated Q saying (given different contexts by Matt. 8.20 and Luke 9.58) describes the Son of Man (the group whose leader Jesus is) as having nowhere to lay his head. He dwells in a sense permanently in the wilderness, that is, has cut adrift from normal personal ties and possessions (Mark 3.34 f. pars.). Jesus, with an urgency greater than that of Judas Maccabaeus, demanded in his time the same renunciation (Mark 10.21 pars.). In Qumran we see but one example of a well-established tradition.

authority of the sons of Zadok The legitimacy and authority of the Zadokite priesthood is fully discussed on pp. 91–95. CD 4.3 makes it certain that 'Sons of Zadok' was at some time merely one title of the whole sect. Here and in 5.9 below it seems equally clear that they are an honoured and privileged group within the sect. 1QSa 1.2, 24; 2.3; 1QSb 3.22 all suggest that the sons of Zadok were the original group whose decisions were paramount and that other leaders of the sect became equally authoritative after non-Zadokites had joined them and proved themselves by their conduct. 1QSa 2.3 shows the Zadokites as those in whose presence the others are admitted while 1QSb 3.22 is particularly clear: here 'the sons of Zadok the priests' are blessed as those 'whom God has chosen to confirm his covenant for ever and to make secure all his precepts among his people and to instruct them as he commanded'. (This passage is found in a pointed Hebrew text as lines 45 ff. of *serek habberakoth* in Habermann, p. 161, and is translated by Vermès at the foot of p. 207 under the heading 'The Blessing of the Priests'.)

the priests who keep the covenant Members of the sect who happen to be genuine Zadokites. Their interpretation of the Law is therefore accepted. B. Gerhardsson, *Memory and Manuscript*, p. 86 n. 5, gives a useful list of references to show that the original role of the priests and Levites was that of bearing and preserving the Torah: Deut. 17.8 ff.; 19.16 ff.; II Chron. 19.8 ff.; Jer. 2.8; 18.18; Hag. 2.12 ff.; Mal. 2.1 f.; Ecclus. 45.6 ff.; Josephus, *C. Ap.* 2.21, 23; *BJ* 3.8.3; Philo, *Quod deterius potiori insidiari solet*, 19.1; *Test. Levi* 13; 1QS 5.2 f., 8 f.; 9.7; CD 13.2 ff. In the Mishnah, see *Sanh.* 1.3; in *Ket.* 1.5 there is a reference to 'the court of the Priests' and in 13.1 and at *Ohol.* 17.5 to a body called 'the Sons of the High Priests'. Cf. *R'osh. Hash.* 1.7. See pp. 91–95 for the tradition that only the sons of Zadok remained faithful priests and for the fall and rise in the estimation of Levites. The sect at Qumran clearly held that the sons of Zadok ought to be regarded as the only legitimate priests, but that even they needed to re-establish their position by separating from the men of perversity, no doubt on the ground that the priesthood at the Temple, and the Temple itself, had been irrevocably defiled.

according to the majority Cf. 5.9. Rabin (*Qumran Studies*, p. 105) argues that *rob* does not mean assembly: 'it means "multitude" in Biblical and "majority" in Mishnaic Hebrew'—and on this latter point he is entirely supported by Jastrow. A single letter, *waw*, is written clearly above the line just before *'al pi* ('according to'). If we translate this as 'and', the meaning is left unclear: should the sons of Zadok, the priests, disagree with the majority decision, who has the final word? Rabin argues that with 'and' we should not have expected a second 'according to'. This is cogent, less so Rabin's solution that 'the priests are thus only an executive body'. It seems more likely that the priests initiated legislation (see pp. 70–75) which had to be finally approved in the full assembly and gain majority approval before being regarded as binding. The language of 1QSa 1.2, 24; 2.3 suggests a less democratic régime and these passages may represent an earlier stage of development at Qumran. Maier (*ad loc.*) takes *rob* to mean 'laity', which makes good sense, but is against the evidence from usage.

It does not seem possible to argue confidently from CD 4.1, 3; 5.5 as to the relative age of that work compared with column 5 of 1QS; CD 4.3 may mean either that the original Zadokite founders were still so much a majority that the passage belongs to the early days or that they had become completely absorbed, leaving the title 'sons of Zadok' to be applied to the whole community. Thus CD 4.1 seems to apply it deliberately to the laymen. It may well be that future profitable discussion will turn more and more on the elements from which these works were composed rather than on a direct comparison of the finished works themselves.

5.3. decisive edict   lit. 'decision of the lot'. Josh. 19.1 illustrates the phrase 'the lot went forth' as it is used in the OT for a literal casting of lots. The context here and more clearly still those at 6.16 and 9.7 show that the phrase means in these passages 'the decision is reached' as at CD 13.4. It is possible that Acts 1.24–26 should be interpreted in the same metaphorical way: there a decision is reached after prayer, and this may have been for the Holy Spirit not to influence the way the lot fell, but rather to guide the votes of the eleven. No doubt a considerable history lies behind this change in the meaning of the term. I Macc. 4.44–46 shows that God's will on a particular occasion and for a particular problem may be sought through a prophet; I Macc. 3.48 (where Abel's emendation should be accepted) shows that Judas and his men enquired from the law concerning those things on which Gentiles consulted their idols. 1QS 6.6 applies this principle to everyday practice. The present passage shows that the final decision is made by the Council of the Many, or full assembly, whose voice is like that of God in such cases. This explains the use of a phrase ('the lot goes forth') which previously signified an action of God through some sacred object (*urim* or *thummim*, for example) which was regarded as the medium of his pronouncement within the community gathered for this purpose. It is not a long step to the inclusion of a prophet's utterance from a trance among the media through which God will make known his decision; nor from this to the conscious decision of a sacred assembly after debate. Because such decisions are thought of as reached by divine operation within the assembly, it follows that a novice or a member under punishment cannot take part in the deliberations: he might be a mouthpiece of Belial.

5.4–5. the stubbornness of his heart . . . Seitz (*NTS* 6, 1959–60, p. 94), aptly remarks:' Here echoes of Jer. 3.7 and Ps. 95.10 have been brought into harmony with others from Jer. 4.4 and Deut. 10.16, which call for a circumcision of the "uncircumcised heart". The substitution of *yeṣer* for *lebab* in the *Rule* is significant and instructive, in view of later rabbinic exegesis connecting the two *yeṣarim* with the double heart (*Midr. Tehillim* on Ps. 14, sec. 1). It would appear that the compilers of the *Rule* were already well on the way to the kind of exegesis which discovered in Deut. 10.16 "uncircumcised" as one of seven biblical names for the *yeṣer haraʿ* (*Sukkah* 52a).'

The evil *yeṣer* is a *yeṣer* of flesh in 1QH 10.23 and *yeṣer* used by itself is by implication evil in 1QH 5.6, 31 f.; and perhaps elsewhere (see Mansoor's note on 1QH 7.3 [note 11]). In CD 2.16 we find 'guilty inclination', Rabin comparing *Pss. Sol.* 4.13, where the phrase 'lawless desire' (ἐπιθυμία παράνομος) occurs. The *yeṣer* of flesh in 1QH 10.23 is perhaps the most interesting parallel for the present passage of the *Rule*. It is as though the *yeṣer* were a physical organ surrounded by fleshly skin and so closed against the revelation of God, like the 'uncircumcised' heart or ear (Acts 7.51 echoing Lev. 26.41; Deut. 10.16; Jer. 4.4; 9.26; Ezek. 44.7; and Jer. 6.10). Thus it clings to its own *machshabah* (here in singular, but often found in the plural). The idea of the wilful thoughts of men, not brought under divine discipline and rebelling against evidence of divine revelation, is an important conception in the NT, expressed often by the term διαλογισμοί (Matt. 15.19; Mark 7.21; Luke 2.35; 5.22; 6.8; 9.47; 24.38; I Cor. 3.20; James 2.4).

foundation of truth See on 8.5 ff. and for the vocabulary cf. I Tim. 3.15.

for Israel Wernberg-Møller remarks that Israel stands for 'the

true Israel' and compares Gal. 6.16 and Rom. 9.6; but there is a very
important difference between the concept of the true Israel as understood at Qumran and as understood by Paul. For the latter Israel
can now include men and women of all races, and their entry into it
is by way of unity with Israel's already revealed Messiah (e.g. Gal.
3.28 f.), but the men of Qumran contemplated an Israel only of
Israelites, and their intention was to restore Israel as she was of old
by purifying Israelites of today according to that ancient Law which
plays either no part or a very subordinate part in the salvation of the
new Israel according to Paul (e.g. Rom. 3.21 f.).

5.6. make atonement   See on 2.8 (**forgive by covering thine
iniquities**). Here it appears that the sect is conceived of as making
atonement by its pure life (pure both morally and ceremonially) for
all who join it with the intention of attaining holiness or truth, or
both (see below). It is a cleansing community which purifies those
who join it by absorbing them into its life. The idea that men can
thus themselves effect atonement is found also in 3.6 and 8.6. In 2.8
and 11.14 it is God who atones or 'covers' as in all the CD passages,
2.4 f.; 3.18; 4.6 f.; 14.19; 20.34 (Wernberg-Møller). Mansoor's note
quoted in the comment on 2.8 seems indeed to be justified: in
Qumran men are regarded as effecting atonement when they observe
those conditions of repentance and purification which bring them
within the atonement which God alone, properly speaking, provides.

holiness in Aaron or . . . truth in Israel   Guilbert is no
doubt right in commenting that the members who belong to priestly
families seek a restoration of holiness, while those who belong to other
tribes seek that of faithfulness—or loyalty to the Law, called here
truth. Either priest or layman would by attaining his own appropriate aim necessarily find also the other. See note on 8.4 ff.

those who join them   This seems at first to mean the same as
those **who offer themselves** (above). The difference can easily be
explained. Those **who offer** are literally 'those who volunteer', a
phrase used of those who enter the covenant at 1.7, 11; 5.1; that is
those who have served their two years' novitiate and now of their own
choice join the sect at the ceremony held for the purpose. **Those who
join** translates a Hebrew word (*hannilvim*) which elsewhere (Isa. 14.1;
56.3) is used of non-Israelites who attach themselves to Israel, who
in these later days of Qumran would be called proselytes. That is
hardly the meaning here, since all recruits are to come from Israel,
but the expression can be used by those who regard themselves alone

as the true Israel and who regard unpurified Israelites as in a position like that of the 'strangers' of old. The phrase means, then, the novices, those who are joining but have not yet 'volunteered', i.e. not yet formally joined the ranks at the prescribed ceremony.

5.6–7a. in dispute and in judgment to pronounce guilty Wernberg-Møller refers to II Sam. 15.4; CD 14.12; 1QSa 1.13 f.; these terms belong to the sphere of legal practice (not particularly, as Wernberg-Møller thinks, to jurisprudence) and remind us that the Council of the Many sometimes sat as a court, as 6.24–7.25 shows.

It was thus like the later rabbinic *yeshibah* in being both a *beth din* (court) and a *beth midrash* (assembly for interpretation). As the first it judged cases, as the second it legislated.

transgress Here, in 5.14 and 8.22, as in 1QH, the verb *'abar* is used in its common OT meaning of transgress (from the literal meaning of cross or cross over). In columns 1 and 2 it is used nine times in its neutral sense of 'passing over towards'. This may be an indication of the present sections (5.1–7.25; 8.1–9.16), being due to a different author or different authors from that of columns 1 and 2. The word is not used in columns 3 and 4.

This is the course of their ways There is no break in the text, but this sentence seems to point forward to **all these ordinances** which are now set out in the following passage 5.7b–7.25.

THE WAY OF THE COMMUNITY ALONE TO BE FOLLOWED:
MEMBERS NOT TO ASSOCIATE WITH OTHER ISRAELITES:
5.7b–20a

7b Everyone who approaches the council of the community 8shall enter the covenant of God in the sight of all who offer themselves; and he shall take upon his soul with a binding oath to return to the Law of Moses, according to all that he commanded, with all 9his heart and all his soul, and to all that has been revealed from it to the sons of Zadok, the priests who keep the covenant and who seek out his will, according to the majority of the men of their covenant 10who offer themselves in community to his truth and to walk according to his will.

By the covenant he shall take upon his soul to be separate from all the men of perversity who walk 11in the way of wickedness, for they are not reckoned in his covenant because they have not enquired nor sought among his ordinances to discover the hidden things in which they have erred 12to their guilt, while in the things revealed they have acted with a high hand; so that wrath arises for judgment and to wreak vengeance by the curses of the covenant, to bring upon them great punishments 13to annihilate them for ever without remnant.

(Such a man) shall not enter the waters to approach the purity of the men of holiness, for men will not be purified [14]except they turn from their wickedness, for uncleanness clings to all transgressors of his word. So too no member shall be united with him in his work or in his property lest he defile the member [15]with guilty iniquity, but distance shall be kept from him in every matter, as it is written, 'From every false thing keep away!' (Ex. 23.7).

No member [16]of the community shall respond to their authority on any teaching or decision;

no member shall eat from any of their property nor drink from it, nor take anything from their hands [17]except by payment, as it is written, 'Turn away from man whose breath is in his nostrils, for what account shall be taken of him?' (Isa. 2.22). For [18]all who are not accounted as in his covenant—keep them separate and all that belongs to them.

No man of holiness shall rely upon any deeds [19]of vanity, for vanity are all that do not acknowledge his covenant; and all who spurn his word he shall destroy from the earth and all their deeds shall be filthiness [20a]before him and uncleanness in all their property.

5.7b–7.25, a passage of *halakah*, that is of regulations or laws belonging to the way, may be compared with CD 4.19–5.11; 9–16 and with *Jub*. 50.7–13, all being examples of *halakah* from non-Pharisaic sources. Rabin, *Qumran Studies*, p. 82, accepts 'Ginzberg's demonstration of the Pharisaic character' of CD, based on the halakic portions just given. Yet Rabin recognizes the existence of more than one ancient system of Jewish Law covering law and ritual, and that 'we possess full knowledge only with regard to the Rabbinic one, as formulated between *c*. 100 and 200' (i.e. the Mishnah). It seems then that CD can be called Pharisaic in the general sense of being like and often agreeing with what we know of Pharisaic principles, and, especially if we judge by its sabbath laws, lying in the direct line of development from earlier severe rabbinic practice. It is not necessary to conclude that CD belongs to a Pharisaic group.

Foerster (*NTS* 8, 1961–2, p. 122) argues for a common ancestry for Qumran and Pharisaism in early Hasidism and instances as points on which they later diverged the adoption of a solar calendar, prohibition of marriage of uncle and niece (not only—on the basis of Lev. 18.13—between aunt and nephew) and direct opposition to wealth as such.

On the stricter marriage law Rabin is illuminating. The prohibition of uncle marrying niece is clearly expressed in CD 5.7–11. Here many would suppose that Pharisees are being attacked, but

Rabin, while he agrees that in the later rabbinic evidence—usually supposed to represent developed Pharisaism—this type of marriage is applauded, believes that the accusation in CD is levelled against Sadducees (*Qumran Studies*, p. 93) and that the approval given in later rabbinic sources does not represent Pharisaism but has grown up to counteract an exaggerated hatred of such marriages in the breasts of those whose principles condemned a number which they had themselves known to take place in their own time. There was one in the Tobiad family (Josephus, *Ant.* 12.4.6) and many in that of Herod the Great (including two contracted by Herod himself). Whether or not Rabin is right, it is clear that CD can hardly be classed unequivocally as Pharisaic on this point, and we may take it that CD as well as the present *Rule* passage provides examples of Qumran *halakah*. Lines 7–9 do little more than summarize what has already been enjoined in lines 1–2. Significant additional points can now receive comment.

5.8. in the sight of all who offer themselves   The insistence on entering the covenant by the public ceremony of the Renewal of the Covenant is familiar to us from I Chron. 28.8; Neh. 8.5 ('in the sight of all the people') and from 1QS 1.16 ff., where they must enter 'in the presence of God' at a ceremony in which priests and Levites solemnly lead the performance of a rite at which the only laymen present are those who are 'offering themselves' or 'entering the covenant'. The present passage is entirely consistent with this picture.

he shall take upon his soul with a binding oath   Num. 30.3, 5, 7, 9, 11, 14, 15 uses the same kind of language.

to return to the Law of Moses   The covenant into which each member enters is virtually identical with that which Moses effected for Israel, and is therefore a renewal of a covenant; this is clear already from 1.3; cf. CD 15.8–10, 12; 16.1 f. To enter the covenant therefore obviously implies a promise **to return to the Law of Moses**; cf. 8.15, 22; CD 5.8, 21; 1QH 17.12.

5.9. all . . . revealed from it to the sons of Zadok   See on 5.2 above and pp. 70–75. The other passages in the *Rule* which show that the sect enjoined on its members new regulations discovered through their study of the Law are 1.7–9; 8.14 ff.; 9.17 ff. This passage reminds us that the chief reason and motive for Law study is **to seek out his will**. It is necessary not only to be willing to obey, but also to know what is the will of God.

5.10. Hence each member offers himself **to his truth, and to**

walk according to his will, i.e. to the study of Torah and the performance of *halakah*.

5.11. they are not reckoned   CD 19.21. The reasons why the men of Qumran boldly held that Israelites outside their number did not belong to the covenant are entirely consistent with the foregoing: they have not engaged in Torah study in order to discover how they have transgressed laws of which they were ignorant. Cf. 8.1, 11 f.; CD 3.14; Deut. 29.29; Pss. 19.12; 90.8; Job 34.32, especially Ps. 19.12, for the idea of guilt incurred unknowingly. This is quite distinct from the guilt of known but concealed sins as in Ps. 44.21.

they have not enquired nor sought   The phrase is from Zeph. 1.6b, where the object is the LORD. It is typical of the sect to take this as meaning enquiry of the Law.

5.12. the things revealed   The clear commandments of the Law known to all Israelites.

with a high hand   8.17, 22; 9.1; CD 8.8; 10.3; cf. 1QS 10.15; 11.1; CD 11.6; 20.30; 1QpHab 8.10. The classical OT passage is Num. 15.29 f., where one regulation applies to a man who has incurred guilt *bishegagah* or unwittingly (*ibid.*, v. 24, etc) and another who has sinned with a high hand, i.e. deliberately.

curses of the covenant   See 2.5 ff.

5.13. annihilate . . . without remnant   See 4.14.

5.13b–20a. Regulations which define more specifically the thorough measure of separateness which must exist between members of the sect and Israelites outside it. In the previous section the necessity of entering anew into the covenant was emphasized; and the present section teaches the same as 2.25–3.12, which denounced those who refused to enter the covenant. The insistence that **men will not be purified except they turn from their wickedness** recalls 1.11–18 with its important emphasis on inner sincerity in those who agree to enter the covenant and on its indispensability for ceremonial purity.

men of holiness '*anshe haqqodesh*, which could mean men of the Holy One, that is of God, recurs at 8.17, 20, 23; 9.8 and at 5.18 in the singular. Rabin (*Qumran Studies*, p. 41) thinks the full name of the sect probably 'was '*adhath* '*anshe temim haqodesh*, "Congregation of Men of Perfect Holiness" (CD 20.2), but this is abbreviated in various ways'. Cf. CD 7.5; 20.5, 7. One abbreviation is '*adath qodesh*, 'community of holiness', at 5.20 below. This recurs at 1QSa 1.9, 12; 1QSb 1.5; cf. DSW 12.7; 1QH frgt. 5.3. Rabin claims that the normal term is simply *ha'edah*, 'the community', which is found throughout CD and DSW and many times in 1QSa. This could be an abbreviation of the full and grandiose title of CD 20.2, but it does not occur in the *Rule* and a few other titles are found which cannot be abbreviations of it: 'community of Israel', 1QSa 1.1, 20; 2.12; 'community of men of the name' (i.e. of renown ?), 1QSa 2.8; 'community of the congregation', 1QSa 2.21; 'house of holiness', 1QS 8.5 f.; 9.6; 'dwelling of holy of holies', 8.8; DSW 12.2; 1QH 12.2; 1QSb 4.25. There was probably no one official title; or, if there was, it was never written down. All the phrases which occur could well be periphrases for this purpose. See also on 2.25 and 6.1–7.

5.14. in his work or in his property Wernberg-Møller compares CD 20.7. That passage deals with renegades from the sect, whereas it seems that here Israelite non-members are the subject. Association in work or property would defile the member with ceremonial uncleanness or **guilty iniquity**. See 1QpHab 8.12, and Lev. 22.14 ff., which suggests the right pointing of the verb here, *yaśśi'ennu*, lit. 'cause to bear' (Lev. 22.16). Guilt is thought of as a contagion which can be carried and caught like a disease.

This portion of *halakah* clearly envisages a life in which it was physically possible for members of the sect to associate with Israelites who were not members; Josephus's account of the Essenes in his main passage on this subject (*BJ* 2.8.2 ff.) certainly does not exclude the interpretation that they could meet other Israelites during the working hours of the day although they dwelt in communities and ate together apart from all non-members. Philo, in his lost *Apology for the Jews* (Eusebius, *Praep. Ev.* 8.11), says that 'they dwell in many cities in Judaea and many villages, and in large and populous societies'. Pliny's description in *HN* 5.17 is part of a geographical gazetteer and clearly does not imply that the Essenes, whom he places so interestingly at a site which can be identified easily with Qumran, lived only here. Again, CD 14.3, 9, as Rabin notes in his commentary, imply that there were a number of communities, and that there was an overseer who wielded authority over the entire movement ('all the camps'). It is a natural conclusion from all this evidence, including the present passage, that Qumran was the headquarters either of the whole movement or of one branch of the Essenes, and not the sole place where they lived. All this would be agreed by every student of the matter, but the further conclusion with regard to the *Rule* has not always been drawn. It seems that the *halakah* before us was drawn up for Essenes living still at relatively close quarters with other Israelites and that the whole section 5.1–6.23 may date from a time before the withdrawal into the desert, or be the work of a group originally 'in the world' and subsequently absorbed into the Qumran literature, perhaps when its authors were absorbed into the desert community. Again, it might be *halakah* drawn up by the men of Qumran for their brethren still in contact with other Israelites. In view of the manifesto for a pioneer community which seems to be comprised in 8.1–9.16, it may well be that the creation of this *halakah* passage (5.1–6.23) precedes the foundation of the 'monastery' at Qumran.

as it is written   The Hebrew formula (*ki ken katub*) occurs only here in the scrolls. Rabin regards it as 'corresponding to the very rare *shehare katub*' and notices that it occurs in the same form as here in the late *midrash*, *Deut. Rabbah*, *Nissabim* 1.

5.15. 'From every false thing . . .'   Ex. 23.7. A good example of midrashic thinking: the context and original meaning of a scripture is disregarded and the phrase made to serve an entirely different argument from that in which it was employed by its author. This is justified when the point to be made is already based upon Torah and the passage quoted out of context is used solely as illustration; but often a rabbi showed ingenuity by taking the extra step of applying a passage in a sense in which it had never before been considered. Here the main teaching could have been found more obviously in Lev. 18.3, 24, 30; 20.23; cf. Ex. 23.24; Deut. 9.5; 12.29–31; and the passage may have been a *midrash* upon one of these, it being typical of *midrash* to start from one scripture and illustrate rather fancifully by another. II Cor. 6.14–7.1, which is the sole passage in the NT to use the name Beliar (i.e. Belial), and which is justly suspected as an interpolation, and even as non-Pauline, uses a number of scriptural passages in very much the same way, without too scrupulous a regard to their original context and meaning. It is, in fact, a typical piece of *midrash*.

5.17. except by payment   The reasoning may be that purchase renders the object the property of the member, which alters its status with regard to cleanness. Parallels in rabbinic *halakah* would be naturally sought among regulations governing commerce with Gentiles. In this regard perhaps Mishnah *Neg.* 11.1 and 12.1 are relevant, since they suggest that garments or houses bought of a Gentile once bought undergo a change in status. *'Ab. Zar.* 1.1 f. is the passage in the

Mishnah which perhaps gives the clearest indication that commerce with Gentiles was common and indicates most concisely some of the main principles governing it. Cf. *Dem.* 6.1 ff.; *Hall.* 3.5.

'Turn away from man . . .'   Isa. 2.22 is a gloss in the *MT* and is found only in the margin of one LXX manuscript, but appears in the text of 1QIsa. It was congenial to the sect; cf. 11.21 f.; 1QH 3.24, etc; Job 25.6 for similar devaluation of man on account of his earthy origin. But the application here implies that there is a difference between the **man whose breath is in his nostrils** and a member of the sect. Gaster believes the writer meant ' "whose spirit lies only in his breath", i.e. not in his "soul" '; but it is hard to see how, if breath is equivalent to spirit, nostrils can be equivalent to breath. If the writer intended this he risked being misunderstood by the majority of his readers and the interpretation takes too much for granted the belief of the men of Qumran in the immortality of their own souls and the mortality of all others (see p. 61). It is better in view of other passages (e.g. 11.21 f.) to assume that a contrast is drawn in a general way between unregenerate Israel and members of the sect. If a reference to the doctrine of spirits, with the further addition of a doctrine of immortality, had been intended, the term *ruach* could hardly fail to have been introduced into the exegesis. In fact, as Wernberg-Møller points out, there is a play on *neshamah* as meaning breath and *hebel*, which means either breath or vanity, in line 19.

5.18. all who are not accounted   The phrase containing the verb translated **accounted** was in the original Isa. 2.22 meant to imply that man as such was 'of no account'. This word is applied quite out of context to describe those **who are not accounted** or reckoned in his covenant.

man of holiness   See on 5.13 above for this phrase and for **community of holiness** (20b).

RULES FOR LIFE WITHIN THE COMMUNITY: 5.20b–6.8a

20b When a man enters the covenant to act according to all these statutes, to be united with the community of holiness, they shall examine in community [21]his spirit as between a man and his neighbour, according to his intelligence and his deeds in the law interpreted according to the sons of Aaron who devote themselves in community to restore [22]his covenant and to heed all his statutes which he has commanded men to practise, according to the majority of Israel who devote themselves to return in community to his covenant.

23 They shall register them in order, each before his neighbour according to his intelligence and his deeds, for each to listen, every man to his neighbour, the small to the great. There shall be [24]examination of their spirits and their deeds year by year, to raise each according to his intelligence and the perfection of his way and to lower each according to his defection; for each man to rebuke [25]his fellow in truth and humility and loving mercy towards mankind.

He shall not address him in anger or with grumbling [26]or with a [stiff] neck [or a hard heart or] spirit of wickedness and he shall not hate him [and conceal it in] his heart; but on the same day he shall rebuke him and not

COLUMN SIX

[1]heap iniquity upon him.

No man shall bring against his fellow a matter before the many which has not been subjected to rebuke before witnesses.

By these principles [2]they shall walk in all their dwellings, every man with his fellow:

they shall listen the small to the great in regard to work and money; and together they shall eat and [3]together they shall bless God and together they shall take counsel.

In every place where there shall be ten men from the council of the community there shall not be lacking among them [4]a priest; and each according to his rank shall they sit before him, and thus they shall be asked for their opinion on every matter.

And it shall be when they prepare the table to eat or the grape-juice [5]to drink, the priest shall be first to stretch forth his hand to bless at the beginning the bread or the grape-juice (to drink the priest shall be first to stretch forth his hand [6]to bless at the beginning the bread or the grape-juice).

There shall not be lacking in a place where there are ten men a man expounding the Law day and night [7]continuously . . . each man to his fellow. And the many shall keep vigil in community for a third of all the nights in the year to read in the Book and to study its decree [8a]and to bless God in community.

5.20b. they shall examine The procedure for training and examination of novices is fully set out at 6.13b–23 and is discussed in the commentary on that section.

5.21. his spirit as between a man and his neighbour The whole passage recalls Ex. 18.16, but here the emphasis lies not on the necessity to judge a particular issue but on a man's whole character, which 'spirit' seems to mean here. This is consistent with the views expressed above in 3.13–4.26 which would explain a man's disposition according to the proportion of each kind of spirit within him (4.16). For this use of the term see 6.17 and 9.14. In 6.17 *ruach* (spirit) replaces *śekel* (intelligence). Josephus in *BJ* 2.8.7 says of the Essene about to be admitted after two years' novitiate, 'But before touching the communal food he must swear terrible oaths, first that he will revere the Godhead, secondly that he will deal justly with men, will injure no one either of his own accord or at another's bidding, will ever hate the wicked and co-operate with the good, will keep faith at all times and with all men—especially with rulers, since all power is conferred by God' (Williamson). (On the question of hating the wicked see note on 1.3.) No doubt the examination concerned conduct in daily life as well as these weightier matters, as is implied by the latter part of the phrase now under comment.

his intelligence and his deeds in the Law   For *śekel* (intelligence) see I Chron. 22.12. It is clear that understanding of the Law's requirements such as leads to its proper obedience is the subject here. Cf. 6.18. In 5.23 below and 6.14 **in the Law** is left understood. In CD 13.11 the examination is entrusted to the inspector overseer (see 6.12, 20 and notes) and the novice is to be examined as to action, understanding, strength, courage and property. Rabin comments: 'We have here the Rabbinical contrast of *limmudh*' (learning) 'and *ma'aseh*' (deeds) '('*Aboth* 1.17; 5.17) "actions" being the strictness of religious observance'. This part of the examination therefore covers the novice's performance of his duty towards God, although not clearly marked off from his duty towards his neighbour. Cf. 1QSa 1.17.

interpreted according to the sons of Aaron   and

5.22. according to the majority   See 5.2, 9 above. Sons of Aaron is no more than a variant for sons of Zadok here. The scholars of the priestly recension of the Pentateuch modified the exclusive claims of the Zadokites and made all the sons of Aaron priests (e.g. Num. 3.3). Zadok himself, originally a priest of a local sanctuary in pre-Davidic Jerusalem (II Sam. 8.17), was provided with a place in the Aaronid genealogy as a descendant of Eleazar, son of Aaron (I Chron. 6.1–8). Once this was accepted and had become part of the canon in *c.* 200 BC sons of Zadok would be well content to employ at times the title 'sons of Aaron'.

5.23. in order   It was noted above that the whole passage about the examination of a man (5.20 ff.) recalled Ex. 18.16. Ex. 18.12 ff. describes the organization of Israel recommended by Jethro. Yadin (pp. 59 ff.) points out the correspondence between the division of Israel in Ex. 18.21 and the organization of the sect according to the *War Scroll*, showing by reference to I Macc. 3.55 that this was not an isolated archaism. CD 14.3 ff., cited by Yadin, certainly seems to illustrate this fact, but the present passage of the *Rule* does not mention any of the customary divisions (priests, Levites, thousands, hundreds, etc); and seems rather to belong to the regulations for the placing of each member in his individual position, organized as he was no doubt also on a military basis, though that is not discernible here. It is different with 2.19 ff., where both civil and military aspects are apparent, showing Yadin to be fundamentally right in his conception of the sect's organization. For its religious significance see p. 135.

the small to the great   Just as there was a gradation of purity (see 6.16), so also a parallel gradation of authority in matters of Torah.

5.24. examination . . . year by year   There was then an annual examination even for full members, to re-allot their status within the community **according to his intelligence and the perfection of his way.**

5.24–25. to rebuke his fellow   CD 7.2; 9.2–8; Lev. 19.17 f.; Ecclus. 19.13 ff.; Matt. 18.15; Luke 17.3; Rom. 15.14; Gal. 6.1; Eph. 5.11; II Tim. 4.2; Titus 3.10; Heb. 10.25; *Test. Gad* 6.3 ff.; *Siphra* 89a on Lev. 19.17; *b. Bab. Mez.* 31a. The passages in Ecclesiasticus and CD, esp. 9.2–8, are clearly expositions of the principle laid down in Lev. 19.17 f. that admonition must be given without anger or delay.

5.26. stiff neck or a hard heart   The text is that of Habermann. Milik (*RB* 67, 1960, pp. 410 ff.) restores on the basis of the reading of 4QSd a text which would be translated, 'or with a stiff neck or with the complaint of an evil spirit'. The point is that the rebuke must arise from a fault objectively observed (hence in part the insistence on witnesses in the following section) and not from a grumbling disposition in the accuser.

on the same day   CD 9.2 ff.; 9.22; Lev. 19.17; Ecclus. 20.2; Eph. 4.26; Heb. 3.13. There is clearly a strong tradition that a rebuke should be carried out promptly so that the sun does not go down on a situation or an action that has called forth anger (παροργισμός in Eph. 4.26 is best explained thus on the basis of the LXX passages, I Kings 15.30; II Kings 23.26; II Esdras 19.18 [Hebrew and EVV

Nch. 9.18]). The other passage which has influenced Eph. 4.25 f. is Zech. 8.16, which is clearly concerned with matters of judgment. Eph. 4.25 seems indeed to be an exhortation to 'speak truth' in the sense of 'openly rebuke' without hesitation, as in the present *Rule* passage. *b. Bab. Mez.* 31a describes how Raba (b. Joseph b. Chama) assures a disciple that Lev. 19.17 implies that a disciple has a duty to rebuke his master no less than that the master has a duty to rebuke his disciple. Heb. 3.13 also suggests that the early Church adopted the same practice of mutual rebuke.

and not heap iniquity upon him   This translation is suggested, against the consensus of translators not only of this passage and CD 9.8 but of Lev. 19.17. Lev. 22.16 shows that *nasa'* can be used in the *Hiph'il* to mean 'cause to bear' (guilt); the present phrase, where the *Qal* is used along with the preposition *'al*, may well mean the same. The prohibition is not against incurring guilt on oneself by failing to rebuke a transgressor but against prolonging his guilty state by not bringing his fault into the light so that atonement can be made for it. Behind this there probably lies the fundamental day-night conception according to which it is felt that the man with an unatoned fault upon him will fall more deeply under the dominion of Belial when darkness (the sphere of Belial) supervenes upon light. The thought of Eph. 5.13 f. is very close to this. In support of the translation it may be urged that Amos 5.1 uses the *Qal* of *nasa'* and *'al* in the same way as is suggested here, the object which is 'lifted upon' the house of Israel in that passage being a complaint. It is indeed possible that the vocabulary of Amos 5.1 has influenced the *Rule* here. The idea that one may prolong or increase God's wrath on a transgressor is frankly acknowledged and even recommended in Prov. 25.21 f., which Paul has used with a presumably more moral application, at variance with its original meaning, at Rom. 12.19 f. It may be urged finally that the interpretation offered here makes excellent sense of the prohibition against taking vengeance in the context of Lev. 19.18: the vengeance would take the form of allowing wrath to fall upon a transgressor which a rebuke would have prevented.

If other translators are right and the prohibition is the rather obvious one of not incurring guilt in oneself by the failure to rebuke, it is perhaps relevant to compare Rom. 1.32; I Tim. 5.22; II John 11.

6.1. before the many   To produce a sudden accusation would mean that the accuser had allowed the guilt of the accused to affect him longer than necessary. This is therefore prohibited; but if the accused can be shown to have disregarded the first neighbourly rebukes, an accusation in full assembly becomes a duty. CD 9.2 ff. is a good commentary on the whole conception as well as a closely parallel passage.

before witnesses   CD 9.3; the classical passage about witness is Deut. 19.15 ff. Cf. Isa. 8.2; Jer. 32.10 ff., etc. Brownlee's comment seems to be right. The first duty is to rebuke a transgressor oneself, 5.25 f. and Matt. 18.15; if this is unsuccessful, take witnesses, 6.1 and Matt. 18.16; if this is also unsuccessful, report it to the assembly, 6.1 and Matt. 18.17. It is relevant that a further step is envisaged both at Qumran and in the Syrian church which produced Matthew: 1QS 6.24 ff. and Matt. 18.17b show that in both cases complete excommunication was envisaged (cf. I Cor. 5.5). See K. Stendahl, *The School of St Matthew*, Gleerup, Uppsala, 1954, pp. 23 and 138 f., where comparison is made also with II Cor. 13.1 and I Tim. 5.19.

6.1–7 legislates for the life of the sect as it was lived in small scattered groups, kept together by acknowledging some central authority as well as by their own community lives. This is clear from the reference to dwellings (1) and the injunction to act together (2 f.), surely superfluous at Qumran (cf. Josephus, *BJ* 2.8.4). **The council of the community** (3) is a title of the sect (see on 5.13 above) and wherever there are ten to form a *minyan*, a *chaburah* of members, there must be a priest to preside, a reflection of the fact that the Sons of Zadok were the nucleus of the movement.

By these principles . . .   This seems to have been originally a separate heading or introduction. As part of a larger continuous work the whole sentence is superfluous.

6.2. dwellings   The word is used always in the plural in the OT and usually suggests a more or less temporary lodging, whether actually or because of a sense of the transitoriness of any mortal dwelling on the earth.

the small to the great   Or junior to senior, reckoning by length of membership in the sect, as is obvious from the laws governing new members (6.13b ff.).

work and money   It may well be that in the smaller scattered groups, the discipline imposed on members included obedience to the group's decision on the work which a member undertook. It is almost certain that the group decided upon the use of money earned as wages by the members in their work in the world. 4QSi reads here the word *hon* instead of *mamon* (1QS). The latter is relatively rare in the scrolls so far discovered (elsewhere CD 14.20 and the fragment 1Q 27.1.2.5) while *hon* is frequent. Both mean property or wealth. *Mamon*, the mammon of Matt. 6.24; Luke 16.9, 11, 13, was sometimes used in the sense of money dishonestly obtained (as in a bribe) by the Targums, but it is unlikely that the use of *hon* here in the variant is due to anything more than the unthinking use of the commoner word.

together they shall eat Rabin (*Qumran Studies*, pp. 33 ff.) explains that a meal shared by ten men is communal in Judaism and believes that such *chaburoth* must have met on communal ground or in special buildings; he observes that *Ẓab.* 3.2 in the Mishnah suggests that the synagogue was the place for such meals. 'The classic example of such a meal is the Passover lamb.' For some regulations showing the close connexion of *chaburoth* with the Passover see *Pes.* 7.13; 8.1, 3, 4; 8.3 implies that a man who is in a *chaburah* when the lamb is killed must remain in that company for the Feast. Mark 14.15 (cf. Luke 22.12) emphasizes the correct use of a large and properly prepared room, and 14.17 (cf. Matt. 26.20; Luke 22.14) seems to imply that the *chaburah* consisted of thirteen on the occasion of the Last Supper.

6.3. ten men CD 13.1 In later Hebrew this quorum of ten males over the age of thirteen, the minimum required to constitute a congregation for public worship, is called a *minyan*. The early occurrence of this rule can be seen in the Mishnah, *Meg.* 4.3, where a number of liturgical acts are said to require the presence of ten men. Josephus, *BJ* 2.8.9, says of the Essenes that 'Obedience to older men and to the majority is a matter of principle: if ten sit down together one will not speak against the wish of the nine.' The Mishnah tractate *Sanhedrin* 1.3, dealing with the sale of pieces of land, says that such matters are dealt with before nine and a priest. *Sopherim* 10.7 f. is sometimes quoted as showing that in Palestine at the time of this work seven men were allowed to hold public services; but according to *JE* VIII, p. 603, this seventh-century work is really dealing with a technical point in connexion with late comers to a synagogue service and is not relevant to the present issue. The same authority connects the *minyan* with the 'tens' of Ex. 18.21, 25, and points out that the Babylonian Talmud comments on *Meg.* 4.3 to the effect that Num. 14.27 provides the scriptural authority for ten forming a congregation: Caleb and Joshua were the only faithful men among the twelve spies; therefore the murmuring 'congregation' consisted of ten. This reasoning is found already in *Sanh.* 1.6 in the Mishnah. Cf. *'Aboth* 3.6.

6.4. a priest   It should be noted that the priest is required not only to preside at the meal but at a formal assembly when the members take counsel together. CD 13.6 suggests that this is a matter of ritual significance rather than because the priest might be assumed to have greater knowledge than others.

according to his rank   That is, his seniority in the sect (see above on 2 **the small to the great**).

when they prepare the table   1QSa 2.17–22. The context shows that the normal meal, taken communally, is meant (cf. **together they shall eat** in lines 2–3 above). Heroic attempts have been made to see in this simple injunction a connexion with, even the origin of, the Christian eucharist. See for an excellently clear example K. G. Kuhn, 'The Lord's Supper and the Communal Meal at Qumran' (in *The Scrolls and the New Testament*, pp. 65 ff.). E. F. Sutcliffe discussed the whole question with balance in 'Sacred Meals at Qumran?' in *The Heythrop Journal* 1 (1960), pp. 48 ff., and may be taken as a good antidote to less moderate theories. Kuhn refers from the outset to 'the daily cult meal of the community'. That it was a cult meal is just what has to be proved. Kuhn proceeds quite rightly to compare Josephus, *BJ* 2.8.5, and the general agreement between the two passages may be conceded; but Josephus is here describing the daily routine of the Essenes without giving so much as a hint that the meal which they took with such due order was a cult meal. Kuhn proceeds to adduce 1QSa 2.17–22, which, as he claims, describes a very similar situation, except that the 'Messiah of Israel' is there expressly mentioned as allowed, should he have been born by then and be present, to touch the bread and grape-juice after the priest and before the rest. This subordination of the Messiah to the priest shows that the men of Qumran thought of the Messiah in a very different way from that of the early Christian Church. In 1QSa he is the expected chosen secular leader indeed, but without any divine attributes, holding a position comparable to that which the mysteriously fated Zerubbabel held in partnership with Joshua the high priest in Hag. 1.1, 12, 14; 2.2, 4; perhaps in the original text of Zech. 6.11; and in Ezra 3.2, 8; 4.3; 5.2. Kuhn then refers to NT passages in the eucharist and concludes, 'The relation between the Marçan and the Pauline text in their description of Jesus' last meal would then be quite similar to the relationship of the formulae of the Qumran texts to the text of Josephus in his description of the cult meal of the Essenes, the Qumran formula and Mark reporting the peculiar usage of the "sect", while for Josephus and Paul the common Jewish custom has to provide the framework.' In spite of this astonishing statement Kuhn continues, 'Neither of the two Qumran passages we have considered so far has given us any information about the religious (or perhaps even the sacramental) significance which the Essenes attributed to their cult meal' (p. 74). Undeterred by the truth of this admission Kuhn proceeds to discuss the Egyptian-Jewish legend *Joseph and Aseneth* which he believes to give such an interpretation of the significance of a Jewish cult meal, holding that the legend is originally Jewish and that passages from it (8.5, 9; 15.5; 16.6; 19.5, given on p. 75) warrant his declaration: 'When we recognize the striking similarity between this formula and the formulations in the Qumran texts, a connection between the two must be postulated.' The argument need hardly be taken further, because many will never recognize any similarity whatever; Kuhn himself rightly says, 'The similarity between these five passages [from *Joseph and Aseneth*] shows that the expression "to eat the blessed bread of life and to drink the blessed cup of immortality" is a technical formula'; but nothing like these phrases occurs in the Qumran passages and Kuhn is on much safer ground when (p. 76) he says, 'The terminology reminds us of Jn. 6 . . . We are also . . . reminded of Ignatius' *Epistle to the Ephesians* (20.2), where the Eucharist is "a medicine of immortality".' Kuhn himself admits indeed that 'great caution is advisable in transferring the sacramental understanding of the meal in *Joseph and Aseneth* to the meal of the Essenes at Qumran, since nothing of the sort is found in the Qumran texts themselves.' But he continues, 'Nevertheless, it is obvious from the central position of the cult meal of the Essenes that they must have attributed to it a deep religious significance, perhaps even a sacramental one' (p. 77). Enough has been quoted to reveal the weakness of this interpretation, which seems to arise from the unexamined assumption *a priori* that the passages in the *Rule* and 1QSa describe a cult meal.

In contrast to such elaborate theory a few sentences may be quoted from the article by Sutcliffe, especially as they express a number of important facts: 'The purpose of the regulation . . . is to secure the due observance of the pious custom of asking God's blessing on the good things He provides before they are taken. And as the opening phrase "to arrange the table" is the regular biblical expression for the preparation of a meal and as there is nothing in the context to indicate that the regulation envisages anything except the daily meals of the Community, there does not seem to be any reason here for supposing the word to mean other than a meal whatever the viands that might be provided' (p. 51). 'The prayer preceding the repast was a pious act in recognition of the fact that it is God who "grants food to all flesh", Ps. 135(136).25. Such a prayer is still offered in Jewish and Christian circles but is never considered to alter the simple domestic character of the meal' (p. 52).

6.5 the priest shall be first . . . to bless Rabin (*Qumran Studies*, p. 33) compares *Git.* 59b and summarizes the rabbinic Law, 'If a priest is present he has the first right to pronounce grace (cf. *Shulhan 'Arukh* 1.167.14; 201.3) and anyone else who says grace in his presence must say "by permission of the priest".'

grape-juice The word is quite different from the common Hebrew word for wine, and shows that unfermented juice was the drink taken. After this word the scribe of 1QS has accidentally repeated all the words which followed **grape-juice** in line 4 above as far as its second occurrence, a splendidly clear example of dittography due to the scribe's eye falling on an exactly similar word in a different line of his exemplar from that at which he had arrived. That the repetition may be polemical emphasis (Maier's tentative suggestion) is improbable.

6.6 expounding the Law 8.1, 15; 11.1. For this central activity of the sect and its place in their life see pp. 69 ff., and for a full treatment of the whole subject, O. Betz, *Offenbarung*. Gerhardsson, *Memory and Manuscript*, pp. 235 ff., aptly quotes Josh. 1.8; Ps. 1.1 f., but does not emphasize the closeness of the vocabulary of this passage of the *Rule* to that of the Joshua passage. He follows Betz in taking the **man** as always the same man, whose special task it is thus to expound the Law for his fellows, and in imagining him to be necessarily a priest. It seems rather that the sect attempted to fulfil the ideal of Ps. 1.2 as nearly as possible. A literal fulfilment would be out of the question, but a community could meditate in the Law day and night by having always one representative who was doing so.

6.7. continuously . . . The gap after **continuously** represents a Hebrew word *'aliphoth* which has not been explained. Habermann in his note accepts the theory that it is a variant of *chaliphoth*, for which the translation would be 'by turns'. This interpretation would make certain that the Law interpreter was not necessarily a priest.

keep vigil   Rabin (*Qumran Studies*, p. 44) refers to *Soṭah* 9.15, where a number of gnomic utterances in praise of famous rabbis is collected, and include 'When Ben Azzai died there were no more diligent students. When Ben Zoma died there were no more expounders.' 'Diligent students' translates *shaqdanim* from the root whose verb is translated *keep vigil* here. 'Expounders' renders *darshanim* from the root *drsh*, the verbs being the common word for interpret or expound (as in 6.7), from which also the term *midrash* is derived.

and the many   Possibly **and** should be **but**; the dispersed communities must have one man occupied with Torah study every hour of day and night, but the main body, the headquarters community at Qumran, are to study **in community**. How this was fitted into their time-table is not quite clear. See next note.

a third of all the nights   The natural explanation that a third of every night was so spent (rather than the whole of a number of nights amounting to a third of a year) is supported by the fact that the sect divided the night into three watches (10.2). S. Talmon ('The Manual of Benedictions' in *RQ* 2, 1960–1, p. 483) remarks that this agrees 'with the opinion of R. Nathan, which became authoritative in normative Judaism, against the opinion of Rabbi Jehuda Hannasi, who divided the night into four watches, as stated in *Talmud Babli Berakhoth* 3b.' Again, *Midd. Rabb. Eccles.* 9.9 speaks of a certain Jewish community, called 'the holy congregation', which 'divided the day into three parts, a third for study of the Torah, a third for prayer, and a third for work'. The division into four is due to Roman influence and is found in Matt. 14.25; Mark 6.48, while Luke 12.38 seems (though not certainly) to imply the division into three (cf. Judg. 7.19; *Jub.* 49.10, 12). Both Wernberg-Møller and Talmon mention the opinion of Rabinowitz (*Vetus Testamentum* 3, 1953, p. 180) that this threefold division reflects the fact that the *Rule* was composed before AD 70.

the Book   That is, of the Law. Ezra 6.18; Neh. 8.1, 3, 5, 8; 9.3; 13.1; Mark 12.26.

6.8a. to bless God   The Hebrew does not contain the word 'God', which is, of course, implied. Probably the prescribed prayers opened and closed the watch of the night (10.2) which was devoted to the study of the Torah.

This last regulation serves as a link between the regulations for small dispersed communities and similar regulations for the larger community at Qumran. There also the priests (of whom there must be, as we have seen, at least one in each small community) take precedence.

RULES FOR A SESSION OF MEMBERS: 6.8b–13a

8b The order for a session of the many, each in his rank.

The priests shall sit first and the elders second and the rest [9]of all the people shall sit, each in his rank. And in this order they shall be asked for judgment and for any counsel or matter which is the concern of the many, for each to respond with his opinion [10]to the council of the community.

No man shall speak during the words of his fellow before his brother ceases to speak. Again he shall not speak before a rank registered [11]before his. A man who is asked shall speak in his turn.

In a session of the many a man shall not speak on any matter which is not according to the wish of the many.

When there is a man who is acting as [12]inspector of the many or any man who has a matter to speak of to the many who is not in the *ma'amad* of the man who is asking the counsel of the [13a]community, the man shall stand on his feet and say, 'I have something to say to the many.' If they tell him, he shall speak.

6.8b–13a seems to be as clearly a piece of legislation for a large community as the previous section (6.1–8a) was legislation for small dispersed communities. This is concisely indicated by the first sentence, which reads like a heading; but the two sections are linked by the last regulation in the previous section (6.8a).

6.8b. The priests shall sit first See on 6.4.

the elders second CD 9.4. The term **elders** (*zeqenim*) is frequent in both Old and New Testaments, and the following note is based on Bornkamm's article in *TWNT* VI, pp. 651 ff.

The original character of elders as heads of families or clans is revealed by Ex. 12.21, but this has already become for the most part obscured by the time of the composition of J and E, in which strata elders appear already as representatives of all Israel. Thus Moses must report to them and enlist their services, Ex. 3.16; 4.29. They receive the revelation of Yahweh on Sinai from Moses (Ex. 19.7), support him when he strikes water from the rock (Ex. 17.5) and are granted a vision of Yahweh along with him (Ex. 24.1, 9), besides being present on other important occasions. In a still later tradition they are one stage of the transmission of the oral law (*'Aboth* 1.1).

The biblical narratives reveal the imprint of the later age which envisaged Israel's settlement in Canaan as a conquest carried out by an already unified nation organized on a pattern familiar to the historians from their own day. The story in Num. 11 illustrates this fact, but also the real antiquity of the elders by accepting their existence and firmly subordinating them as spiritual authorities to Moses (11.17). This is an E passage. Ex. 18 (also E) accounts for the military aspect of Israel's organization in a way which subordinates the officers to Moses and assigns to these captains of thousands, hundreds, etc, functions elsewhere discharged by elders, but without mentioning this latter term.

In the view of the biblical historians the time of the Exile saw the elders maintaining some kind of authority as the natural and accepted representatives of the people. In Jer. 26.17 they support the prophet against his highly placed opponents and in Jer. 29.1 Jeremiah sends his letter to those who were left of the elders of the captivity, the priests, and prophets and all the people, in that order. Ezekiel has elders for company while in exile (Ezek. 8.1) and sees seventy elders of Israel at idolatrous worship (8.11). Cf. Ezek. 14.1; 20.1, 3. Indeed, from this time onwards the elders no doubt in actual fact achieved enhanced status, through the destruction of all other forms of political authority, as functionaries of a restricted self-administration of the people; but their position was much changed: with the dissolution of the tribal organization the meaning of the word elder as head of a single family came to the fore, and it was in this sense that the elders supplied the foundation for the organization of a new community in the time of the restoration. Accordingly the Hebrew term elder now tended to disappear and we find 'heads of families', 'chiefs', 'presidents', with an occasional use of the Aramaic equivalent for the old Hebrew term.

Consistently with their earlier history the elders eventually formed with other elements an aristocratic senate or γερουσία, which later developed into the Sanhedrin familiar to us in the NT (called πρεσβυτέριον in Luke 22.66 and Acts 22.5). The earliest reference to it as a constituted body is in Josephus *Ant.* 12.3.3, in the time of the Seleucid King Antiochus III (the Great), 223–187 BC, the father of Antiochus Epiphanes, but it no doubt existed before then, in the Persian period. In connexion with this assembly *elders* at first meant all its members, but gradually came to signify the laymen as distinct from the priestly families (whose most powerful representative, the high priest, presided over this assembly) and the scribes. The three groups are mentioned together in Mark 11.27; 14.43, 53; 15.1; Matt. 16.21; 27.41; Luke 20.1, in all of which instances the elders come last, reflecting the relative lack of importance of these 'laymen' in NT times. Luke is sometimes influenced in his use of the word by the practice of appointing elders in churches in his own day. Thus in Luke 7.3 we find Jewish elders assumed as friendly to Jesus and in 9.22 the order is elders, chief priests and scribes.

It is unnecessary for our purpose to pursue the history further; it is enough to add that in the Sanhedrin at Jamnia after the dissolution of the state as a political institution following on the destruction of Jerusalem with its Temple, scribes took the leading part and the conception of the whole body as a council of elders was restored; Num. 11.16 f., 24 f., served as a model for its composition and size, and provided the scriptural text for the ordination of rabbis. *The Apostolic Tradition* of Hippolytus (d. 225) 8.3 also refers to the same passage in the prayer used at the ordination of a presbyter in the Christian Church.

It seems that here in the *Rule* there is a perhaps unconscious reflection of the constitution of the γερουσία as known to the author in Hasmonaean (i.e. later Seleucid) times. At 1.19 f. Levites follow immediately after the priests. It may be also that the writer regarded *elders* as an alternative title for the heads of the thousands, hundreds, etc., which would make the present passage more consistent with 2.21; but the omission of Levites here is remarkable. Wernberg-Møller calls it a 'small discrepancy' (p. 56 in his note on 2.20) and is more to the point when he adds that it 'appears to favour the view that 1QS has been compiled from different sources; still another tradition is contained in CD 14.3 ff., according to which the community was divided into four classes: priests, Levites, Israelites, and proselytes'. Wernberg-Møller is right in adding that the proselytes are recruited by the sect from Jews (see the note on 5.6 above).

6.10. during the words of his fellow   Josephus, *BJ* 2.8.5, says of the Essenes: 'Neither shouting nor disorder ever desecrates the house: in conversation each gives way to his neighbour in turn.' This passage occurs shortly after 'The priest says grace before meat: to taste the food before this prayer is forbidden.' Here Josephus is particularly close to the information derivable from the *Rule* in columns 5 and 6.

6.11. When there is a man who is acting as inspector   The

Hebrew has 'and' before this phrase, but it may be disregarded in translation as a way of passing from one regulation to the next; yet this 'and' is important in justifying the interpretation here given: without it, those translators would certainly be right who translate 'except the man who is acting as an inspector' and attach the phrase to the previous sentence.

6.12. inspector   Heb. *mebaqqer*. 6.20; CD 9.18, 19, 22; 13.6, 7, 13, 16; 14.8, 11, 13, 20; 15.8, 11, 14. The term is not found elsewhere in OT or later Hebrew, although the participle of a common enough verb. In CD 9.18 ff. and 13.6 ff. this official seems to be an indispensable camp overseer acting as a kind of public prosecutor for the whole community in cases of transgression of the Law. Rabin, in his note on CD 9.18, distinguishes him from the 'Overseer of All Camps' in CD 14.8; this latter could be the overseer of the headquarters 'camp' at Qumran and *ex officio* administrative head of the whole movement. His position is clearly not like that of the Teacher of Righteousness who appears in CD and 1QpHab, nor that of the author of 1QH (if these are different persons), but an administrative post which he holds under the authority of the many, or full assembly. There is nothing to indicate whether or not he was one of the elders. The 'overseer of all the camps' had to be from thirty to fifty years old (CD 14.9).

A review of these facts reveals better than any argument how far such an office may rightly be compared to that of the bishop *(ἐπίσκοπος)* of the early Church. This comparison has often been made with more zeal than discretion. There is a purely general likeness in that both have administrative functions; but the *mebaqqer* seems to have no pastoral duties, such as were without question the main work of the bishop, and we cannot imagine that the latter counted among his chief duties the presentation of a case against an offender. Most important of all is the history of the episcopacy, indeed that it had a history. The bishop evolved from being a kind of chairman among the elders (Titus 1.5 ff. suggests this, while Acts 20.17–35 equates bishop and elder) to being at least in the eyes of one Apostolic Father a monarchical representative of Christ (Ign. *Eph.* 3.2; 4.1 ff. etc.). There is no history of the office of *mebaqqer*. See also on 6.14 (**the officer at the head**).

ma'amad   See the note on 2.22 (**the place of his standing**) for an explanation of the term and its use in the *Rule*. The following is a possible interpretation of the present passage and of other evidence bearing on this question. The sect in full assembly reflected its composition by a number of smaller communities. Some at least of these may have originally existed elsewhere and at different points in the history of the sect eventually gone into the wilderness to join the headquarters community at Qumran, each in a body. Such corporate additions to the numbers would explain the considerable expansion of buildings on the site which is a characteristic of Period Ib. Since these constituent parts were already organized in association with at least one priest, they could be regarded as *ma'amads*. Within one *ma'amad* it was sufficient to rule that each should wait for his fellow member to cease speaking before he began to speak himself (line 10); thus Josephus, *BJ* 2.8.9, says of the Essenes: 'Obedience to older men and to the majority *(τοῖς πλείοσιν)* is a matter of principle: if ten sit down together one will not speak against the wish of the nine.' The rule still applied when each group or *ma'amad* was sitting in the assembly, but occasions would obviously arise when the *mebaqqer* or some other member had something to say on the subject under discussion. Whether it was relevant or not, or whether he might intervene in a debate which had begun in and might concern solely a particular *ma'amad* to which he did not belong, had to be decided by the assembly after he had formally signified his wish to speak in the way prescribed here in line 13a.

STEPS BY WHICH A NEW MEMBER ENTERS THE COMMUNITY: 6.13b–23

13b Everyone from Israel who devotes himself [14]to join the council of the community—he shall be examined by the man who is the officer at the head of the many on his intelligence and his deeds; and if he passes the test he shall bring him [15]into the covenant to return to the truth and to turn away from all iniquity; and he shall instruct him in all the decrees of the community.

And afterwards, when he has come and stood before the many all shall be asked [16]about his affairs; and according to the way the lot goes forth at the council of the many he shall approach or retire.

At his approaching the council of the community he shall not touch the purity [17]of the many until they have examined his spirit and his deeds upon his having completed a whole year.

Also he shall not mingle with the property of the many; [18]but when he has completed a year among the community, the many shall enquire about his affairs according to his intelligence and deeds in the Law, and if the lot go forth for him [19]to approach the company of the community on the authority of the priests and the multitude of the men of their covenant, they shall commit both his property and his possessions into the hand of the man who is acting as [20]inspector. He shall enter it with his hand in the account with the possessions of the many but he must not spend it on the many.

He shall not touch the drink of the many until [21]he has completed a second year among the men of the community, and when he has completed the second year he shall examine him on the authority of the many; and if the lot go forth for him [22]to approach the community, he shall enter him in the order of his rank among his brothers for the Law, justice and purity, and to mingle his wealth; and his counsel and [23]judgment shall be for the community.

6.13b–23 describes the steps by which a new member may enter the community. The passage demands a general explanation before comments upon specific points are made.

Brownlee (in his notes on this passage) and Rabin (*Qumran Studies*, pp. 1 ff.) agree in their interpretation of these rules laid down for entry into the sect: there is an indefinite period of probation *outside* the sect. At its beginning the candidate is given a preliminary examination by the *paqid* (14) and at its end by the full assembly or Many (15). Then follows a year's probation after which he is admitted to the **purity of the many** (16–17). A further year is required before admission to full membership, which allows his approach to the **drink of the many** (20).

This **drink of the many** is of greater exclusiveness than the **purity of the many**. Gaster makes the distinction by translating **drink of the many** by **common board**: only on attaining completely full membership is a candidate admitted to full table-fellowship with the rest. (For a full note on both these phrases see pp. 193–95.)

Josephus, *BJ* 2.8.7, says of the Essenes that 'Persons desirous of joining the sect are not immediately admitted. Excluded for a whole year, a man is required to observe the same rule of life as the members, receiving from them a hatchet, the loin-cloth mentioned above, and white garments. When in this period he has given proof of his temperance, he is associated more closely with the rule and permitted to share the purer waters of sanctification, though not yet admitted to the communal life. He has demonstrated his strength of purpose, but for two more years his character is tested, and if then he is seen to be worthy he is accepted into the society. But before touching the communal food he must swear . . .' 'The purer waters of sanctification' translates a Hebrew phrase which means literally 'waters of uncleanness', but which is generally rendered in some such way as here to indicate that they are really waters *for* (the removal of) uncleanness. The novice after a year is admitted evidently to the same ritual baths whose water if properly prepared cannot be rendered impure. This explains away the apparent inconsistency with the fact that liquids were held to be specially susceptible to uncleanness (see below in the following section).

Gaster reconciles Josephus with the *Rule* by his comment (p. 107, n. 61): 'There is no real discrepancy between his statement and our author's, for the latter starts, as it were, from the moment the postulant has entered "within".'

Such is the widely accepted view; and Brownlee and Rabin are certainly faithful to the text of the *Rule*; but if it is necessary to compare it with Josephus, this may be done in a somewhat different way.

According to the interpretation offered here, the preliminary examination by the many (15) follows very soon after that by the officer (*paqid*) (the Hebrew merely says 'afterwards'). The novice then completes a whole year before he touches **the purity of the many**. (He cannot yet touch **the drink of the many**.) Josephus expresses this by saying that he shares 'the purer waters of sanctification' (purer, presumably, than those provided by Israel outside the sect).

The novice may not touch the final purity (the drink) until he has completed **a second year**. This implies *one* more year of probation before full admission. Josephus writes clearly of *two* more years being required. If he was writing about the same sect (i.e. if the men at Qumran were Essenes), two alternative ways of reconciling his account with the *Rule* are possible: (*a*) Josephus was misinformed and should have omitted 'more' (ἄλλοις) in the phrase 'for two more years his character is tested' and should have said that although the novice has demonstrated after one year his strength of purpose, for two years (in all) his character is tested; i.e. he must undergo one more year's test; or (*b*) the phrase **until he has completed a second year among the men of the community** in the *Rule* (6.21) means 'until he has completed two years among the men of the community'.

Neither of these ways of attempting to reconcile Josephus with the *Rule* is satisfactory, but there are weaknesses in the apparently natural interpretation of Brownlee and Rabin, which is indeed adopted by many scholars. The phrase *and afterwards* (15) is taken to imply a previous period of probation outside the community. It is true that Josephus refers to the candidate as 'remaining outside', but it is difficult to envisage the situation. How could a man practise the essentials of the life enjoined while remaining in the world? Even those who joined one of the small dispersed communities could hardly practise the rule of life required of him without considerable general (not necessarily close physical) contact with those whom he wished to regard as his fellows. How could he join in the Law study or hear the priest say grace? (See the section 6.1–6.) Ought not Josephus' words 'remaining outside' to be taken to mean 'excluded from membership'? Again, the language of lines 15–16 implies a definite admission to or rejection from the novitiate, rather than to a pre-novitiate period which seems on the usual theory indefinite not only in length but also in character.

Whether or not the *Rule* can be reconciled with Josephus, it seems possible to interpret the former as follows; one **who devotes himself to join** is examined first by the *paqid*, then by the full assembly, and enters immediately on a two-year novitiate which has an examination in the middle admitting the novice to a higher grade, but not yet to full membership, to which he attains after two whole years from the time of his admission. During the first year he practises all the rules of the sect, but carefully avoids any action which would endanger the levitical purity of a full members. The 'purity' which he can approach after this first year comprises objects not capable of transmitting uncleanness (see the following section). At the end of the second year he can, if accepted at his examination, become a full member.

Note: 'The purity of the many' (6.16 f.) *and 'the drink of the many'* (6.20)

The admission of the novice after one year to the **purity of the many** and his exclusion for a further year from **the drink of the many** prompts consideration of grades within the sect and of the meaning of the phrases themselves. At 2.19 f. and 6.8 ff. there seem to be three grades, either priests, Levites, laymen; or priests, elders, laymen (see the notes on these passages); CD 14.3 gives four grades, priests, Levites, Israelites, proselytes. Josephus, *BJ* 2.8.10, says of the Essenes: 'They are divided into four grades, according to the stage they have reached in their preparation; and so far are the juniors inferior to the seniors that if they touch them the persons touched must wash as though contaminated by an alien.' If Josephus is right and describing the same body as that prescribed for by the *Rule* his four grades cannot correspond to the priests, Levites, Israelites and proselytes of CD 14.3; for a priest or Levite was so by heredity, nor could a proselyte become, though he might become like a born

Israelite. There could be no question of passing up through these orders. There is another explanation with which Josephus's account would be quite consistent: according to 5.23 ff. an annual examination determined the 'raising' or 'lowering' of each member. Nothing is said there or anywhere else in the *Rule* about the resultant grades being grades of purity, but it would be quite natural that this should be the case. See also CD 10.5.

It remains to explain why a novice after a year might touch **the purity of the many**, but must await his full membership before touching **the drink of the many**.

To appreciate this aspect of the life at Qumran it is necessary to understand two distinct but closely related lines of thought about 'cleannesses' (the Hebrew word is *Tohoroth*, the title of the sixth and last division of the Mishnah, comprising twelve tractates). The first is that certain things convey uncleanness directly, and that other things are susceptible to uncleanness in very varying degrees. In his edition of the Mishnah in English, Danby included as Appendix IV (p. 800) 'The Rules of Uncleanness' from a commentary on the Division *Tohoroth* by Elijah of Wilna (1720–97). From this summary it can be seen that the things which convey uncleanness directly are called 'Fathers of Uncleanness'. Other things convey uncleanness by contact with the 'Fathers of Uncleanness'. To take one example from what is an extremely complex system: a corpse is a 'Father of Uncleanness'; it can also convey uncleanness 'through seven removes' by touching vessels which touch a man who touches vessels. All these become 'Fathers of Uncleanness'. They in turn render common food unclean at four different removes, bestowing first-, second-, third- and fourth-grade uncleanness.

The second line of thought is closely related: Israelites who strictly obey the Law observe those prescriptions which avoid or remove uncleanness. The priest and Levite of Luke 10.31 f. avoided the uncleanness of what might have been a corpse or of something issuing from an injured man ('flux', or morbid discharge or excrement). The Samaritan, regarded as himself a Father of Uncleanness, need have no such scruples; for the Samaritan or Gentile was unclean for the Jew largely because suspected of uncleanness through contact with the uncleanness of women. Thus the tractate *Niddah* 4.1 says, 'The daughters of the Samaritans are deemed unclean as menstruants from the cradle; and the Samaritans convey uncleanness . . .'

The strict schools, forming themselves into *chaburoth* for corporate keeping of the Law, saw even fellow Jews as unclean. Thus *Niddah* 4.2 reveals Pharisaic hostility to others less scrupulous than themselves: 'The daughters of the Sadducees, if they followed after the ways of their fathers, are deemed like the women of the Samaritans.'

Flusser draws attention (in' The Baptism of John . . .', pp. 212 f.) to the instructive passage in the Mishnah, *Chag.* 2.7, which clearly illustrates the relativity of uncleanness even among those who observed ceremonial laws carefully: 'For Pharisees the clothes of an *Am-haaretz*' ('people of the land') 'count as suffering *midras*-uncleanness' (uncleanness conveyed by pressure such as sitting or lying on anything normally so used); 'for them that eat Heave-offering' (i.e. priests) 'the clothes of Pharisees count as suffering *midras*-uncleanness; for them that eat of Hallowed Things the clothes of them that eat of Heave-offering count as suffering *midras*-uncleanness; for them that occupy themselves with the Sin-offering water the clothes of them that eat of Hallowed things count as suffering *midras*-uncleanness' (Danby). Flusser refers also to two passages of Josephus about the Essenes: *Ant.* 18.1.5 describes them as sending offerings to the Temple, but performing sacrifices 'with degrees of purifications according to a system of their own' (διαφορότητι ἁγνειῶν ἃς νομίζοιεν) and for that reason debarred from the common precinct, performing sacrifies by themselves (ἐφ'αὑτῶν); *BJ* 2.8.12 says of them that 'some of them claim to foretell the future, after a lifelong study of sacred books and degrees of purifications (διαφόροις ἁγνείαις) and the utterances of prophets'.

We have seen that the men of Qumran held that breaches not only of ceremonial laws but also of moral laws conveyed uncleanness, and that the latter type of uncleanness required for its removal the addition of sincere resolution within the heart to the prescribed ceremonial enactment. A candidate or novice therefore might convey uncleanness to a full member if he were not yet thoroughly purified by the spirit of holiness in the community. Such uncleanness clearly might be contracted by direct touch; but it might be contracted also at a remove. As liquids were the most powerful conveyors of uncleanness at a remove, a doctrine based upon Lev. 11.38, the purity of the full members must be protected by prohibiting anyone other than a fellow full member to touch the drink which they shared. Lev. 22.2 may well provide the basis for this careful distinction.

6.14. the officer at the head   The Hebrew for **officer** is *paqid*.

He is probably the same as the 'camp overseer' of CD 13.7 whose
function seems the same (CD 13.11); probably he is the same also
as 'the priest at the head of the many' of CD 14.7 (cf. CD 15.7–11).
The 'overseer of all the camps' of CD 14.9 is evidently different,
though he might be the same as the overseer of the headquarters, the
main camp at Qumran. See on 6.12 (**inspector**).

6.16. the lot   See on 5.3 (**decisive edict**). Cf. 6.18.

6.17. he shall not mingle with the property of the many   See
the notes on 1.12 and on 5.2. **The property of the many** would
include vessels used for food and cooking; the novices are barred
for a year from table-fellowship with the full members and exclusion
from use of their kitchen ware is a natural extension of this. It no
doubt extended also to reading and writing material. Cf. John 4.9.

6.20. inspector   Hebrew *mebaqqer*; see note on 6.12 and on 6.14,
the officer at the head.

he must not spend it on the many   If the novice's wealth was
registered but kept separate, it could be used for his food or any
other necessary commodity during his probationary year. The
arrangement perhaps lends some slight support to the argument put
forward above that novices lived this year within the community
while avoiding close contact with full members, eating and working
at different tables and no doubt sleeping in separate quarters. Once a
man was a full member the purity laws would enable him to share
in all the commodities purchased by and on behalf of the community,
and no separate cooking vessels would be necessary. It would therefore be no longer necessary for his capital to be kept separate from
that of the community, and **his wealth** can be 'mingled' (22).

the drink of the many   See pp. 191–95. S. Lieberman (*JBL*
71, 1952, p. 203) believes the phrase refers (as its literal sense
would suggest) to drink only. Sutcliffe (*Heythrop Journal* 1, 1960,
p. 53) strongly criticizes Gaster's translation **common board** and
rightly insists that drink is here literally meant. 'The regulation is a
safeguard of levitical purity.' Burrows supports Gaster in *Oudtesta-
mentische Studien* 8, 1950, pp. 163 f.; while Gaster's translation is too
free, it is very probable that the levitically based prohibition from the
drink of the many would imply separation from the table or tables
at which full members sat. Betz (*Offenbarung*, p. 114) rather fancifully
connects with the water metaphors in the scrolls. With God there is
an eternal well (1QH 10.31), a well of power (1QH 1.5; 12.13), of
righteousness (1QS 11.5) and above all of all knowledge (1QS 11.3;

1QH 12.29). This, like the light from its divine source, is absorbed by the inner man (cf. 1QH 10.31). The idea is based on the well of Num. 21.18 interpreted as the well of the Law in CD 6.2 ff. This is what lies behind the phrase **drink of the many** in 6.20 (here) which Betz takes to include the community meal of all full members, but to extend to other specific times of assembly (those for study, reading and learning) when the divine knowledge is proffered to the thirsty. It seems safer to accept the simpler explanation that it is entirely a matter of levitical purity.

21. the lot See on 5.3.

22. order of his rank See above, pp. 191 ff.

for the Law Perhaps 'for instruction'. If *torah* here means the Law, it probably means for study of the Law, in which the new member is assigned a rank assessed according to his expertise in it.

justice His rank determines his place also in the assembly when it acts as a *beth din* or court of justice.

purity As briefly explained above (p. 194), the laws governing degrees of purity were very complicated among the Jews at this period; and Josephus (see pp. 191 f.) testifies to the scrupulosity of the Essenes in avoiding the contraction of ceremonial uncleanness.

22–23. counsel and judgment No less than the member's worldly wealth, his mental abilities were likewise to be at the service of the community. Cf. Rom. 12.5 ff., where Paul acknowledges grades of faith (v. 6) in a way parallel to that in which the men of Qumran acknowledged grades of knowledge and understanding in the Law.

PENITENTIAL CODE OF THE COMMUNITY
6.24–7.25

24 These are the rules by which they shall judge at an enquiry of the community, on the authority of the words.

If there be found among them a man who speaks falsely ²⁵about property, and does so knowingly, they shall cut him off from the purity of the many for one year and he shall be deprived of a quarter of his rations.

Whoever has answered ²⁶his fellow with obstinacy and spoken with short temper so as to reject the discipline of God's truth, by rebelling against the word of his fellow member who is registered above him, ²⁷and has taken the law into his own hand, shall be punished for one year . . .

Whoever makes an oath in the honoured name for any . . .

COLUMN SEVEN

1 If a man has cursed either through terror at affliction or through anything that happens to him while he is reading the book or praying, they shall separate him off ²and he shall not return any more to the council of the community;

if he has spoken in anger at one of the priests who are registered in the book he shall be punished for one year ³and be excluded for his soul from the purity of the many;

but if he spoke thoughtlessly he shall be punished six months; one who lies deliberately ⁴shall be punished six months.

The man who harms his fellow without just cause and with intent shall be punished one year ⁵and be separated; and whoever speaks deceitfully or deliberately acts deceitfully against his fellow shall be punished six months.

If ⁶he defrauds his fellow he shall be punished three months, but if it be the property of the community which he has defrauded so as to cause its loss, he shall restore it ⁷in full; ⁸but if he has no power to restore it he shall be punished sixty days.

Whoever bears a grudge against his neighbour (which is unlawful) shall be punished one year; ⁹and thus for one who takes vengeance for himself for any matter.

Whoever utters an improper word, three months;

for one who speaks in the midst of the words of his fellow, ¹⁰ten days.

Whoever lies down and sleeps at a session of the many—thirty days.

Similarly for the man who leaves a session of the many ¹¹without permission and for no good reason, up to three times in one assembly: he shall be punished ten days; but if they are standing ¹²and he left he shall be punished thirty days.

Whoever walks before his fellow naked, and this was not through illness, he shall be punished six months; ¹³and a man who spits among a session of the many shall be punished thirty days; and whoever brings his member out under his garment and the garment is ¹⁴ragged so that his nakedness is seen shall be punished thirty days.

Whoever laughs foolishly and makes the sound heard shall be punished thirty ¹⁵days; and he who brings out his left hand to lean on it shall be punished ten days.

The man who goes about slandering his fellow ¹⁶they shall separate him one year from the purity of the many and he shall be punished.

The man who goes about slandering the many—he is to be expelled from them ¹⁷and not return any more; and the man who murmurs against the authority of the community—he shall be expelled and not return. If he murmurs against his fellow ¹⁸(which is unlawful) he shall be punished six months.

The man whose spirit so quakes at the authority of the community as to betray the truth [19]and to walk in the stubbornness of his heart, if he return, he shall be punished two years; and in the first he shall not touch the purity of the many, [20]and in the second he shall not touch the drink of the many, and he shall sit behind all the men of the community. When he has completed [21]two years, the many shall enquire into his case, and if they bid him approach he shall be registered in his rank, and after this he shall be asked about judgment.

22 But every man who belongs to the council of the community as long as ten full years [23]and whose spirit has turned back to betray the community, and he goes out from the company [24]of the many to walk in the stubbornness of his heart, he shall not return any more to the council of the community. And everyone from the men of the community who associates [25]with him in purity or property . . . the many —his sentence shall be like the first man's . . .

The section 6.24–7.25 is a rather miscellaneous collection of legal enactments and in 1QS reveals gaps, not only those caused by damage to the ms. but also others not easy to explain, particularly the considerable space between line 6 and the single word in line 7, and the larger space between this word and line 8. There the sense seems continuous; a much less obvious space, namely the residue of a line in which only two words are written, occurs at 6.23, and can be reasonably taken as designed to mark a change of subject and as betraying the composite nature of the work. There is, in fact, a slight connexion between the two sections: the new member must contribute three things to the community, wealth, counsel, judgment (his opinion on a legal matter). This last term (*mishpaṭ*) suggests to the composer the place to insert his collection of *mishpaṭim*, i.e. judgments or decisions which, once made by the appropriate authority, have the force of law and guide the assembly in any new case with which they have to deal.

6.24. rules by which they shall judge The Hebrew contains a natural word-play—*mishpaṭim* by which they *yishpeṭu*.

on the authority of the words Heb. *debarim*. Wernberg-Møller urges that *dabar* is a judicial term at 6.1 and quotes Van der Ploeg and Delcor as adducing Gen. 43.7; Ex. 18.16, 22; 22.8. This is relevant, and it is important to recognize that the **words** are words of the Law. Some commentators miss this point and provide only vague translations. Habermann in a note takes *debarim* to be an abbreviation of *'eleh haddebarim*, the title of the book called in English Deuteronomy. To support fully this interpretation would demand demonstration that all the *mishpaṭim* could have been arrived at by midrashic exegesis of Deuteronomy. In view of the difficulty of such a task, and since the full title of that book is not used here, it is perhaps safer to suppose that the sect possessed a book to which they gave a similar title to that of the fifth book of Moses, a book which could rightly be called a *midrash*. On the other hand, it is relevant to observe that the Hebrew which we translate by 'Chronicles' is literally 'the words of the days', but above all that at 1QS 1.14 we find the phrase 'all the words of God' (cf. 3.11), which means of course the Torah. Cave 4 at Qumran has yielded another work with a similar title, namely *The Words of the Luminaries* (*RB* 68, 1961, pp. 195–250). Again, in Talmudic Hebrew 'the words of the Torah' are biblical laws and 'the words of the scribes' are rabbinical laws. **The words** here therefore means either the words of God, i.e. the Law or Torah, or the words of the scholars of the sect, their authoritative interpretations of the Law, possibly gathered into a book with a title which could be shortened into *The Words*.

6.24–25. speak falsely about property   CD 9.11 f.; 14.20; Lev. 5.1; Judg. 17.2 (Acts 5.1 ff.). Lev. 5.1 and Judg. 17.2 both refer to the custom by which an owner put a curse on the thief when he discovered that something had been stolen from him. Anyone who heard him utter the curse was held to be obliged to give any relevant information which he might possess. The procedure is prescribed in CD 9.11 f. The present passage also is based on this custom and condemns the man who gives false testimony when he knows the truth about some matter of property which is under investigation. Wernberg-Møller is perfectly right to say that Acts 5.1 ff. is no parallel. The sin of Ananias and Sapphira consisted in attempting to deceive the Holy Spirit (vv. 3, 4b, 9); its gravity did not derive from its being a lie about property, for Peter expressly draws attention to the fact that the lie to the Holy Spirit was inexcusable partly because before the sale the property and after it the proceeds were both at Ananias's disposal (4a). He was evidently under no compulsion to give the proceeds to the Church.

6.25. they shall cut him off   The verb meaning to separate is used in this punitive sense in 2.16; 7.1, 3, 5, 16; 8.24; CD 9.21, 23; Deut. 29.21; Isa. 59.2; Josephus, *BJ* 2.8.8, narrates the same punishment in the Essenes, and we should perhaps refer also to the obscure passage I Cor. 5.5. The whole temper of this form of punishment reflects not only Deut. 29.21, where God himself is regarded as the extractor of the penalty, but also the exclusive attitude of Ezra 10.7 f.

he shall be deprived   The culprit is cut off from **the purity of the many** and must look after himself. Rabin (*Qumran Studies*, p. 26) wonders if the stewards prepared special unclean meals for those undergoing punishment. It seems more probable that an offender was relegated to the position with regard to eating and cooking which he occupied as a novice: he could not use, we have suggested, the facilities and ironmongery of the community's kitchen, but he might manage well enough in company with others who were of the same status whether through punishment or still being novices. The deprivation **of a quarter of his rations** is more serious, since we do not know whether or not all the food produced at the Qumran 'home farm' at 'Ain Feshka was reserved for **the purity of the many**, i.e. for full members only. 7.18 ff. is instructive: here an offender is punished in a way which very clearly relegates him to novice status, yet, as Rabin notes (*ibid.*), he is able to return to the community; his exclusion has not meant starvation, and we may assume therefore that he was able to obtain food without great difficulty. Probably the man who was deprived of a quarter of his rations had to choose to do without that much or to make it up by his own efforts; he was not prevented from obtaining food, but given only a proportion of the communal stock. Josephus's grim tale of those who were expelled altogether by the Essenes (*BJ* 2.8.8) and who die as a consequence has been manifestly overdramatized by him: the obvious course for such an expelled member to take would be to resume eating the world's food which as a member he would have regarded as unclean, but which now befits him, since he has been cast out of the purity of the many himself. If there were any, as Josephus relates, who were received back at their last gasp, it was no doubt because they had demonstrated their fidelity to the order by refusing to eat 'common' food. If any actually died, it was their own voluntary act, since they could if they wished find food, though this would imply returning to the world. Cf. *b. Ber.* 56a; *RH* 166; *b. Sanh.* 37b.

6.26. discipline   Reading with Brownlee *yissur* rather than *yasod* ('foundation'). The difference in the Hebrew letters is insignificant. See 3.1.

6.27. an oath in the honoured name   and

7.1. If a man has cursed   CD 15.1–5.

The command not to swear falsely by the name of God (Lev. 19.12; Ex. 20.7; *Did.* 2.3) gave rise to a quite distinct and more radical command not to use the name of God at all in a solemn oath. Thus Matt. 5.33–37 represents very strict *halakah* derived from Lev. 19.12 by means of Isa. 66.1 and Ps. 47.2.

Such prohibition is distinguishable from that against actual blasphemy or cursing God by name, Lev. 24.15 f. This might be deliberate, and Job refuses to commit the offence (Job 2.9 f.), avoiding it when he relieves his feelings by cursing his day instead (Job 3.1). According to Mark 3.22–29 and Matt. 12.25–31, Jesus condemned as deliberate blasphemy something which was recognizable as such not by the specific uttered words but in the rebellious response which they betrayed to a divine challenge. Luke 12.10 applies the same saying differently (see below).

Most blasphemy is not deliberate but thoughtless, and thus represents perhaps as certainly the disposition of the heart (Luke 6.45), justifying the extreme statement of Matt. 12.37. Thoughtless use of the name of God is condemned in Ecclus. 23.7–11, which makes the Greek version of 47.18 (translated in the EV) the more surprising, since it turns into an oath what was in the original Hebrew a simple statement that Solomon was called by the honoured name (a reference to his original name Jedidiah, II Sam. 12.25). The Greek text of Ecclus. 47.18 is the sort of expression prohibited along with more solemn oaths in Matt. 5.36 f.; it illustrates and indeed helps to date another well-known development.

This was the prohibition not only of the use of the name in oaths but of pronouncing at any time, even in religious contexts, the name of God represented by the tetragrammaton YHWH. This is clearly formulated in *Sanh.* 7.5; 10.1, the only exception being the pronunciation of the name on the Day of Atonement by the high priest in the holy of holies, *Yoma* 6.2; cf. 3.8; *Tamid* 3.8; *Sotah* 7.6.

One possible situation envisaged in the present passage of the *Rule* seems to be like that contemplated by Luke at 12.10, blasphemy under stress, perhaps torture. The halakic strictness of the sect is illustrated by the same extreme punishment of irreversible expulsion being awarded for blasphemy in such a situation as for blasphemy which might be thoughtless or even deliberate.

James 2.7 apparently reveals the existence of deliberate blasphemy against the name not of God but of Christ. Cf. I Peter 4.14.

the book See following note.

7.2. priests who are registered in the book The Chronicler gives a register of priests in their twenty-four courses (see pp. 91 ff.)

at I Chron. 24.1–19; 25.9–31, and there is a brief summary by family names in Ezra 2.36–39 and Neh. 7.39–42; cf. Ezra 10.18–22. The twenty-four courses of the Chronicler's register are attested as historical by *Taʿan.* 4.2; *Tos. Sukk.* 4; *Tos. Taʿan.* 4; Talmud *b. Taʿan.* 27ab; *j. Taʿan.* 4.2; *Num. Rabbah* 3; and Josephus in *Ant.* 7.14.7. These lists would be known by the sect, but it is unlikely that they are meant, partly because their own list appears to have extended to twenty-six courses; a more formidable difficulty is presented by the phrase **the book** here and in the previous line. It seems natural for the meaning to be the same in each case. In 7.1 it apparently means the book of the Law, a common phrase in Talmudic Hebrew which also knows the abbreviation 'the book' with the same meaning. The books of Chronicles do not belong to the Law; if a brief list such as the names in Num. 3.1–4 is meant, **priests who are registered in the book** will mean 'priests whose names (or possibly whose ancestors' names) are found in the Law', and the crime is regarded as serious because committed against one whose sacerdotal status is due to divine ordinance. The alternative is to suppose that **the book** in line 2 refers to a list drawn up by the sect; this may seem a very natural explanation, but involves taking the phrase here in a sense different from that which it seems to bear in line 1.

7.3. for his soul i.e. for the good of his soul; based on the similar phrase in II Kings 7.7 which means 'for their lives'. So Guilbert. Alternatively the phrase means 'separated to his own self' i.e. placed in solitary confinement (Brownlee, Wernberg-Møller, Gaster). CD 12.3 ff.; 13.6 show that imprisonment was among the punishments meted out by the sect.

thoughtlessly 8.24; 9.1; Lev. 4.2, 22, 27; 5.15, 18; 22.14; Num. 15.25, 29; Josh. 20.3, 9; Eccles. 5.6; *Shab.* 11.6; *Hor.* 3.3, etc etc. Num. 15.28–31 expresses very clearly the distinction between sins done unwittingly (or **thoughtlessly**) and those done 'with a high hand' (**deliberately**). The priest is to make atonement for the former; the perpetrator of the latter 'shall be cut off from among his people' and 'his iniquity shall be upon him'. Unwittingly committed sins are to us not sins at all; in a world where ceremonial defilement was real they were sins and they must be expiated. Deliberate sin could not be expiated, but an individual might supplicate the LORD for forgiveness, as, for example, David apparently did in II Sam. 12.13–16, and as Amos did on behalf of Israel (Amos 7.2, 5). In the sect's view sins of inadvertence incurred ceremonial guilt, but, though it was ceremonial, the responsibility lay upon the 'offender' and he must atone for it, albeit by a relatively light penalty; this attitude was no doubt largely fostered by estrangement from the Temple, where normally the necessary levitical sacrifices would be made. Deliberate sins incurred, as we have seen (pp. 139 f.), both ceremonial and moral guilt and must be expiated by a severer penalty.

who lies deliberately   From this point to line 6 reflects Lev. 6.1–5 (Hebrew 5.20–24).

7.4. without just cause   Cf. 7.8, 18, which illustrate the difficulty of translating the phrase into English without banality, avoidance of which perhaps introduces a wrong shade of meaning; for Wernberg-Møller is probably right in his note *ad loc.* in saying that the action is in any case atrocious and the phrase merely stresses the fact, as in Jer. 17.11 and Ezek. 22.29. There is no suggestion that harm could be inflicted justly.

7.5–6. if he defrauds his fellow   The penalty in this case is severer than if the offender has deprived the community of property. Was this because there was scriptural warrant (in Leviticus—see note above) for restoration to a 'neighbour', but not to the community? In Leviticus ceremonial expiation also is required; for this the *Rule* substitutes punishment for **three months** or **sixty days**; that is exclusion from the **purity of the many** for this period, a natural substitution for a community which believed in the reality of ceremonial defilement, but had no contact with the Temple. **Sixty days** is written above the line.

in full   Lev. 6.5 (Hebrew 5.24). The single Hebrew word stands alone and is followed by a gap, but the verse runs on and there is no change of handwriting.

7.8. whoever bears a grudge   The verb is not absolutely clear, but the facsimile seems to show that the last letter has been written above the line only because a mark already on the leather had rendered the space below it unusable. It seems clear that the passage is based upon Lev. 19.18. The severity of some regulations obscures the attractiveness of others which show a genuine concern for love and kindness between the members. The original command in Leviticus was not universalist, for the crucial question 'Who is my neighbour?' was not answered in that sense until the second century of our era. The scholar who raised it in Luke 10.29 might have been trying to win the argument after the conservative and unexceptionable answer of Jesus to which Luke has attached it (Mark 12.28–31;

Matt. 22.34–40; Luke 10.25–28), but he asked an important question which received from Jesus a subtle and penetrating reply which invited him to abandon the laws of Levitical purity and be not like priest or Levite, but like the Samaritan whose uncleanness actually helped him to keep the commandment.

'Thou shalt love thy neighbour as thyself' (Lev. 19.18) was not always treated as the chief scripture on which to base the ethics of society. In *Ned.* 9.4 R. Meir quotes commands of apparently paramount importance in this connexion, since his opinion is that a vow which contravenes any of them may be regarded as invalid. The passage quotes 'Thou shalt not take vengeance', or 'Thou shalt not bear any grudge', or 'Thou shalt not hate thy brother in thy heart', or 'Thou shalt love thy neighbour as thyself', or 'That thy brother may live with thee'. The first, second and fourth are from Lev. 19.18, the third from Lev. 19.17, and the fifth from Lev. 25.36. The present passage 7.8–18 may be said to apply these commandments to the community at Qumran.

7.9. one who takes vengeance CD 9.2–5. See also end of previous note. The Old Testament reflects clearly the state of primitive society in which the vendetta even for an accidental killing was a duty, and legislation is introduced at various dates to regulate or to prevent it: Num. 35.12; Deut. 19.4–6 illustrate these facts, and Deut. 19.12 (cf. Josh. 20.2 ff.) shows clearly that the avenger's right was acknowledged even though it was restrained by the community. Gen. 4.15 firmly insists that the duty of vengeance must be left to God. He will take it on behalf of his people or himself (e.g. Deut. 32.35, 43; I Sam. 24.12; Ps. 94.1; Luke 18.7 f.; 21.22; I Thess. 4.6; II Thess. 1.8; Heb. 10.30). This essential modification does not always proceed from a high ethic of forgiveness, as is shown by Prov. 24.17 f.; 25.21 f., which advise leaving vengeance entirely to God, so as not to lessen its devastating effect on one's enemy. If the obscure passage Gen. 4.23 f. could be regarded, in spite of the main teaching of the OT, as a warrant for taking vengeance, or at least for desiring it (Ps. 79.12), the saying in Matt. 18.21 f.; Luke 17.4 may be in deliberate verbal opposition to it, as is the general sense of Matt. 5.38 ff.; Luke 6.27 ff. In Rom. 12.19 f. Paul uses Prov. 25.21 f. in the service of this higher ethic, but with the positive suggestion that God will exact retribution from a wrongdoer, for he recalls Deut. 32.35 and goes on to approve of justice being exacted by the State (Rom. 13.4). So also here in the *Rule* the prohibition is against private vengeance (**for himself**), not against punishment administered by the community. It is wrong to try to understand the extreme ethic of the 'Sermon on the Mount' (Matt. 5.39; Luke 6.29) without setting it in the context of a community. Jesus no less than the rabbis acknowledged the authority of the state (Mark 12.17 pars.) and warned often against the severe retribution which God would exact from those in debt to him (e.g. Matt. 5.26; Luke 12.59).

improper word   CD 10.18. Kuhn, tracing a connexion between Qumran and the epistle to the Ephesians, compares this passage, line 14 below and 10.21–24, with Eph. 5.4 (*NTS* 7, 1960–1, p. 339).

in the midst of the words of his fellow   See on 6.10. The language recalls the Hebrew of Ecclus. 11.8.

7.11. if they are standing   Rabin has given the only likely explanation (*Qumran Studies*, p. 105): the verb is a Mishnaic *Niph'al* and means 'to stand up from a sitting position'; it thus means the same as *'amad*, to stand in order to vote. The offence would in this instance be absence from voting and more serious than absence at other times.

7.12. naked   In contrast to Greeks, who regularly took athletic exercise naked, the Semite regarded it as natural to man in his fallen state to feel shame if seen naked (Gen. 2.25; 3.7); moreover, nakedness was associated with immoral behaviour; Ex. 32.25, whatever its true meaning, includes the fact that the people were naked (cf. Lam. 4.21). The objection to nakedness is certainly part of the hostility to Greek customs shown in II Macc. 4.13 ff.

7.13. a man who spits   Num. 12.14; Deut. 25.9; Job 30.10; Isa. 50.6; Matt. 26.67; 27.30; Mark 10.34; 14.65; 15.19; Luke 18.32 all suggest the insult implied in spitting, although Mark 7.33; 8.23; John 9.6 see nothing reprehensible in the use of spittle. Although the regulation perhaps demands no explanation, it is possible that its specific inclusion here is based on obedience to the laws of levitical cleanness. Josephus, *BJ* 2.8.9, finds it worth mention that 'They are careful not to spit into the middle of other people or to the right' immediately before describing the strict sabbatarianism of the Essenes. Lev. 15.8 may provide the basis, for *Toh.* 4.5 f. shows that not all spittle was unclean. The Mishnah *Sanh.* 10.1; *T. Sanh.* 12.9 and the Talmud *b. Sanh.* 101a; *j. Sanh.* 28b denounce those who whisper a magical formula over a wound. This formula is associated with spitting, which was a mode of healing usual at the time. The prohibition is made only in connexion with this 'spitting'—and apparently because the Divine Name is not to be recorded while 'spitting'. See also on 15, **his left hand.**

7.14. laughs foolishly   See on line 10 (**improper word**) above.

7.15. his left hand   Dupont-Sommer notes (*ad loc.*) that Philo (*De vita contemplativa*) tells of the Therapeutae that they showed their disapproval of an orator by a sign with the right hand. To use the left would be insulting. We have seen that Josephus says that the Essenes were prohibited from spitting to the right (line 13), which is the honourable side. *Benjamin* may mean 'Son of the right hand'. According to the evidence of the Mari letters a desert tribe of unruly warriors who were skilful left-handed bowmen were so called, perhaps to avoid calling them left-handed. If it is indeed a matter of the left hand being unacceptable, we may compare the *Gospel of Thomas* log. 62, which takes the last part of Matt. 6.3 from its context. B. Gärtner, *The Theology of the Gospel of Thomas*, p. 115, expounds the passage clearly: 'It is usual in Gnostic literature to connect the work of the demiurge, the material world, with the left side, and the heavenly world with the right . . . Man must not allow the material—or for that matter anything belonging to this world—to encroach upon the heavenly.'

Another interpretation of the whole passage is possible, that from 13b onwards (the stricture on the sectarian who allows his member [male organ, in Hebrew euphemistically called here 'his hand'] to be seen because his garment is ragged) the regulations are concerned with correct behaviour when relieving oneself. Yadin (pp. 74 f.) points out that Josephus tells us (*BJ* 2.8.9, after the mention of the prohibition of spitting) how exactly the Essenes obeyed the injunctions of Deut. 23.12–14, and that they refrained from relieving themselves on the sabbath because this involved digging.

7.16. who goes about slandering   Lev. 19.16; Ezek. 22.9. In the latter there is a similar juxtaposition of ceremonial with moral fault.

he shall be punished   It is uncertain what constituted the punishment. Very probably a fine in the form of deprivation of rations, for the first time this verb is used (6.25) this is explicitly stated.

slandering the many   Similarly derivable from Lev. 19.16; Ezek. 22.9. In this instance the crime against the community is regarded as worse than that against the neighbour, in contrast to fraud connected with property (76–7). This is no doubt because the community in itself is regarded as holy and the crime as a religious one.

7.17. murmurs 1QH 5.25; Ex. 15.24; 16.2, 7, etc.; Josh. 9.18; Ps. 106.25; Matt. 20.11; Luke 5.30; 15.2; 19.7; John 6.41, 43, 61; 7.32; I Cor. 10.10; Phil. 2.14; Jude 16.

7.18. to betray the truth By ceasing to live by it.

7.19. to walk in the stubbornness of his heart means to live as before when not a member; as is clear from 1.6; 2.14, 26; 3.3; 5.4; 7.24; 9.10; CD 2.17; 3.5, 11; 8.8, 19; 19.20; 20.9; 1QH 4.15 the phrase describes the way of life of all who are not members of the sect.

7.19–21. punished two years For a discussion of the regulations which follow see pp. 191–94. Evidently the member who sought readmission was subjected anew to the same probation as when he first applied for membership. During his probation he has no rank, for he sits **behind all the men**, but after enquiry he is **registered in his rank**; it is not clear if this means that to which he had attained before his defection or that to which he is now assigned after deliberation. That he is **asked about judgment** indicates his full status as a member of the full assembly, to which he must contribute his opinion on any matter under debate.

7.22. ten full years The concessions with regard to penitent defectors just given do not apply when the offender has been a member so long. The rest of this column shows two gaps due to fragments missing from the bottom of the scroll, the smaller affecting virtually only the last line, the larger the last two lines.

7.24. 4QSe supports the restoration, **of the community who associates**, only partly surviving in 1QS.

MODEL OF A PIONEER COMMUNITY
8.1–9.26

CONSTITUTION OF THE PIONEER COMMUNITY: 8.1–9.11
[There shall be]

¹in the council of the community twelve men and three priests, perfect in all that has been revealed from all ²the Law, for the practice of truth and righteousness and justice and love of mercy and walking humbly each man with his neighbour, ³for the preserving of faith in the land with a lowly disposition and a broken spirit, and making amends for iniquity by the practice of justice ⁴and the endurance of the trial of affliction; for walking with all men according to the standard of truth and the regulation of time.

When these exist in Israel [5]the council of the community will be established in truth for an eternal planting, a house of holiness for Israel, a company of holy [6]of holies for Aaron, witnesses to truth for the judgment and chosen by good will to atone for the land and to requite [7]the wicked with their reward. It shall be a trusty wall, a precious cornerstone: their foundations will not [8]shift nor shall they move from their places. A dwelling which is a holy of holies [9]for Aaron in the knowledge of all, for a covenant of justice and to offer a pleasant savour, and a perfect house and truth in Israel [10]to establish a covenant on eternal statutes. They shall be acceptable to make atonement for the land and to determine judgment upon wickedness, and iniquity shall be no more.

When these are established in the foundation of the community for two years in perfection of way—[11]they shall be separated as a holiness within the council of the men of the community. And all the matters which were hidden from Israel and revealed to the man [12]who enquires —they shall not conceal them from these through fear of a spirit of apostasy.

And when these exist as a community [13]in Israel, according to this programme they shall be separated from among the settlement of the men of iniquity to go into the desert, to prepare there the way of Him, [14]as it is written,

In the wilderness prepare the way of . . . in the Arabah they shall make straight a highway for our God (Isa. 40.3).

15 This means study of the Law [which] he commanded by the hand of Moses, to act according to all that is revealed from time to time [16]and according as the prophets revealed by the spirit of his holiness.

No man from among the men of the community, (in) the covenant [17]of the community, who turns from anything that is commanded, acting with a high hand, shall touch the purity of the men of holiness [18]and he shall not know any of their counsels until his deeds are purified from all iniquity to walk in perfection of way, and they have bidden him approach [19]the council on the authority of the many; and afterwards he shall be registered in his rank. According to this precept it shall be for everyone who is added to the community.

20 These are the rules by which are to walk the men of perfection and of holiness each man with his fellow: [21]everyone who enters the council of holiness, of those who walk in perfection of way as he commanded, every man from among them [22]who transgresses a word from the Law of Moses with a high hand or by negligence—they shall expel him from the council of the community [23]and he shall return no more; and no man from among the men of holiness shall mingle his property nor his counsel with his for any [24]purpose.

But if by inadvertence he do it he shall be separated from the purity and from the council; and they shall consult the regulation [25]which says 'He shall not judge anyone and he shall not be asked for any counsel for two years'. If he perfect his way [26]in session, in study and in council . . . if he has committed no further accidental offence during his completion of the two years

COLUMN NINE

[1]since for one accidental offence he shall be punished two years but for him who commits it with a high hand the penalty is that he return no more. Only the one who commits an accidental offence [2]shall be tested two years for the perfection of his way and counsel at the authority of the many and afterwards he shall be registered in his rank in the community of holiness.

3 When these exist in Israel according to all these plans for founding a spirit of holiness in eternal truth [4]to atone for the guilt of transgression and the treachery of sin and for favour for the land more than by flesh of burnt-offerings or by the fat of sacrifice; and the offering [5]of the lips according to precept is like a sweet-savoured offering of righteousness and perfection of way like a freewill offering for favour, at that time the men [6]of the community shall separate themselves as a house of holiness for Aaron and to be united as a holy of holies, and as a house of holiness for Israel who walk in perfection.

7 Only the sons of Aaron shall rule in judgment and in matters of property, and at their mouth shall go forth the lot for every rule which concerns the men of the community [8]and the property of the men of holiness who walk in perfection.

Their property shall not be mingled with the property of the men of deceit, who [9]have not cleansed their way to be separated from iniquity and to walk in perfection of way; and from no counsel of the Law shall they depart to walk [10]in all the stubbornness of their heart, but they shall be ruled by the original precepts which the men of the community began to use for self-discipline [11]until the coming of the prophet and the anointed ones of Aaron and Israel.

At first sight it appears that the passage which now follows (8.1–9.11) regulates part of the constitution of the community at Qumran, stipulating the formation and maintenance of an inner council of twelve men and three priests (Dupont-Sommer; Vermès, p. 26; Brownlee); but 8.12–14 makes clear that the Qumran community was to be formed after this inner *corps d'élite* had been established and tested for two years (10b–11). The community or movement therefore out of which it arose must have been represented by groups dispersed throughout the land, such as we know to have existed (see p. 33).

Further, **the council of the community** does not necessarily mean a smaller body within the wider community, for it is one of the phrases which is used to mean simply the community (3.2; 5.7; 6.13 f.; cf. 8.11; 1QpHab 12.4). Wernberg-Møller is therefore right to say that all that follows 'applies to the community, and not to the twelve or fifteen men exclusively', although it applies to them alone at first, since they for a time are identical with the community.

E. F. Sutcliffe (*JSS* 4, 1959, pp. 134 ff. and *The Monks of Qumran*, pp. 58 f. and 254 f.) seems to have been the first to interpret the whole passage 8.1–9.26 as it is being taken here. It is unnecessary, though not perhaps wrong, to follow him in the details of his theory, which involve association of this exodus to Qumran with the Teacher of Righteousness; for Sutcliffe, rightly remarking that 'The Teacher of Righteousness was not the original founder of the movement that developed into the Essenes' (*op. cit.*, p. 58), nevertheless believes that the Teacher was the founder or first leader of the Qumran community. This is possible, but we have seen (p. 115) that the Teacher of Righteousness may have come to the community when it had already been at Qumran for twenty years.

Sutcliffe seems in any case to be right in his main lines of interpretation of the passage; he is followed by Guilbert and supported by Wernberg-Møller. If we can rely upon this interpretation, which will be further explained in the commentary, we can perhaps correlate this evidence with that of Josephus, taking it that the sentence which begins *BJ* 2.8.4, 'They possess no one city but everywhere have large colonies', describes the movement before the foundation of Qumran, a community which he does not mention, or as it continued to exist after Qumran was established, or both. It is feasible also that *BJ* 2.8.13, the 'second order of Essenes', describes among others the community at Qumran, which was apparently not celibate, since the skeletons of women have been found in its cemetery, and it would be natural for it to be made up at least partly of families if it arose from the movement for which CD 7.6 f. legislates.

Betz (*Offenbarung*, p. 50) regards the passage as arising from Isa. 8.16–18: there the special instruction and teaching are to be sealed and thus hidden from the outside world (cf. 1QS 8.18 and 9.17) and the prophet and his children are to be signs for Israel. Betz argues that the Teacher of Righteousness looks in the same way on himself

and his pupils in beginning this special community. It should be
carefully observed that while the passage in Isaiah may have
inspired the idea of a pioneer community in the wilderness (cf. the
use of Isa. 40.3 in 8.12–14) there is no evidence in the *Rule* and no
certain evidence anywhere in the scrolls which will show that the
leader on this occasion was the Teacher or that if he was he thought
of himself in this way; for the reference given by Betz (1QH 7.20 f.)
recalls different scriptures.

If this part of the scroll is indeed the plan drawn up for the pioneer
community which went out into the wilderness after austere training,
it is clearly another indication of the composite character of the *Rule*.

[There shall be] seem to be the natural words to supply, although
there is no indication of any words having been lost. Sutcliffe argues
for 'when there is', which recurs, for example, at lines 4 and 12, but
these words would be a slightly abrupt beginning for a new section.

8.1. the council of the community I.e. the community. See
the argument in the notes introducing this section.

twelve men and three priests Remarkable nonsense has been
talked about these men; they cannot be directly parallel with the
apostles, who might be regarded as twelve men within whom three
were specially prominent, that is nine men and three leaders (Gal.
2.9), all of whom were certainly laymen. The last point is sufficient
to establish an important difference, even if we interpret the present
passage as meaning 'twelve men including three priests'. It is, however, almost certain that fifteen in all are meant, for a Cave 4
composite fragment described by Milik in *Ten Years of Discovery in
the Wilderness of Judaea*, p. 96, in a passage parallel to 1QS 8.1 ff.,
specifically mentions fifteen (see Milik also in *RB* 54, 1957, p. 589);
moreover, this is the natural interpretation of 1QS.

Habermann interprets the twelve as representing the tribes and
the three as representing the fathers (Abraham, Isaac and Jacob),
but it is very much more probable that while the **twelve** certainly
represent the secular tribes the **priests** represent the Levite tribes
Gershon, Kohath and Merari, for the (unfortunately incomplete)
evidence of DSW 4.1 and the immediately preceding passage suggest
this. See Yadin *ad loc.* and pp. 53 ff.

In spite of the difficulties raised by such questions as whether Levi
should be counted among the twelve tribes, or whether Joseph did
not imply two, Ephraim and Manasseh, the number of the tribes
was always thought of as twelve; this provides the common back-

ground for the twelve men here and the twelve specially called by
Jesus, and the indirect link between the two groups. See Mark 3.14;
Matt. 10.2; Luke 6.13; John 6.70; I Cor. 15.5, and especially the
Q passage Matt. 19.28; Luke 22.30 for a deliberate connexion of the
disciples with the tribes. Rev. 21 shows the way in which twelve
tribes, twelve apostles, twelve gates, foundations, etc., are mingled
in the writer's mind.

perfect   See the note on 1.17 (**all that he has commanded**).
The demand for ethical perfection is made also at CD 7.5; 10.6, the
term being part of the title of the sect in CD 20.2, 5, 7 (see on 5.13).
Ethical perfection is identified with keeping the Torah in all its
injunctions, whether known to all Israel or revealed only to the sect
through their constant study.

8.2. walking humbly   The words recall Micah 6.8, which is
indeed the model for the whole phrase from the word **justice**. In
Micah the phrase ends with the words 'with thy God', for which
with his neighbour is substituted here.

8.3. for the preserving of faith   Isa. 26.1–3; Jer. 5.3; Luke
18.8. Faith here is faithfulness to God and his covenant, which can
be preserved only by steadfast adherence to the Law.

a broken spirit   11.1; Ps. 51.17.

making amends   See on 2.8 and 5.6. In post-biblical Hebrew
the verb means specifically to appease, procure pardon (Jastrow II.
1493B), and it seems that a powerful motive for the establishment
of the community was the desire to work atonement for the sins of
Israel, which the founder or founders believed could be effected by
a body of Israelites cleansed from their past stains and devoted to
perfect obedience to the Law. Such a conception had to be reconciled
with the fundamental doctrine that God alone could forgive sins.
This is explained in the notes on 2.8 (**forgive by covering thine
iniquities**) and on 5.6 (**make atonement**). It is instructive to
compare this high ideal with that in the New Testament: the men of
Qumran apparently believed that such atoning work necessitated
not only **the practice of justice** but also

8.4. the endurance of the trial of affliction (for this phrase see
1.17). Thus they saw the inevitability of suffering as well as the
necessity for righteousness. That the righteous man is destined
to suffer is part of the eschatological belief of devout Judaism at this
time (see the note on 1.17, **trial . . . during the dominion of
Belial**), and allied to it is the general Jewish insight that the righteous

man is in the nature of things doomed to suffering, an insight which the experience of the Jew in every age is unlikely to obscure. The bewildered question of Hab. 1.13 (how can a righteous God tolerate the victory of the unrighteous over the righteous man in this world?) becomes the wholehearted acceptance of Wisd. 1–3; and the over-facile eudaemonism of Deuteronomy and of many Psalms (e.g. 1.3, 6; 5.12, etc.) is abandoned, no doubt in the face of experience which had too often belied it. Even though a well-governed state is designed to discourage the malefactor and reward the law-abiding, society and the world at large do not reflect the construction of the state in this regard.

The righteous may be represented by a remnant large enough to be identified with the essential nation (e.g. Isa. 10.20 f.; 11.11, 16; Micah 2.12) or by individuals such as Moses in Ex. 32.30 ff. and the righteous man in a general sense in Wisd. 1–2; again, the youngest of the seven martyrs in II Macc. 7 associates prayer for his people with his death (7.37), and Eleazar in *IV Macc.* 6.27 ff. prays that his martyrdom may avail for his people. The New Testament makes the concept central: Jesus and his disciples represent the Son of Man, 'the saints of the Most High', destined to inherit the kingdom with the inevitable concomitant of suffering (Mark 10.35–40; Matt. 20.20–28; cf. Dan. 7.13 f., 27), but events lead naturally to the doctrine of atonement being focused on Jesus alone as the one suffer-ing righteous man (e.g. I Peter 3.18).

standard of truth Various teachers and rabbis could enunciate their standards and principles for understanding and applying the Law. For the sect there is only one, an absolute standard by which to live, that is that revealed by God in the first place indeed to Moses, and now in more detail to the sect by their study.

regulation of time See on 1.9, and p. 89.

8.5 ff. an eternal planting The general sense of this whole passage is excellently summarized by Vermès in *Scripture and Tradition in Judaism*, pp. 32 f.: 'The Temple of Jerusalem, fallen into the hands of wicked priests, was to be considered defiled (CD 6.11–20; 1QpHab 12.7–9) until its purification at the return of the Sons of Zadok in the last days. The War Scroll prophesies that this capital event will occur in the seventh year of the eschatological war against the Sons of Darkness (DSW 2.1–7). In the meanwhile, the Council of the Community is the one true sanctuary in which God is to be wor-shipped.' Vermès then quotes the present passage of the *Rule*. For the

actual metaphor of **planting** see 11.8; CD 1.7; 1QH 6.15, 8.6 ff.;
Isa. 60.21; 61.3; Ezek. 17.23; 31; Dan. 4; *I Enoch* 10.16 (cf. 62.8;
84.6; 93.2, 5, 10); *Jub.* 1.16; 7.34; 21.24; *Pss. Sol.* 14.3; 17. (3–4), 5.
The most remarkable passages are perhaps Ezek. 31 with its elabora-
tion of the cedar metaphor, and 1QH 8.6 ff., which is given by
Mansoor's notation. Licht's edition (1957) made two poems, 8.4–37
and 9.3–36 (Hebrew edition, pp. 131 ff.) of a long and important
psalm published already by M. Wallenstein as *The Nezer and the
Submission in Suffering Hymn from the Dead Sea Scrolls*. Both Licht and
Wallenstein rightly see the subject of these passages as the Messianic
Woes, but the imagery is manifold and includes at the beginning the
lines which may be quoted from Wallenstein:

> 'I [thank thee, O Lord,
> For] thou hast set me at a streaming fountain in dry ground,
> And (at) a well of water in a parched land,
> And (at) garden-irrigating water [in the desert.
> I thus tu]rned, for the sake of thy glory, into a plantation of
>   the fir tree and the pine and the box-tree together.
> Trees of life at a secret fount, hidden amongst all the trees by
>   the water,
> are about to blossom forth a branch to become an everlasting
>   plant.
> It will strike roots ere they will blossom forth,
> And ere they will spread out their roots by the river.'

The author, if he wrote as seems likely at Qumran, has here given
evidence of a poetic vision not wholly based upon Scripture, although
some lines recall Isa. 35.6 f.; 37.31; 60.13; the actual geographical
situation is invested with spiritual significance. He lived near 'Ain
Feshka—'at a streaming fountain in dry ground, a well of water in
parched land, garden-irrigating water in the desert'. He vows to
turn the community, which he compares to this natural phenomenon,
into God's planting. But even in a time of great disturbance such a
planting needs time to develop, to 'strike roots'.

   a house of holiness for Israel   9.6; 10.4; 1QSb 4.28; 1QH
6.26 ff.; 7.8 ff.; Gen. 49.24; Isa. 8.14; 28.16; Ps. 118.22; Dan. 2.34 f.,
45; Zech. 3.9; 4.7, 9; 12.3; Rom. 9.33; 10.11; Eph. 2.20; I Peter
2.4–8; *Ep. Barn.* 6.2–4.

   Betz (*Offenbarung*, pp. 158 ff.) discusses this passage carefully,
showing that it is founded upon Isa. 28.16 taken out of its context,
so that we are unaware that the original oracle is reported as spoken

by God, who will himself bring about the result of which he speaks. The stone laid by God in the Isaiah passage becomes a building, that is the community, grounded in truth and holy in character. The strong foundation is an important theme of both passages.

In Isa. 28.16 the word 'stone' is repeated, the second time receiving the epithet 'tried'. In I Peter 2.6 the first occurrence of 'stone' is omitted, in the present passage of the *Rule* the repetitive phrase is paraphrased: *'eben 'eben bochan* becomes *chomath habbachan*. Thus 'a stone, a tried stone' becomes 'the wall of a tower', although the meaning 'tried' is still operative and the phrase can be rendered **trusty wall**. After the manner of some rabbinic exegesis both meanings are accepted. A wall of a tower is necessary for defence, and a tested community—tested in the wilderness—is necessary for Israel. Remains at Qumran include the lower courses of a substantial tower which stood at the main entrance of the community buildings (R. de Vaux, *L'Archaéologie et les manuscrits de la mer morte*, p. 5), illustrating the literal interpretation which existed side by side with the metaphorical. Not only constant spiritual warfare but an actual military war was expected; but against the tower the forces of Belial will not prevail (1QH 6.24 ff.; cf. Matt. 16.18, 23). The community is then to be **a house of holiness** which is the fulfilment of the stone planted by God. Hence it is **for Israel**, that is, to re-found and re-create Israel. See further the note below on **a trusty wall, a precious cornerstone**.

8.5–6. a holy of holies for Aaron   5.6, 21; 8.9; 9.6 ff.; 11.8; CD 1.7; 6.2. The community is to take the place of the sanctuary of the Temple, an idea which is linked in the New Testament with that of the Body of Christ, the new people of God, I Cor. 3.16; 6.19; II Cor. 6.16; cf. John 2.21; Rom. 8.9. See also the opening of the comment above on **an eternal planting for Aaron**, i.e. to re-establish the high priesthood, since the official high priesthood had been defiled. The Hasmonaeans were Levites and are reproached as such in *Test. Levi* (see note below on **to atone for the land**). The defilement of the high priesthood had begun with the murder of Onias III (II Macc. 4.34). *Jub.* 23.21 f. reflects the disgust at the subsequent degradation into which the office fell no less surely than the Qumran *Habbakuk Commentary*, and *Ass. Moses* 5.4 speaks of the pollution wrought by those who offer gifts to the LORD, while they 'are not priests but slaves, sons of slaves'. Cf. Josephus, *Ant.* 13.10.5, where one Eleazar taunts John Hyrcanus with being the son of a mother who was a captive and demands therefore that he should repudiate the high priesthood, already in his day the title covering a position analogous to that of a Greek 'tyrant' and soon to be openly called kingship. Reproaches and taunts of these falsely so-called high priests form the substance of the *Pss. Sol.* 2.4, 8.

8.6. to atone for the land   1QSa 1.3; 1Q22 24.1. See on 2.8; 5.6, and especially 8.3 above; and cf. 8.10 below. **For the land** means 'for the land of Israel', the land and nation combined in one concept, a usage developed from such passages as Gen. 12.1, 6, 7; 31.3; Deut. 17.4; 18.9; and it includes the meaning, 'for the earth' (Gaster, Vermès and Wernberg-Møller). The latter carries with it the notion that the ground itself must be cleansed from defilement. See Lev. 18.27 f.; Num. 35.33; Joel 3.17 (Hebrew 4.17); *Jub.* 50.5; *Or. Sib.* 5.264; *II Bar.* 66.2 and a Cave 4 fragment published by Allegro in *JBL* 77 (1958), p. 351, for the idea of the land's pollution; and *Kel.* 1.6 for the holiness of Israel as a land. Pollution had been brought upon the land partly by the association of Hasmonaean rulers with heathen women and other sexual transgressions. *Test. Levi* reproaches them for their lax sexual morality at 14.6; cf. 9.9 f., and for similar reproaches of the tribe of Judah see *Test. Jud.* 13.7; 23.2.

Later writings reflect these convictions. The Tosephta to the Mishnah Tractate *Sanhedrin* 4.2 says of the king, 'He may choose for himself wives wheresoever he please from among the priestly, Levitic, and Israelitish families.' Danby comments *ad loc.* that the Israelites must be 'of pure descent who are eligible for marriage into priestly families' and refers to *Kid.* 4.1, 4, 5.

The sect or its founder took to heart the injunction of Num. 35.33, 'Ye shall not pollute the land', and the fact that it had been so terribly disobeyed. The new community would spiritually fulfil the intention of the sacrifice enjoined in Deut. 21.1–9. For reflection on the moral innocence implied by the performance of such a sacrifice and the pronouncement of forgiveness by the Holy Spirit see *Soṭah* 9.6.

8.6-7. requite the wicked   CD 7.9; DSW 11.13 (cf. 4.12); Ps. 94.1 f.; Prov. 21.18; Joel 3.4, 7; Obad. 15; Dan. 7.22; Ecclus. 12.6; 35.18 f.; Matt. 21.41; 25.31 ff.; Luke 18.7 f.; I Cor. 6.2; I Thess. 4.6; Rev. 20.12. Prov. 21.18 seems to imply that the punishment of the wicked constitutes the atonement on behalf of the righteous and Wernberg-Møller would connect this thought with the present passage. This may be right, for the emphasis seems to fall on the duty which the new community will carry out on behalf of Israel. In practice this punishment of the wicked would be, in their eyes, wrought by God through their agency as a holy army in the final war. In the New Testament this final requital is reserved for the coming of the Lord as judge (e.g. Matt. 25.31 ff.; Rev. 20.12), and only one unexpected passage suggests that the righteous will play any part in this judgment (I Cor. 6.2).

8.7. a trusty wall, precious cornerstone   See the note above on **a house of holiness for Israel** for relevant passages, of which the most important is perhaps Isa. 28.16, and for an explanation of the handling of the text. The history and meaning of the metaphor has been brought out by S. H. Hooke, *The Siege Perilous*, ch. 17, pp. 235 ff. In Gen. 49.24 the Stone of Israel is probably the LORD, and in Isa. 8.14 it is the word of the LORD which supports the man of faith and is a cause of stumbling to the faithless (cf. Matt. 16.18 and 23). Isa. 28.16 Hooke plausibly connects with the situation revealed by Isa. 10.5–34, the Assyrian 'flood' upon the land of Israel: he suggests that 'Isaiah here expresses in vivid symbolism his belief that Jahveh intends to bring out from the fires of purgation and establish in Zion a godly and righteous remnant to be the basis and nucleus of the restored order and the coming kingdom of Jahveh'. This certainly connects well with the use made of the passage here in the *Rule* and Hooke's quotation of Zephaniah's oracle three-quarters of a century later is very apt: 'I will leave in the midst of thee an afflicted and poor people, and they shall trust in the name of the LORD. The remnant of Israel shall not do iniquity, nor speak lies, neither shall a deceitful tongue be found in their mouth, for they shall feed and lie down, and none shall make them afraid' (Zeph. 3.12 f.).

The **corner-stone** Hooke explains as a fixed and pivotal point of a building, as in the late passage Zech. 10.4, so that it may mean metaphorically the rallying-centre for a restored community. In this connexion the emergence of the metaphor in Zech. 3.9; 4.7, 10 is significant, whatever meaning be given to the other imagery in these difficult passages. Like Haggai, Zechariah is seeking to rekindle enthusiasm for rebuilding the Temple in the hearts of a small body of people who are the true representatives of Israel, and Hooke is surely right to claim that the prophet 'is setting forth in symbolic form his belief that Jahveh is now about to establish a new order, with a purified priesthood, a pure worship, a people cleansed from iniquity and emerging from the fires of purgation, under the leadership of a Messianic king, a shoot from David's line, in the person of Zerubbabel'. It seems very probable that the author of the present passage, well versed in exposition of scripture by scripture, received inspiration from passages associated with previous great attempts to restore a purified Israel, that under Haggai and Zechariah and that under Nehemiah and Ezra; and the sect's preoccupation with water symbolism and the spirit lend some support to Hooke's view that the LORD's 'opening of the opening of the stone' in Zech. 3.9 should be connected with Zech. 13.1, 'And in that day a fountain shall be opened for the house of David and for the inhabitants of Jerusalem for sin and for uncleanness.'

Ps. 118.22, often and very aptly quoted in the NT (Mark 12.10; Matt. 21.42; Luke 20.17; Acts 4.11; I Peter 2.7) as a symbol of the rejected Messiah, seems to have been originally that of a rejected and restored Israel.

8.9. to offer a pleasant savour   3.11; 9.5; 1QSb 3.1; DSW 2.5; Gen. 8.21; Ex. 29.18; Lev. 1.9; Num. 15.13. Metaphorical: the sect by their correct conduct will be the equivalent of a properly constituted priesthood. In the NT it is Christ who offers himself as the perfect sacrifice, but in one passage he is envisaged as presenting, after cleansing, his bride the Church to God (Eph. 5.26 f.). The metaphor of 'an offering and sacrifice to God for the savour of a sweet smell' is used of Christ's sacrifice at Eph. 5.2 and Phil. 4.18, the vocabulary being taken from Ex. 29.18. Cf. also Ezek. 20.41, which is close to the ideal of the sect as expressed in this passage.

8.10. they shall be acceptable . . . iniquity shall be no more   This whole phrase is written above the words which follow, **when these are established . . . perfection of way**; it is added by the same hand, and 4QSd, though not 4QSe, appears to have contained it. The same is true of the first word of line 11, **they shall be separated.**

for two years   See 6.13b–23, esp. 6.21. The period of probation there prescribed evidently reproduced the original preparatory period of the pioneers.

8.11. separated as a holiness within the council   If we are right in interpreting **the council of the community** as the community, this phrase must mean that the pioneers, recruited from members of the movement in its original dispersed state, will form

the nucleus of the sect in its new condition in the desert (see line 13);
their **holiness** would be shared by all subsequent new members
who then formed the **many**, all the full members of the community,
into which the pioneers would in time thus grow.

   matters which were hidden from Israel   9.17. Rabbinic
Judaism shows evidence of what was probably a very old tradition in
Chag. 2.1; *Meg.* 4.9 f.; according to this, certain passages of Scripture
were not expounded, one reason being for fear of loss of faith. Philo
in *Quod omnis probus liber* 12 says that when the Scriptures were
publicly read to the Essenes, the interpreter passed over what was
unintelligible to the ordinary man. It is therefore possible that our
passage is relaxing this rule in the case of the new community to be
found in the desert. There is indeed evidence that within such
esoteric groups withholding revelations from fellow members was
forbidden. Josephus, *BJ* 2.8.7, says Essenes neither hide anything
from fellow members not reveal their secrets to outsiders. 1QS 6.6
may describe the occasion when such communication or reticence
could occur and 9.17 forbids such communication to non-members;
Test. Reub. 3.5 attributes 'concealments from kindred and friends'
(i.e. fellow members) to the sixth of the seven spirits of deceit. The
stricter rule persisted in Judaism and was known to Origen when
he wrote the prologue to his *Commentary on the Song of Songs* (PL 13.63),
giving the traditional passages about which reserve was exercised:
'The beginnings of Genesis, where the creation of the world is
described; the beginning of the prophecy of Ezekiel, where the
doctrine of the angels is expounded; the end [of the same book]
which contains the description of the future temple; and this book
of the Song of Songs' (from G. G. Scholem, *Jewish Gnosticism, Merkabah
Mysticism, and Talmudic Tradition*, p. 38; for further references see
Neusner, *A Life of Rabban Yohannan ben Zakkai*, p. 99 n. 3).

   8.11–12. the man who enquires   6.6 shows that provision was
made in the movement for constant exposition of the Scripture in
any group of ten or more, even as early as the days when the movement existed only in dispersed communities; but it is hard to believe
that revelation resulting from such exposition had ever to be
concealed. The phrase here therefore (differing from that in 6.6 by
the addition of the definite article before the participle) probably
carries a technical meaning—the student or seeker, with the implication that his subject was the deeper revelation contained in the
passages not expounded to the public (see previous note). It seems

that any full member of the sect was regarded as fit to receive such esoteric revelation. 1QS 1.1; 5.9; 6.6 all suggest this is the right interpretation here; and 1QH 2.15, 32, 34; 4.14 ff. with their plurals further support it. The reference is to someone carrying out one of the functions of the sect and who may be a different person at any particular time. The *doresh hattorah* (expounder of the Law) of 4QF1 seems to be an expected historical figure who will arise at the end of the days with the 'shoot of David'. CD 6.7 identifies the *mechoqeq* (the lawgiver) and CD 7.18 the star of Num. 24.17 with him. See below on 9.11 **anointed ones of Aaron and Israel.**

a spirit of apostasy Elisha ben Abuyah, a pupil of R. Meir, became famous for the fact that, having become a great scholar, he entered too deeply into esoteric speculation and eventually apostatized. Danby in his note on the mention of his name at *'Aboth* 4.20 gives his date as about AD 90–150. No doubt he was but one example of defection to gnosticism.

8.13. into the desert 9.19 f.; DSW 1.2 f.; 2.12; 10.13; (cf. CD 6.5); 4QpPs37.2.1; Ex. 2.15; I Sam. 23.14; 24.1; 27.1 ff.; I Kings 19.4; Isa. 40.3; 62.10 ff.; Jer. 48.6, 28; I Macc. 2.27 ff.; 5.27; Mark 1.3, 12; 13.14 pars.; Matt. 3.3; 4.1 ff.; Luke 3.4–6; 4.1 ff.; John 1.23; Acts 7.38; Heb. 11.38; Rev. 12.6, 13 f.; *Asc. Isa.* 2.8–12. For the part played by the wilderness in the history and the religious psychology of Israel see Hengel, *Die Zeloten*, pp. 255 ff., and Mauser, *Christ in the Wilderness*, esp. pp. 15–58. The wilderness is the place both of refuge (as for David and the Maccabees) and of turning back to the LORD in penitence and for restoration (Elijah), especially under the conviction of a crisis in world-history or of the imminence of the end of the age. Betz (*Der Paraklet*, pp. 57 f.) emphasizes with justice the motive of desiring to be separate from the realm of evil (a motive certainly present at Qumran) and compares *Jub.* 12.21, where Abraham begs to be defended from the evil around him in Ur.

It is Isa. 40.3; Matt. 3.3; Mark 1.3; Luke 3.4–6; John 1.23 which chiefly concern us here. As often already remarked, the sect fulfilled both metaphorically and literally Isa. 40.3 cited in line 14; the literal obedience was due not merely to the desire to fulfil the text of Scripture but also because separation from defiled Israel was necessary for a cleansed community. Talmon, *SH* IV, pp. 166 f., suggests that conflicts arising in everyday life between the observances of the movement and those of other Jews brought its members to recognition of the fact that they could 'no longer be a part of the house of Judah but each *Side* must mount guard for himself' (CD 4.11 f.; Rabin in his commentary translates a little differently). It was in these circumstances that they formed the decision expressed here in 1QS 8.13–15.

to prepare there the way Betz (*Offenbarung*, pp. 155 ff.) has explained well the use made by the sect of Isa. 40.3 in comparison with the Gospels. The sect's use of Scripture here is of particular interest, since it is itself about the use of Scripture: for the prophet the Way meant the actual road along which God himself would lead his people back from exile; therefore a road must be built in the wilderness. For the sect the way is *halakah* and obedience to it (cf. 9.19) and this *halakah* must be constructed by study of the Law. In the LXX and the Synoptic Gospels the wilderness is the place where one cries out the command to build a way for the LORD. In the MT, correctly represented at 1QIsa (a) and in the present passage (where, however, the divine name is represented only by dots—see below on the **way of Him**), the wilderness is not the place where one cries but the place where the way of God is to be constructed. The 'one crying' is of the highest importance to the Gospels, but does not appear here in the *Rule*. The Gospels apply the passage to John the Baptist, and this is possible only on the basis of the emphasis on 'one crying'. Qumran and the early Church thus provide two divergent examples of the use of a scripture while they both illustrate the practice of exposition which disregards the original meaning. Lindars (*New Testament Apologetic*, p. 278) draws attention to the neighbouring passage 1QS 8.6 f., where another example of the use of Scripture by the sect different from that of the early Church is to be found (see notes above *ad loc.*)

the way of Him The pronoun is used for God in the scrolls at, for example, 1QS 3.17, 25 and CD 9.5 in its reproduction of Nahum 1.2, but it by no means always applies to him. Its spelling here suggests that it is formed from the first five letters of the Hebrew phrase 'He is God' (cf. Deut. 4.35, 39; 7.9; I Kings 18.39) and since the second is a vowel may be regarded as a surrogate for the Tetragrammaton YHWH (so Brownlee), though less obviously than when, as in col. 3, it consists of only four letters. The Tetragrammaton is constantly avoided in 1QS, in the commentary part of 1QpHab, and in CD; and here in the *Rule*, instead of the elaborate pronoun of 1QS, 4QSe has *ha'emeth* (the truth).

There is much other evidence for the reverence paid by scribes to the written form of the divine name. 1QpHab is written in square Hebrew script, but the Tetragrammaton, where it occurs in the actual text of the prophet, stands out by being written in early Hebrew script. This custom continued into Christian times: in all the five columns of Origen's Hexapla which are preserved the divine name is regularly given as the Tetragrammaton in Hebrew square letters (for interesting details of this scribal custom in the transmission of the text see P. E. Kahle, *The Cairo Geniza*, pp. 162, 218 f., 222, 224). Origen and Jerome say that in 'accurate manuscripts' the Tetragrammaton was written in early Hebrew letters.

In the actual quotation from Isa. 40.3 in line 14 (in the Hebrew, six words farther on from **Him**) the scribe has represented the Tetragrammaton by four bold dots occupying rather more than the space which the four Hebrew letters would have needed. It is usually said that this is paralleled by 1QIsa (a) 40.7 and 42.6, but this is a little inaccurate at least with regard to 42.6: there the Tetragrammaton was omitted and the four bold dots are inserted above the verb and suffix, 'I have called thee'.

8.14. Arabah   In the Bible often the deep cleft or fault which forms the Jordan valley. The word means primarily desert or steppe and is used for arid land near the Jordan. The Dead Sea is sometimes called the Sea of the Arabah as at Deut. 3.17; Josh. 12.3.

8.15. This means study of the Law   9.13. For the whole subject in this and the following line see on Revelation at Qumran (pp. 63 ff.) and note above on **to prepare there the way.**

8.16   the prophets revealed by the spirit of his holiness The spirit's work is seen with regard to the Scriptures in two complementary ways: the prophets have been divinely led to write mysteries or secrets (*razim*); and the Teacher of Righteousness and his sect have been given the equally divine ability to reveal the true interpretation (*pesher*) of them. When these things are revealed the sect must obey them. (See Bruce, *Biblical Exegesis in the Qumran Texts*, pp. 1–11.)

8.16–17. the community, (in) the covenant of the community This seems the best way of translating 1QS, assuming that **in** (Hebrew *b*) has been accidentally omitted before **covenant** (*berith*), and that the two phrases are in apposition and that to belong to the community is the same as to be in the covenant of the community.

4QSd probably has the correct text, which omits the first **the community**. For the conception of **covenant** see the notes on 1.8 and 1.16.

8.17. a high hand 8.22. See the note on 7.3 (**thoughtlessly**).

shall touch the purity For a full discussion of this idea see the note on **the purity of the many** (6.16 f.) and **the drink of the many** (6.20), p. 191.

8.18. until his deeds are purified The offender in this original prospectus for the beginning of the community appears to have been obliged to act as though no longer a member and regain his membership by passing through a period of probation here left as of unspecified length. The fact that line 22 enjoins much more drastic punishment for transgressing **a word from the Law of Moses** shows that **anything that is commanded** in line 17 refers to the rules of the community. The more specific and detailed rules of 6.24–7.25 may well represent the later days of the well-established sect when experience had developed more rules.

8.20. These are the rules The section 6.24–7.25 opens with the same phrase.

8.24. by inadvertence See on 7.3, where **thoughtlessly** translates the same term in Hebrew. Rabin (*Qumran Studies*, p. 108) argues that Qumran terminology differs from rabbinic partly from the occurrence of the phrase only here in the sect's *halakah*, but he has overlooked the occurrences at 7.3 and 9.1.

they shall consult the regulation which says The Hebrew contains only the word **which** of the last two English words; but something like this appears to be the meaning, especially in view of what follows. The sentences are rather disconnected, partly owing to the loss of about two words by a gap in the last line of the column; but they seem to represent a number of *mishpaṭim* (decisions or judgments) applying or modifying this principle of relegation for two years.

9.3–6 is a variation on the theme of 8.1–11. For the main points it will be enough to refer to previous notes.

9.4. to atone See on 2.8; 5.6 and 8.3 (**making amends**).

favour for the land See on 8.6 (**to atone for the land**).

offering of the lips [9.26]; 10.6, 9, 14; Deut. 12.11; Job. 2.10; 27.4; Pss. 45.2; 51.15; 63.3, 5; 119.171; Prov. 10.21; Isa. 6.5, 7; Hos. 14.2; Heb. 13.15. Deut. 12.11 and Ps. 119.171 have expressions close to this one in the *Rule*, whose meaning is clear from the context

which compares the system of sacrifice in the Temple, abandoned
by the men of Qumran, with the worship of praise offered by them.
Here the latter is regarded as better than actual sacrifices and no
question is raised about the value of praise compared with deeds, a
theme too common in the Bible to need illustration here. Heb. 13.15
concisely expresses the sentiment, following the LXX of Hos. 14.3,
which in its turn probably translates the correct Hebrew text.

9.6. house of holiness for Aaron   See on 8.5 ff.

9.7. Only the sons of Aaron   For the position of the Zadokite
priesthood see pp. 91–95 and the notes on 5.2, and for the alternative
title **sons of Aaron** see on 5.21 f.

shall go forth the lot   See on 5.3 (**decisive edict**).

9.8. property   See on 1.12 and 5.2.

Their property shall not be mingled   See on 6.17.

9.11. 4Q Testimonia quotes Deut. 5.28 f., followed by 18.18 f.;
Num. 24.15–17; Deut. 33.8–11. These last three passages are the
standard texts which are taken to prophesy the coming of a prophet
like Moses, a Davidic Messiah, and a priestly Messiah, respectively.
The prophet promised by Moses in Deut. 18.15, 18 f. was often
identified with Elijah *redivivus* as in Mal 4.5 (Hebrew 3.23); Mark
15.35 f., cf. Matt. 27.47 ff.; as Elijah he is connected with John the
Baptist in Mark 9.11 ff., cf. Matt. 17.10–13; Matt. 11.14; Luke
1.17, 76; John 1.21; and with Jesus in Mark 6.15; 8.28 pars.; Luke
9.8; 9.54. He is not—at least not necessarily—identified with Elijah
at I Macc. 4.46; John 1.21, 25; 6.14, 7.40, 52; Acts 3.22–26.

The flexibility of the concept is further illustrated at John 6.14,
where the prophet is apparently identified with the Davidic Messiah;
nor is this necessarily a mere untaught popular confusion, for Ps.
105.15 (I Chron. 16.22) makes 'anointed ones' (so RV correctly;
the 'mine anointed' of AV is misleading) and prophets parallel
conceptions. This flexibility should help our understanding of the
problem discussed in the following comment.

anointed ones of Aaron and Israel   The translation 'anointed
ones' is to be preferred to 'messiahs', since it begs no questions. Thus,
too, in the OT the past participle *mashiach* (it never stands alone in
the OT, but always with a suffix meaning 'his' or 'my', or in the
phrase 'the LORD's anointed one') could be translated messiah only
by committing a misleading anachronism.

How securely or how permanently the sect believed in the future
appearance of two anointed ones, one priestly, the other secular, or

in what way such expectation is related to that of the prophet—these questions are somewhat obscure. The present passage does not occur in 4QSe, which omits 8.16b–9.11 inclusive, but perhaps this is accidental and has no significance for the history of these ideas. Starcky ('Les quatre étapes du messianisme à Qumran' in *RB* 70, 1963, p. 481) has elaborated a different view. The absence of the passage from 4QSe he regards as significant, since the script of this manuscript suggests that it is the more ancient: the exemplar, which he dates between 150 and 130 BC, would also not contain it. Equally significant is the absence from 4QSe of the quotation from Isaiah in 8.14. On these and many other facts Starcky builds an interesting theory of the development of messianic beliefs at Qumran, dating 1QS (with its additions, especially 9.11) to the time of Alexander Jannaeus (103–76). This is the time of a new generation of Essenes which include the author of the *Commentary on Nahum* and the scribe of 1QS, of 1QSa and 1QSb, of 4Q Testimonia and other works found in Cave 4. It is perhaps a weakness of the view that 4QSd and 4QSe must be excluded. The *Damascus Document* is held to be later, for in it the two messiahs have become the sole 'messiah of Aaron and of Israel' (19.10 f.; 20.1; 12.23; 14.19, the last reference being supported by 4QDb). A rather different view, taking into account the composite character of the *Damascus Document* and interpreting the messianic references differently, is suggested here.

The history of the hope for two anointed ones begins about 520 BC, when Haggai and Zechariah look forward to the early re-establishment of the state of Judah under a dual leadership, Joshua the high priest and Zerubbabel, scion of the house of David, the anointed secular ruler (Hag. 1.12 ff.; 2.2 ff. etc.). In Zech. 4.14 they are the 'two sons of oil', i.e. two anointed ones. This dual notion is not found elsewhere in the OT, no doubt because of the severe discouragement given to secular messianic hopes when the widespread rebellion in the Persian Empire (522–520) was successfully quelled by Darius I. The high priest is called 'the anointed' in Lev. 4.3, 5, 16; 6.20, 22 (Hebrew 6.13, 14), but for the dual conception we have to wait until the second century BC, when the *Testaments of the Twelve Patriarchs* provide remarkably clear examples of this aspiration, notably in *Test. Levi* 18, which prophesies the appearance of a priestly messiah, in *Test. Reub.* 6.7–12; *Sim.* 7.2; *Levi* 2.11; 8.11 ff.; *Dan* 5.10; *Gad* 8.1; *Jos.* 19.11, where both anointed ones are expected (cf. *Jub.* 31.13–20). *Test. Judah* 21.2–5 sums up the matter: 'To me God has given kingship, to him (sc. Levi) the priesthood; and he has subordinated the kingship to the priesthood.'

In the scrolls the evidence of the sect's belief is not uniform. 1QSa 2.12, 14, 20 speak of one messiah in the singular, as also does the fragment 1Q30 1.2. It is the *Damascus Document* which is puzzling: 6QD 3.4 (a Cave 6 fragment of the *Document*) seems to have 'anointed ones of the holy one', but the plural is far from certain. In the Geniza text we have to consider CD 2.12; 6.1; 12.23; 14.19; 19.10; 20.1. In 2.12 and 6.1 Kuhn emends *m-sh-y-ch-v* to *m-sh-y-ch-y*, supported by the manifest mistake at 12.23 where the ms. reads *mashuach* for *mashiach* (K. G. Kuhn, 'The Two Messiahs' in *The Scrolls and the New Testament*, p. 59, and *Konkordanz zu den Qumran-texten*, p. 135). 12.23; 14.19; 19.10; 20.1 all have the singular, but with the qualification 'of Aaron and Israel'. The singular in 14.19 is supported by what Milik regards as the oldest exemplar of the *Damascus Document*, 4QDb; and J. F. Priest, writing in *JBL* 81, 1962, pp. 55 f., holds that the fragment proves conclusively that the *Document* expected only one messiah, as Starcky also holds; but Milik is surely justified in remarking that CD 7.18 ff. shows that the idea of the old dyarchy continued under new names (*Ten Years of Discovery* . . ., p. 126).

As became clear in connexion with 8.12 (**the man who enquires**), 4QFl expects a *doresh hattorah* to arise with the 'shoot of David', that is, associates with the Davidic Messiah a teacher who is not necessarily a priestly anointed one, but probably is to be identified with him. CD 6.10 f. suggests the belief in the return of the Teacher of Righteousness *redivivus*, and therefore that he is regarded as the expounder of the Law and as in some way associated with messianic coming. According to CD 20.14 f. there will be forty years between his death and the anointed one or messiah. This would be consistent with regarding him as a forerunner of the anointed one or anointed ones; and here in the *Rule* he is closely associated with both.

If it is correct to see the present section of the *Rule* (1QS 8.1–9.26) as an originally independent early document, the unequivocal evidence of this passage suggests that when the sect was first established its members were taught to expect the coming of **the prophet** followed eventually by **the anointed ones**, whose forerunner he would be. Other evidence suggests that when the Teacher of Righteousness arose after twenty years of the existence of the community at Qumran (CD 1.9–11) he was regarded, as Betz puts it,

as God's gift to the community (1QpHab 2.8 f.), able to deliver the
message which he has received from the mouth of God (1QpHab
2.2 f.; cf. 7.4 f.; Ex. 4.12, 15). Betz cannot go farther and say that the
Teacher is also **the prophet** in the eyes of the sect, because he thinks
that the Teacher is the author of the *Rule*; but if the *Rule* is composite
and the part now being considered is an early document written
by the founder (as already observed, not to be identified with the
Teacher) at least twenty years before the rise of the Teacher, then it
becomes possible that when the latter did arise he was identified with
the prophet, and after his death was expected to return, perhaps
now re-identified with the priestly anointed one.

On this theory it may be conjectured that the original text of the
Document (as represented by 6QD 3.4, for example) looked forward
to two **anointed ones** and that this accounts for the remarkable
juxtaposition at CD 12.23, etc, of *mashiach* with 'Aaron and Israel'. If
this work originally looked forward to two anointed ones, such
passages as expressed this expectation might well be corrected if the
sect had in the meantime become convinced that the priestly anointed
one had already come, leaving only one still to be awaited.

GUIDANCE FOR THE INSTRUCTOR OF THE PIONEER COMMUNITY: 9.12–26

12 These are the statutes for the instructor for him to walk in them,
with everyone who lives according to the rule of each time and the
weight of each man.

13 To do the will of God according to all that is revealed from time
to time; and to learn all the wisdom which has been discovered in
relation to the times and the [14]order of the time.
To separate and weigh the sons of Zadok according to their spirits
and to hold fast to the chosen of the time according to [15]his will according as he commanded; to form his judgment of each according to his
spirit and to advance each according to the cleanness of his hands and
to bring each nearer according to his intelligence. [16]Thus shall be his
love with his hatred.
Not to contend or dispute with the men of destruction [17]but to
conceal the counsel of the Law among the men of iniquity;
to contend for knowledge of truth and righteous judgment for those
who choose [18]the way, each according to his spirit according to the
disposition of the time;
to comfort them with knowledge and thus to make them wise in

the secrets of wonder and truth among [19]the men of the community, that they may walk perfectly each with his fellow in all that has been revealed to them.

This is the time to prepare the way [20]to the wilderness and to instruct them in everything which has been discovered to be done at this time, and to be separated from every man who has not turned his way [21]from all iniquity.

These are the rules of the way for the instructor in these times for his love and for his hatred: eternal hatred [22]for the men of destruction in a spirit of secrecy, leaving to them property and toil of the hands like a slave for his master, and humiliation before him [23]who lords it over him.

To be a man zealous for the ordinance and its time, for the day of vengeance, and to do (God's) will in all that which he sets his hand [24]and in all the exercise of his authority according as he has commanded.

In all that befalls he will delight with willingness and save in the will of God he will take no pleasure; [25][and in al]l the words of his mouth he will delight and he will not covet anything which he has not comma[nded]. For the judgment of God he will always long, . . . [26]he will bless his creator and in all that shall be he will re[cite] . . . of his lips he will bless him.

9.12. These are the statutes   The sentence as far as **weight of each man** forms here a heading for lines 13–20. Such introductory headings are legion in the OT and other Hebrew literature. Almost the same words are found at CD 12.20 f., but at the end of a long collection of *halakah* (CD 10.1 ff.). There *mishpaṭ* takes the place of *tekun* here, justifying the translation of the latter by **rule**, in the phrase **rule of each time**.

the instructor   See on 1.1 and p. 72. If 8.1–9.26 is the original manifesto, the mention of this official here and at 9.21 prompts speculation on whether he is a unique historical individual or an official occupying a position only for a time and destined to be succeeded in it by others. Vermès (Pelican) identifies him with the Guardian, that is the *mebaqqer* whom he thinks the same as the *paqid* and the *doresh hattorah*. For a summary of his view see p. 72. On the *doresh hattorah* see on 8.11, where it is suggested that the phrase **the man who enquires** (*'ish haddoresh*) means whoever is expounding the Law at any particular time, while the full title *doresh hattorah* in the singular in 4QFl is an expected historical personage. The *mebaqqer* or **inspector** is discussed in the note on 6.12 and *paqid* (**the officer at**

the head) in that on 6.14, which implies the probable identity of *mebaqqer* and *paqid*. It seems that there the **instructor** has a definite part to play in establishing the community (see lines 19–20) and the word does not mean (as Wernberg-Møller, for example) simply a well-instructed and therefore wise man in general, although this makes good sense and remains possible. Neither *mebaqqer* nor *paqid* appears in this pioneer manifesto and the terms may be alternatives for an official who discharged the functions of an instructor and who was still sometimes so called (as at 3.13 and conjecturally at 1.1) when the community had been established. In this manifesto, though always in the singular, it may refer to a select number of men who were able to train the rest. If there were only one such he would presumably be identified with the author, who would not naturally write of his own duties in this fashion, but more probably thus refer to others, his relation to them being rather like that of the author of the book of Daniel to his *maśkilim* (Dan. 11.33; 12.3, 10).

according to the rule of each time   The reference is probably not to keeping the correct calendar and not therefore parallel to 1.15; nor is it a piece of 'wisdom' like Eccles. 3.1–9 or Ecclus. 4.20; 20.5 f., but rather is amply explained by the first part of line 13. See 1.9 with the note *ad loc.* and p. 89.

the weight of each man   A conception with a long history. From the time of the eighteenth dynasty paintings on papyrus in Egypt frequently illustrate an underworld scene in which the dead man's heart, representing his moral and spiritual worth, is weighed in a balance against *ma'T*, righteousness, represented by a feather (which is a determinative sign for the word *ma'T*). This seems to be the origin of the Egyptian-sounding 'negative confession' of Job 31 and especially of v. 6. Cf. line 14 below; Prov. 16.2; Ps. 62.9; Dan. 5.27; *I Enoch* 41.1; 61.8.

9.13. in relation to the times   Lit. 'according to the times'. The most probable explanation is that the secrets in the Scriptures concerned with historical events are here referred to: they are part of what had to be learnt by members, the scriptural commentaries found at Qumran furnishing examples of the necessary textbooks.

9.14. the order of the time   Presumably the time present to the student: each point in the unfolding of history demands a particular recognition and appropriate action. The responsibility falls in the first place upon the instructor, who has to form the community and obey the behest of the time in the way clearly stated in 19b–21 below.

The community which he forms is naturally described as **the chosen of the time.**

the sons of Zadok   Here a title for the whole community.

according to their spirits   Cf. 3.14 and the note *ad loc.* According to Prov. 16.2 the LORD 'weighs' the spirits of men.

9.16. his love with his hatred   The context suggests that the phrase means that the instructor is to show favour and therefore give advancement to some and to show disfavour to others only on the basis of his judgment of their character. See on 1.4.

not to contend nor dispute   The sense though not the vocabulary is reminiscent of Isa. 42.2. The whole section seems to be inspired by themes derived from the book of Isaiah, made obvious by the quotation of Isa. 40.3 at 8.14.

9.17. conceal the counsel   Cf. line 22 below (**in a spirit of secrecy**). It is very intelligible that the founder of the sect should seek to fulfil the idea suggested by Isa. 8.16 ff. According to 1QH 15.20 the sect, the author's disciples, are to be like Isaiah's 'children' —for signs and examples, using the terms in Isa. 8.18 (a point apparently missed by Licht and Mansoor in their editions of the *Psalms of Thanksgiving*). 4QSd has **his counsel** for **counsel of the Law.** Josephus, *BJ* 2.8.7, says that Essenes will not reveal their secrets to outsiders even on pain of death. Cf. Matt. 7.6; II Cor. 6.14.

those who choose the way   The way is the way of the LORD. See 8.14 and notes.

9.18. to comfort them with knowledge   In Isa. 40.1 the prophet's message is that God desires the people to be comforted, but the book (considered no doubt by the sect to be a unity and arising from one prophet only) opens with the complaint that Israel 'does not know' (Isa. 1.3).

9.19. This is the time   The writer speaks with authority: he is convinced from his study of Scripture and no doubt from signs of the times in events around him that this is one of the times demanding specific action. No phrase in the whole of the *Rule* reads more like a manifesto nor gives so unmistakable an impression of being written by the actual founder of the community. There is no need, with the punctuation adopted, to follow Maier in regarding the sentence as far as **wilderness** as a gloss.

to prepare the way to the wilderness   1QS is supported by 4QSe against 4QSd, which has **in the wilderness.** 4QSd has probably been influenced by the exact text of Isa. 40.3, which is quoted at 8.14. The adaptation here seems the more likely reading.

9.20. to be separated from every man . . . The reading of 4QSd is adopted as alone making sense in the context.

9.22. a spirit of secrecy See on line 17 above.

leaving to them property and toil Guilbert construes as though these were desirable objects for the natural man which the instructor must abandon and make himself humble like a slave; but he must then be God's slave and the phrase in line 23 **who lords it over him** could hardly be a description of the proper sovereignty of the divine Lord of such a slave; and **toil of the hands** suggests something which may gladly be left. Doubt as to the meaning seems to have arisen very early because 4QSd has 'profit' for toil ('*amal*), supporting indeed Guilbert's interpretation of the passage. Wernberg-Møller refers to Ps. 105.44 and Eccles. 2.19 as examples of '*amal* meaning the fruits of toil; but each context shows that the emphasis must fall on the toil by which another than the toiler profits. So exactly in John 4.38 with the corresponding Greek word. The interpretation adopted here is that the instructor and his followers should abandon the life of servitude to worldly ideals in which labour serves no end in which the labourer has any real interest, since his work serves an alien master. The same thought lies behind Rom. 6.18. See also the following note.

9.23. To be a man zealous This and 10.19 illustrate neatly the concept of zeal in Judaism; see the note on 4.4 (**zeal for the precepts of righteousness**). To be zealous for God is good, but it must be with discernment, as Paul implies in Rom. 10.2 (cf. Acts 22.3). According to 1QS 10.19, zeal could be shown even with an evil spirit. Phinehas is called zealous for God in Num. 25.6–15 and is the first to be called a zealot (*IV Macc.* 18.12). Mattathias' enthusiasm marks him as zealous in I Macc. 2.26. But St Paul is not the first to judge even such zeal for God by other standards than the mere intensity of the zeal shown. Whether the exploit of Jacob's sons in Gen. 34.25 ff. was praiseworthy or not is clearly already in Scripture regarded as debatable (Gen. 34.30; 49.5–7) and was, in fact, often debated. It is condemned in a fragment of a scroll described as messianic by Allegro in *JBL* 70, 1951, pp. 182–6; 4.23–30. Phinehas' barbarity is evaded and a more edifying action ascribed to him in Ps. 106.30, which may reflect and certainly gave assistance to a long process of elaboration of the story in *midrashim* which set Phinehas' action in a much more favourable light than the story in Numbers.

The whole matter is lucidly expounded by Hengel (see on 4.4). Licht is probably right (in his edition of 1QH, p. 50 n. 38) to regard zeal here **for the ordinance and its time, for the day of vengeance** as a special requirement of members of the sect, namely willingness to fight in the war of the sons of light against the sons of darkness.

day of vengeance   10.19; DSW 7.5; Isa. 34.8; 61.2; 63.4. At Deut. 32.35 the MT reads 'To me (is) vengeance' and much teaching in Judaism (including the OT) and in the NT is founded upon this principle. See the note on 1.11. But the Samaritan version reads instead 'to the day of vengeance' and the LXX rendering is very like it. Gaster in his note on this passage in the *Rule* says the Samaritan type reading is found in a fragment of Deut. discovered at Qumran and that the term is standard among the Samaritans for Doomsday (*sic*—the OT phrase, Day of the LORD, would be more appropriate).

to do (God's) will   The Hebrew has only 'to do the will', but the vocabulary here seems to be taken from Isa. 61.2 and the meaning is therefore clear.

9.24. he will take no pleasure   The phrase **save in** leads one to expect a negative with the verb in such a context. It seems therefore better to assume that *lo* is an error for *lo'* than to translate *lo* as 'for him'. The instructor will face severe trials and must be ready to desire only that God's providence is being fulfilled in the birth-pangs of the new age. Such is the moon of 1QH.

CLOSING HYMN
10.1–11.22

1 . . . with the times which he has ordained, at the beginning of the rule of light, at its turning-point; and at its being gathered to the dwelling decreed for it;
at the beginning of ²the watches of darkness, when he opens his treasury and sets him above, and at his turning-point, when it is gathered from before the light; at the appearance of ³the luminaries from the holy realm and at their being gathered to the abode of glory.

At the introduction of the seasons at the (first) days of the month as well as at their turning-points when ⁴one succeeds to other. At their renewals great is their glory for the holy of holies and a sign for the renewal of his eternal mercies at the beginnings of ⁵the seasons at every time which comes.

In the beginning of the months at their set times, and holy days in their order as memorials in their proper times.

6 With the offering of the lips I will bless him as a statute engraved for ever;

at the beginnings of the years and at the turning-point of their seasons by fulfilling the law ⁷of their order, each decreed day duly following the other, the season of wheat harvest passing to summer and the season of sowing to the season of herbage, (at) feasts of years according to their seven-year periods ⁸and at the summit of their seven-year periods at the feast of release.

As long as I live shall the engraved statute be on my tongue for the fruit of praise, and an offering of my lips ⁹will I sing with understanding; and all my music shall be for the glory of God; and my lyre and my harp shall be in tune with the order of his holiness and the flute of my lips I will raise to the string of his decree.

10 With the coming-in of day and night I will come into the covenant of God and at the going-out of evening and at morning I will recite his statutes; and while they exist I will set ¹¹my bounds without returning; and his decree will I declare to be according to my iniquity, and my transgression is before my eyes like an engraved statute. And to God I will say, 'My righteousness!' ¹²and to the highest, 'Author of my good, source of knowledge and well of holiness, height of glory, might of all with eternal majesty!'

I will choose according to ¹³what he teaches me and I will delight in what he decrees for me.

Before the putting forth of my hands and my feet I will bless his name, before going out and coming in, ¹⁴when I sit down and when I rise up; and on the couch of my bed I will praise him, and I will bless him with the offering which comes from my lips from the table set for my companions; ¹⁵and before I raise my hand to be nourished with the delightful fruits of the earth.

At the onset of fear or terror or in a condition of need and destitution ¹⁶I will bless him for his great wonders and I will meditate upon his might; and upon his gracious mercies I will trust through the whole day. And I will testify that in his hand is judgment ¹⁷for all that lives and all his deeds are truth. When the hour of need begins I will praise him no less than I will sing his praise in the time of his salvation.

I will return to no man evil recompense ¹⁸but for good will I pursue my fellow, for with God is judgment over all that lives and it is he that shall pay to a man his recompense.

I will not show jealousy with a spirit ¹⁹of evil, and my soul shall not covet wealth got through violence; and in the strife of men of destruction I will take no part till the day of vengeance, but from men of iniquity I will not ²⁰retract my wrath and I will take no pleasure until judgment is accomplished. I will bear no grudge in wrath against those who return from transgression but I will offer no comfort ²¹to those who turn from the way. I will not console the smitten until they have perfected their way and Belial I will not cherish within my heart.

There shall not be heard from my mouth ²²any obscenity nor wicked deceit neither shall cunning nor lies be found upon my lips; but the fruit of holiness shall be on my tongue and abominations ²³shall not be found there.

In thanksgiving I will open my mouth and the righteous acts of God shall my tongue ever tell, and the treachery of men until the completion ²⁴of their transgression. Vanities I will repel from my lips, uncleanness and crookedness from the knowledge of my heart. With wise intent, I will conceal knowledge ²⁵and with prudent knowledge I will fence [it] in with a firm boundary, to keep faith and a strong decree. For the righteousness of God I [will apportion] ²⁶the statute with the measuring-line of the times [and practise truth and] righteous [decrees]—(to show) loving mercy to the humbled and strengthening of hands for the feeble [and to teach]

COLUMN ELEVEN

¹understanding to those who err in spirit, to instruct those who murmur, and to respond with humility to those who are haughty in spirit, and with a broken spirit to men ²of authority who point the finger and utter iniquity and are zealous for wealth.

For, as for me, my judgment is with God and in his hand is the perfection of my way; with him is the uprightness of my heart ³and in his righteousness he will blot out my transgression.

For from the source of his knowledge he has opened up his light and upon his wonders mine eye has gazed and the illumination of my heart is in the secret ⁴of what shall be and of that which is, for ever. The support of my right hand is on a strong rock; the way of my steps shall not be shaken by anything; for the truth of God is ⁵the rock of my steps and his might is the support of my right hand. From the source of his righteousness are the decrees of light in my heart; from his marvellous secrets mine eye has gazed on what is for ever, ⁶wisdom which is hidden from man, knowledge and a skilful plan hidden from the sons of men, a well of righteousness and reservoir ⁷of might with the spring of glory from the assembly of flesh; those whom God has chosen he has given to be an eternal possession and has given them for their inheritance the lot ⁸of the holy ones. With the sons of the heavens he has united their assembly to be a council of community and their assembly is a house of holiness, a planting for eternity in every ⁹age that is to be.

And I belong to the Adam of wickedness and to the assembly of evil flesh. My iniquities, my transgressions, my sins along with the perversities of my heart belong [10]to the assembly of worms and of those who walk in darkness.

For man has no way of his own and mankind shall not direct his steps; for to God belongs judgment and from his hand comes [11]perfection of way; and by his knowledge shall everything happen, and by his design he prepares all that is, and apart from him it will not be made.

But for me, if [12]I falter—the mercies of God are my salvation for ever; and if I stumble in the iniquity of flesh, my judgment is with the righteousness of God, which shall endure for ever.

13 And if my affliction should begin he will deliver my life from destruction and will make my steps firm in the way. In his compassion he has drawn me near and in his mercies he will bring in [14]my judgment.

In the righteousness of his truth he will judge me and in his great goodness he will cover for ever all my iniquities; and in his righteousness he will purify me from the uncleanness [15]of mankind and the sin of the sons of men, that I may praise God for his righteousness and the most high for his majesty.

Blessed art thou, O my God, who openest for knowledge [16]the heart of thy servant.

Direct in righteousness all his deeds and accord to the son of thy handmaid the boon thou hast been pleased to accord to the chosen among mankind, to present himself [17]before thy face for ever.

For apart from thee no way shall be perfect and without thy will nothing shall be brought to pass. Thou hast taught [18]all knowledge and all that is to be has been within thy will; and there is none other like thee, to make objection to thy counsel or to give instruction [19]in any of thy holy design; or to gaze upon the depth of thy secrets or to attain understanding in all thy marvellous works and in the power [20]of thy might.

Who can comprehend thy glory? Or what is the son of man among thy wondrous deeds? [21]Or how shall he that is born of woman dwell in thy presence?

From dust is his forming and the food of worms is his dwelling. He is ejected spittle, [22]clay nipped off, and for dust is his desire. What answer shall clay give, and what counsel shall be understood by him that is formed by hand?

The remainder of the *Rule*, 10.1 (or 9.26b) to 11.22, may be analysed as follows:

10.1–8a	Calendar of Worship;
10.8b–11.15a	Hymn;
11.15b–22	Benediction;

but the author, if composing from a number of already existing elements, nevertheless fused them into a whole. He has, in fact, written a hymn of praise which combines expression of the duty to worship God at certain calendrically fixed times with expression of personal devotion of some depth and eloquence; and the poetic manner suitable to the latter has strongly affected his presentation of the former. Some of the material, especially 10.1–8, may be paralleled elsewhere among the scrolls, the author of the *War Scroll*, for example, having himself used a work which gave the forms of prayer to be used at different phases of the final war. See DSW 9.17–14.15, which contains material at least partly repeated in 15–19 (see Yadin, p. 210). Talmon (*SH* IV, p. 188) thinks that the material used here in the *Rule* belongs to the same book as that used by the *War Scroll*, where it is given the title *The Book of the Order of His Time* (DSW 15.5). This may be correct, but it is early to be certain of the relations between the various liturgical fragments found at Qumran; see further, for example, those conveniently gathered, with brief notes as to their origin and significance, by Vermès, pp. 202 ff., and cf. 1QS 1.8–2.18 mentioned on p. 113.

CALENDAR OF WORSHIP: 10.1–8a

10.1–8a (or with Weise from the last two or three words of 9.26 to 10.8a) forms a passage very difficult to interpret, but which is certainly part of a time-table for worship. The exegesis given here will follow in the main that offered by Weise, *Kultzeiten und Kultischer Bundesschluss in der 'Ordensregel' vom Toten Meer*, which is devoted to this passage and to its close connexion—in his view—with 1.8–2.18, that is the Rite for Entry into the Community. On this latter point it is less important to follow his lead.

The time-table of worship is presented in an elaborate way, partly poetical, partly oratorical, the author displaying his knowledge of Torah by describing the same periods in different ways. The times when prayer and praise should be given to God are laid down as follows:

10.1–3a　　Every day.
10.3b–5a　　The intercalary days of the solar year.
10.5b–6a　　The first day of each month and sabbaths.
10.6b–7a　　The intercalary days of the solar year (expressed in different phrases from those used in 10.3b–5a).

10.7b–8a   Festival years at the end of seven-year periods and
jubilee years.

A considerable literature exists on the basis of a quite different
interpretation of this admittedly difficult and obscure passage. Its
departure-point is the appearance in line 1 of the *'aleph* at the end of
chaqaq and of an alleged *mem* and the apparent phrase *w'oth nun* ('and
the sign *nun*') in line 4. This passage is regarded as an *Amen* acrostic
or the letters are taken to be astronomical signs. See, for example,
Brownlee, Appendix E, p. 50; Dupont-Sommer, p. 97 notes 1 and 2.

The facsimile hardly encourages these speculations. Neither the
'aleph nor the *mem* is in the least prominent: the *'aleph* of line 1 need
be no more than a variant addition to the usual form of the verb;
or it may stand for 'God' (cf. the spelling of the Hebrew pronoun
for 'Him' in 8.13 and see the note below on line 1). The *mem* in line 4
is capable of a number of alternative explanations: it may, for
example, be the last letter of the word *yom* (day) or the third person
plural suffix to a truncated *zayin* and *waw* which form the Mishnaic
word *ziv* (see the commentary); or again it may be the second letter
of the pronoun *hem* (they). The *nun* alone remains. This letter certainly stands by itself with a gap following it large enough for two
letters and a space before the next word, but the *nun* itself is not large
and could easily be the abortive start of some other letter; thus the
gap would be left simply because the leather was here difficult to
write on, as the doubt surrounding the word ending with *mem* has
shown. Several such gaps occur in this ms., one being between the
first and second words of this very column, i.e. between **with** and
the times in line 1. Above this gap an unbecoming smudge has been
left by a scribe in trouble with his pen, ink, the leather, or with all
these. Another gap, apparently caused by erasure, occurs in line 19.
J. Weingreen ('Exposition in the Old Testament and in Rabbinical
Literature' in *Promise and Fulfilment*, p. 188 n. 2) remarks appositely that
'An instance of Biblical manuscripts meant for private use may be seen
in the Qumran Biblical scrolls, as evidenced by the numerous corrections clumsily made. Such unskilled copying and ungainly corrections
would never have been tolerated, if the manuscripts had been meant for
liturgical use.' These remarks apply *a fortiori* to the non-biblical scrolls.
We may conclude in passing that 1QS was certainly meant for private,
not liturgical use, but the main point is the danger inherent in deduc-
ing hidden meanings from what may well be orthographical accidents.

10.1–3a. *Prayer each day*

There are times of prayer for every day which God himself has ordained through the way in which he has constructed the universe and ordered the passage of time in it. In the daytime these are two, (*a*) morning: **at the beginning of the rule of light, at its turning-point** (definitive time); and (*b*) evening: at the end of the 'rule' of light, which is expressed by **at its being gathered to the dwelling decreed for it.**

The same regulation is then expressed from the opposite point of view, now mentioning evening first, in the words **at the beginning of the watches of darkness, when he opens his treasury** (sc. of stars) **and sets him** (sc. darkness) **above**; and then morning, in the words **at his** (sc. darkness') **turning-point when he is gathered from before the light.** The same two points of time are then expressed in a third way, again evening first and morning second. Evening is expressed in the phrase **at the appearance of the luminaries from their holy realm** and morning is expressed by **at their** (sc. the luminaries') **being gathered to the abode of glory.**

This interpretation, that the passage enjoins two prayer-times each day and describes them in three ways, and that it does not enjoin prayer-times by night, is supported by line 10 below and by DSW 14.12–14; 1QH 12.4–11; the injunction is probably founded upon the twice-daily offering of a lamb in the Temple (Ex. 29.38–42; Num. 28.3 f.). *Jub.* 6.14 reflects the same practice, a significant support, since *Jubilees* shares a solar calendar with the sect. Wisd. 16.28, cited by Weise, is evidence only for the practice of prayer at dawn, before sunrise, and does not mention evening prayer; but Philo when describing the Therapeutae (*De vita contemplativa* 27) is perfectly clear, saying that 'they are accustomed to pray twice each day'. If the Therapeutae and men of Qumran were connected by both communities being types of Essenes, Philo may be claimed to throw light on this passage of the *Rule* and on the quality of evidence for the subsidiary but interesting question—was the morning prayer of the sect at dawn or sunrise? For he does not seem to distinguish these times, writing 'at dawn and at evening, when the sun rises . . . and when it sets'. At least it is impossible to interpret this to yield three prayer-times, owing to Philo's explicit opening phrase already quoted.

the beginning of the rule of light Like Wisd. 16.28 this suggests dawn. Josephus, *BJ* 2.8.5 certainly relates that the Essenes prayed

before the sun rose, but implies that the climax of their prayers was
the sunrise (cf. *Jub.* 3.27). *b. Ber.* 9b tells of a body of men, 'the pious',
often identified with Essenes by scholars, who 'used to finish [the
recital of the *Shema*ʿ] with sunrise, in order to join the *geʾullah* with
the *tephillah* and say the *tephillah* in the daytime'. In the passage of the
De vita contemplativa partially cited above Philo says 'at sunrise they
pray for a fine bright day (εὐημερίαν), fine and bright in the true sense
of the heavenly daylight which they pray may fill their minds . . .',
and farther on, at 89, after describing a nocturnal musical liturgy
apparently celebrating Pentecost, he says that at dawn 'they stand
with their faces and whole body turned to the east and when they
see the sun rising they stretch their hands up to heaven and pray for
bright days and knowledge of the truth and the power of keen-
sighted thinking' (trans. Colson in Loeb ed., IX). These passages
from Josephus and from Philo cannot be regarded as simply descriptions and explanations of the practice of the sect at Qumran (Philo's
Therapeutae lived near Lake Mareotis in Egypt), but perhaps
explain what those who venerated the sun hoped to obtain from their
religious observation: Philo calls it εὐημερία and it corresponds to
something like 'inner light' or enlightenment.

Dupont-Sommer, who in *The Jewish Sect of Qumran and the Essenes*,
ch. VI, pp. 104 ff., discusses the same passages, observes that 'the
same custom of venerating the sun was practised by the followers of
the gnostic beliefs of Hermes Trismegistus'. Dupont-Sommer quotes
the Corpus Hermeticum 13.16, 'Then, my son, stand in the open and
facing the south wind, at the moment of the disappearance of the
setting sun make adoration, and likewise again at sunrise, turning
towards the east wind.' This seems indeed to be the only natural
translation of the passage as it now stands, but the injunction to face
the south raises at least the suspicion that the original custom was to
venerate the sun at noon *as well as* at sunset and sunrise. It cannot
fairly be argued that a twice-daily prayer routine expresses respect
for the sun better than thrice daily, since noon might be regarded
as a very suitable third time; and the famous passage in Josephus
which outlines an Essene day is as consistent with a regulation to
pray three times as with a rule to pray twice. Talmon, indeed (*RQ* 2,
1959–60, pp. 481 ff.), would understand the present passage as
implying three prayer-times in the day and three prayer-times in the
night. He regards **at its turning-point** on its first occurrence as
meaning noon, and gives the following rendering: ' "at its (the sun's)

circuit" (orbit), or "in the circuits of day" ', and on its second occurrence as time for 'the night-prayer—"at its (the moon's) circuit" (orbit)'. This interpretation does not explain how the moon— as invisible in the text as she would be at least one night in the sky— regulates the night prayer or prayers; but it has advantages: not treating the passage as poetical repetition, it agrees with the biblical and later orthodox tradition of praying three times a day (Talmon refers to Dan. 6.10; cf. *Tos. Berakoth* 3.6; and Ps. 55.16 f.; and to the reflection of this in the *'Amidah* prayer) and corresponds to the three-fold division of the night explained in the note on 6.7 f.; but if the Hebrew can be regarded as a threefold poetical expression of the same injunction, it may be translated perhaps as naturally in the manner we have adopted. For the word (*tequphah*) here translated **turning point** see, e.g., Ex. 34.22.

10.3b–5a: *Prayer on the intercalary days* (cf. 10.6b–7a)

This paragraph enjoins special observation of the days which have been somewhat loosely called intercalary in the explanation of the solar calendar on pp. 80 ff., where the sacred character of these days is described. Weise shows by reference to Ps. 49.2 and 10 that the construction here is probably a poetic parallelism: **at their turning-points when one succeeds to other** describes well the days which are both the last day of the previous month and the first day of the new month and also the beginning of a new season, the seasons being supposed to enter automatically upon their course on precisely the same day each year, this day being determined by the sun. Two of the days are equinoxes, two solstices. **At the intro-duction of the seasons at the (first) days of the month** ex-presses the same conception. The two parallels are linked together by **as well as,** which means less literally and more logically 'that is . . .'

10.1. with the times which he has ordained Whether or not 9.26 (end) is to be taken closely with this column we must supply something like 'he shall bless God'. See line 6 and cf. 1QpHab 7.12–14. We follow the explanation which takes *chaqaq'* as 'God has ordained', the *'aleph* attached to the end of the verb standing for *'elohim* as in the addition to the pronoun for 'he' at the end of 8.13 (*hu'h'*).

10.4. great is their glory The word for glory is the Mishnaic word *ziv* read here by Habermann (second edition only). The difficulty caused by the bad writing here is described on p. 238 above, but this reading seems likely from examination of the facsimile and makes excellent sense, providing a noun to agree with the adjective **great** in the singular, which follows it.

The reading *yom* of 4QSb and 4QSd is also very attractive. As Milik remarks (*RB* 67, 1960, pp. 410 ff.), the same word could be read here in 1QS if we suppose that the tops of the first two letters have become entangled with one another, to form a defective *hē*. The translation would then be 'At their renewals is a great day for the holy of holies . . .', that is, each of the intercalary days, when it recurs, is a great day.

for the holy of holies   See the extended notes on 8.5 ff., especially on **a house of holiness for Israel** and **a holy of holies for Aaron**, which show that the phrase used here means the community.

10.5. at every time which comes   Whatever happens on earth during the present era, while waiting for God's final action the sect will be comforted by the punctual return of these days in the solar year: observation that the sun has arrived at the vernal equinox, the summer solstice, the autumnal equinox and the winter solstice on the days when these were expected will confirm their trust in God, who has revealed his own calendar and shows that he is still working according to this revelation which he has given to them. The pious expression of the author is somewhat ideal: use of the calendar would have shown the equinoxes and solstices falling on different days in subsequent years, owing to the calendar not really corresponding to the solar year (see p. 85).

10.5b–6a: *First days of each month and sabbaths as prayer-times*

In the beginning of the month at their set times   The last clause (which could be translated 'at their seasons', though less appropriately here) emphasizes that the first day of each month is exactly determined by the solar calendar, and is not to be settled by observation of the moon.

holy days . . . as memorials   Weise rightly draws attention to the connexion between sabbaths and remembering, referring especially to Ex. 20.8. He refers also to Gen. 2.3; Ex. 20.11; Deut. 5.12; Isa. 58.13; Neh. 9.14, and *Jub.* 2.1, 19–32; 50.9. All these further references emphasize the holiness of the sabbath, and the last calls it a 'festival and a holy day'. There seems therefore no doubt that by holy days the sabbaths are intended.

in their proper times Those arrived at by determining the beginning of the month by the sun (by which calculation it fell always on a Wednesday in months one, four, seven and ten, on Friday in months two, five, eight and eleven, on Sunday in months three, six, nine and twelve) and not by the wayward moon. Weise would indeed interpret the Hebrew word as 'in their seasons', arguing that the determination of the sabbaths depends on the seasons which in their turn depend on the special solar (intercalary) days.

10.6. the offering of the lips See on 9.4.

as a statute engraved for ever **As** is loosely used to link the system of worship to the cosmic time-table which regulates that system. The author will bless God with the regularity due to a system of worship divinely ordained; moreover, this system is closely regulated by the sequence of astronomical events which he thinks of as **a statute engraved for ever**. The fixed quality of the behaviour of the heavenly bodies is affirmed in (for example) *I Enoch* 2.1: 'Observe ye everything that takes place in the heaven, how they do not change their orbits, and the luminaries which are in the heaven, how they all rise and set in order each in its season, and transgress not against their appointed order' (*AP* II, p. 189).

10.6b–7a: *Prayer at the four points of the solar calendar* (cf. 10.3b–5a)

In this section the intercalary days are apparently again signified, being described differently from the language in 10.3b–5a. The whole passage 10.1 (or 9.26)–11.22 is expressed with considerable poetic eloquence and may well be a unity, the division between 10.8a and 10.8b being far from abrupt.

at the beginning of the years The Hebrew phrase in the singular means in effect New Year's Day, usually the first day of Tishri. The orthodox calendar celebrated and still celebrates this day as New Year's Day even after adopting a calendar which begins the New Year officially six months before, with the month of Nisan (see p. 24). The tractate *R'osh Hashshanah* explains at its opening that there are four New Year Days. The calendar of the sect seems to have recognized two **beginnings of the years**, that is the spring and autumn equinoxes. As we have seen, these are supposed to fall always on two of the intercalary days of the perfect solar calendar (see the general note at the beginning of the commentary on 10.3b–5a above).

at the turning-point of their seasons These were supposed to fall always on the other two great solar days, that is the summer and winter solstices, the first coming half-way between the spring and autumn equinoxes, the second half-way between the autumn equinox and the following spring equinox. We thus have the four intercalary days, but given a different expression from that in 10.3b–5a.

the season of wheat harvest . . . season of herbage   The four seasons which lie between the four pivotal days are now expressed from an agricultural point of view: they are **wheat harvest** (spring equinox to summer solstice); **summer** or fruit harvest (summer solstice to autumn equinox); **sowing** (autumn equinox to winter solstice); **herbage** (winter solstice to spring equinox). The day when **the season of wheat harvest** passes to **summer** is the summer solstice, the day when **the season of sowing** passes to **the season of herbage** is the winter solstice. The emphasis here falls mainly on the solstices, but also on all the four days, as in *Jub.* 29.16 (see p. 84), and the expressions there may be correlated with the present passage as follows:

Jub. 29.16	Solar event	Date	*Rule* 10.7
between the times of the months	spring equinox	IV.1	
between ploughing and reaping (i.e. reaping and ploughing)	summer solstice	VII.1	when the season of wheat harvest passes to summer
between autumn and the rain	autumn equinox	X.1	
between winter and spring	winter solstice	I.1	when the season of sowing passes to the season of herbage

Each of these four days has a calendrical significance in *Jub.* 29.16 and is a day for prayer according to the present passage in the *Rule*.

10.7b–8a: *Festival years at the end of seven-year periods and jubilee years as prayer-times*

feasts of years   Feasts which are determined by the passage of years, as distinct from feasts within a year determined by the passage of days. The following phrase further explains this.

seven-year periods   The Hebrew word, normally 'weeks', is used here in the same way as in Dan. 9.24–27. The conception is based on Lev. 25.1 ff.

at the summit . . . feast of release   Lev. 25.8 ff. This whole phrase is an elaborate way of saying 'in the jubilee years' when not only the slave but the land was set free from service. For the importance of jubilees and jubilees of jubilees in Qumranite understanding of history, see pp. 102 ff.

10.8. fruit of praise See the note on 9.4: the passages there mentioned show the affinity of this phrase with the **offering of the lips** recurring here.

HYMN: 10.8b–11.15a

10.9. my lyre and my harp The Hebrew says literally 'the lyre of my harp'. This and the phrase 'the flute of my lips' show clearly the purely metaphorical reference to instruments as in 1QH 11.23 (cf. I Cor. 14.15), although Milik (*RB* 67) reports 4QSd reading probably 'I will play upon my harp in tune . . .' The instrument translated **lyre** is the *kinnor*, illustrated on the Israeli stamp 1956 celebrating *R'osh Hashshanah* (30 pr.) and the **harp** (*nebel*) in that for 1955 (250 pr.). Both are plucked stringed instruments. They are mentioned together in Pss. 81.2 and 150.3.

flute Heb. *chalil.* Isa. 30.29. The instrument is depicted as of two pipes on the 1956 Israeli *R'osh Hashshanah* 150 pr. stamp.

I will raise For this musical use of the verb see Ps. 81.2.

string of his decree 1QH 3.27; 6.26 (where, however, the metaphors are not musical). The author will tune his song (**the flute** of his **lips**) to the sound of **the string** as God has tuned it; that is, he will regulate his life of worship to God's cosmic ordinance.

10.10. the coming-in of day and night The phrase is reexpressed by **the going-out of evening and at morning.** Both the poetical repetition and the clear mention of only two prayer-times support the view taken above on 10.1–3a.

I will come into the covenant paralleled by **I will recite his statutes** and meaning the same, that is, probably, the recital of the *Shema'* (Deut. 6.4). See below on line 14.

10.11. without returning Like the bounds set to the sea in Ps. 104.9, they will prevent the author from **returning** to a path which he has now left and to which he must not return, since this would mean living according to a quite different way. It seems possible that this whole passage is reminiscent of Job 33.25 ff.

declare The Hebrew verb is often used of contentious argument, especially in Job (cf., e.g., 19.5). Here the author says in effect that he will convict himself.

my transgression is before my eyes Job 33.27; Pss. 32.5; 38.18; 51.3; Prov. 28.13; Luke 18.13 f.; I John 1.9.

'My righteousness!' Isa. 54.17; Jer. 23.6; 33.16; Ps. 4.1 (Hebrew 4.2); cf. the name Zedekiah, which may mean 'Yah is my righteousness'. The conception that God in himself is the only vindication, redemption and salvation of sinful and limited man is summed up in this concise phrase. For the conception itself cf., for example, Isa. 45.21; 56.1; 62.1–3; Pss. 5.8; 119.142; 143.11; Rom. 1.17; 3.21, etc. In the NT God as righteousness, God as eternal vindication, succour, redemption, salvation is seen and encountered in Christ, a doctrine stated in, for example, II Cor. 5.21. Christ is the divine righteousness personified in I Cor. 1.30. Since in Gal. 2.19 ff. Paul's life in faith is equated with Christ living in Paul, Christ is his righteousness. This means that God has appeared in his character as righteousness in the action which is wrought by and in Christ, which almost *is* Christ (Rom. 3.21 ff.). The present eloquent passage of the *Rule* shows the author sharing with Paul and all other believers in God that act of final trust which is simultaneously the recognition of God as above all other values.

10.12. the highest Heb. *'elyon*. Perhaps originally the name of a shrine in Gen. 14.18 ff., the word was interpreted as 'highest' and used often as a title of the LORD in the OT: Num. 24.16; Deut. 32.8; II Sam. 22.14; Pss. 9.2; 18.13; 21.7, etc; Isa. 14.14; Lam. 3.35, 38; Dan. 7.18 ff.; it appears also in the NT, as at Mark 5.7; Luke 1.32, 35, 76; 6.35; 8.28; Acts 7.48; 16.17; Heb. 7.1—the last being a reference to Gen. 14.18 ff.

source of knowledge It is important to observe that God is in this poetic writing actually identified with the **source of knowledge**. Elsewhere in the scrolls he opens or gives such a source to his chosen, almost always to his chosen one, the author, as in 1QH and in this hymn. The phrases to be found in the scrolls which employ this word source (or 'fount') reveal clearly the essential ideas in the profound thinking of the sect or of its founder: 1QS 11.3; 1QH 2.18; 12.29 again speak of the source of knowledge; the frgt. 1Q 36.12.2 speaks of a well of knowledge; 1QS 11.5 f. of the source of God's righteousness; 1 QH 6.17 of a well of light from an eternal source; 8.8, 20 f.; 10.31; 1QSb 1.3, 6 all of an eternal source. This eternal source, then, is the source for chosen men of their knowledge and of righteousness imparted to them by God and, as here, sometimes identified with God. This is the more intelligible when we reflect that God is or is to

be the bestower of the water which will cleanse for life in the new age
(1QS 4.20 ff.). Thus in 1QH 8.13 f. the waters of holiness are
associated with the source of life in which a man must trust, and
1QH 1.22 and 12.25 both speak of a source of waters for purification.
Reverence for the source of life is reflected in the ritual purity
required in connexion with human genital organs, as, for example,
in DSW 7.6, as well as in the OT. By contrast 1QS 3.19 speaks of a
source of darkness (translated with literary licence **well of darkness**)
from which the generations of perversity arise. See further on
11.3.

well of holiness　8.8; DSW 12.2; 1QH 12.2; 1QSb 4.25. Cf.
1QS 10.1, 3; 1QH 12.5; frgt. 9.7. The word here translated **well** is
often synonymous with the word for **source** and sometimes means a
pool. The phrase here belongs closely to the nexus of images discussed in the previous note.

10.12–13. I will choose . . . what he decrees for me　This
double sentence, using the familiar parallelism of Hebrew poetry,
illustrates very well the Hebraic attitude to the great problem of
moral responsibility before an omnipotent God, the religious form
of the logical difficulty of reconciling belief in the individual's free will
and the pervasive sense of ability to initiate action with a universe in
which the behaviour of its constituent parts is apparently governed
by universal laws to which they are all not only subject but inexorably
bound. For the ethical monotheist not only is God sovereign but
neither may his sovereignty nor his ways be questioned (Rom. 9.20);
yet God demands righteousness of man. Echoes both of this position
and of its difficulties are found, for example, in Isa. 45.7; Amos 3.6;
Wisd. 12.12; 15.7 ff.; Rom. 9.14 ff. In this last famous passage Paul
wrestles with the problem boldly and from a logical point of view
quite unsuccessfully. The believer in God cannot indeed answer the
logical question, but can only state his belief in the form of a description of his own apparent experience. This is to the effect that when
he exerts his will aright and commits himself to right action he fulfils
God's will for himself: he chooses what God ordains. Among NT
writers Luke most clearly believed in a much simpler view, that there
was a plan from God which man could accept or refuse. Thus Luke
7.30; Acts 13.46; but cf. Acts 2.23 for apparent divine predestination
of evil action.

The author of the *Rule* here states with precision the religious
attitude, with words akin to Paul's concise statement in Rom. 6.18

and the description of God in the second collect for Mattins in the *Book of Common Prayer* as the one 'whose service is perfect freedom'.

10.13–14. Before the putting forth of my hands . . . This and the other phrases indicating points of time in everyday life are poetic variants on Deut. 6.7. Talmon (*SH* IV, pp. 187 ff.), drawing attention to this, also points out the parallel between this part of the *Rule*'s closing hymn with the detailed instructions on the same subject of what to pray and when in the Mishnah tractate *Berakoth*. Talmon sees also reminiscences of the *Eighteen Benedictions* (the *Shemoneh* '*Eśreh*) called *Tephillah* in *Ber.* 4.1, 3 (see Danby, *op. cit.*, p. 5 n. 2). The 'benedictions' number, in fact, nineteen, the twelfth, the famous *birkath hamminim*, denouncing heretics, having been added in the first century AD. The prayer, also known as the '*Amidah* because it is said standing, can be studied in Singer's *Authorised Jewish Prayer Book*, pp. 44–54.

10.14. from the table set If **from** is right, the meaning is poetically expressed: the set table gives rise to an offering of praise in the speaker; but the letters *beth* and *mem* look very alike in 1QS and if we read a *beth* here instead of a *mem* we may translate 'at the table . . .' The mention both of table and companions recalls 6.4 f. and suggests that the writer of the *Rule*'s hymn is himself a priest, if we suppose that he is reflecting on his life in the community.

10.15. fruits of the earth Cf. the ninth benediction of the *Tephillah* (*Birkath hashshanim*—the Benediction of the Years).

At the onset of fear or terror *Ber.* 9.5: 'Man is bound to bless for the evil even as he blesses for the good.' The author here mentions the kind of evil specially likely to overtake a member of the sect, subject as he was to the danger of persecution. Cf. line 17 below. The insight into God's providence even when evil befalls is paralleled in Job 2.10 and in a spirit much nearer to the present passage in Matt. 10.26–32 (Luke 12.2–9). The outlook of Matt. 5.10 ff. (Luke 6.22 f.) is a little different.

10.17. to no man evil recompense The very important ethical teaching implied here is fully discussed in the commentary on 7.7, 9. This passage is remarkably like Rom. 12.21.

10.18–19. I will not show jealousy with a spirit of evil show jealousy translates the verb 'to be zealous'. See the commentary on 4.4 and especially on 9.23 (**to be a man zealous**). This makes excellent sense, but the context suggests that possibly *ruach* here should be differently pointed to give the word *revach* (profit), and the

translation would then be 'I will not be desirous of evil profit', fitting
well with the following phrase.

10.19. wealth got through violence   11.2; CD 6.15; 8.5;
1QpHab 8.11; Prov. 10.2; 11.4; Ecclus. 5.8; Luke 16.9, 11; *I Enoch*
63.10. There seems little doubt that the zealots of the day are either
specifically condemned here or at least included in the condemnation.
See next note.

strife of men of destruction . . .   Thus could be described
the activities of the zealots whose attacks upon the wealthy and
conservative members of their own nation caused many Jews who
would otherwise have sympathized with their aims to regard them
as no better than bandits. The author preserved his understanding of
zealot ideals, but his reading of the will of God for the times made
him believe that this included abstention from violence until the final
war which he identifies with **the day of vengeance** (see on 9.23).

10.19–20. I will not retract my wrath   He is careful to make
clear that his abstention from physical hostility towards wicked men is
consistent with preserving detestation of them, as God requires.

10.20. those who return from transgression   Again the
phrase is from Isaiah, viz. 59.20, a verse of great importance for
Judaism in this period. CD 2.5 and 20.17 virtually identify such men
with the community, and Licht, referring to these passages and to
1QH 2.9; 6.6, regards the phrase as a title of the sect. Isa. 59.20 is
quoted at Rom. 11.26 f. and in this connexion is interestingly discussed by Lindars, *New Testament Apologetic*, p. 245.

I will offer no comfort   If it is right to see the influence of the
book of Isaiah in this hymn (see on 9.18 and 9.19 above), there may
well be a reminiscence here of Isa. 40.1.

10.21. Belial   See on 1.18. The author will entertain no secret
hankering to join the world and to use worldly means to gain even
divine ends.

10.22. the fruit of holiness   See 9.4 and 10.8. Wernberg-Møller
(pp. 148 f. n. 70) provides a most ingenious conjecture as to the
origin of this verse. If he is right, it illustrates vividly the use made of
Scripture by the men of Qumran. Lev. 19.24, 'And in the fourth
year all their fruit shall be holy, an offering of praise to the LORD'
(RSV), if slightly altered, some words being little more than repointed
(compared with MT), gives, instead of the plain meaning, 'And on
my tongue . . . there shall be fruit of holiness; profane things shall
not be (there).' One example of the process may suffice: the first

word of Lev. 19.24 is *wbshanah*, 'and in the year' (the MT follows
with the word 'fourth', but the author of 1QS omits it); this is
altered to *blshony* ('on my tongue'). The contrasting phrase 'fruit of
deceit' is found in Hos. 10.13, but not used here, as we might have
expected. A general parallel to the ethical ideals of the passage can
perhaps be seen in Eph. 5.4, as Kuhn suggests (*NTS* 7, 1960–1,
p. 339).

10.23. righteous acts of God   See on 10.11 ('**My righteousness!**'). Judg. 5.11; I Sam. 12.7; Micah. 6.5; Ps. 103.6; Isa. 45.24;
Dan. 9.16 all illustrate very clearly that the phrase means the actions
by which God has in the past rescued and vindicated his people when
they were in distress.

until the completion   Side by side with the history of the
merciful deeds of God the author will recite the parallel history of
the sinful deeds of men, which are **treachery** because they have
ever broken the covenant which God always keeps. But this history is
moving to an end, which God will bring upon it (4.18 ff.).

10.24. uncleanness   Cf. Eph. 5.3, where the author, like the
author of the *Rule*, begs that such things be 'not even mentioned'.
More profoundly, the author of the *Rule* declares he will banish these
evils from his **heart**, reflecting the same outlook as that found in
Mark 7.15 ff. (cf. Matt. 15.10 ff.) and Matt. 5.27 f. The word translated
here is really a plural, the singular *niddah* being the technical word
for the condition of uncleanness and as such the title of a Mishnah
tractate (see on 3.4, **waters for purification**). The present
passage is a remarkable testimony to the extent to which something
originally a taboo could receive a moral interpretation at this
period.

I will conceal knowledge   So Habermann, who remarks that
there is a reference here to the sect's concealment of their teaching.
We may compare 9.17 (see note); but the scribe of 1QS has corrected
the word *'str* by placing a dot under the third letter (*t*) and writing
over it *p*. This would give the opposite meaning, 'I will tell' or
'declare'. It seems possible that the original had **conceal** and that there
was indeed a reference to the secrecy of the sect's teaching; and that
the scribe, after copying it correctly, had misgivings because he did
not see the reference.

10.25. I will fence   For the verb cf. Job 1.10. Wernberg-Møller
remarks on 'the esoteric intellectualism of the society' here expressed
and regards the passage as 'an allegorical interpretation of Isa.

26.1–3'. The phrase 'make a fence round the Torah' ('*Aboth* 1.1) uses different words, but the author may be referring to this principle here as well as to his doctrine of secrecy. In this sense a fence is a further measure the keeping of which ensures the keeping of the main injunction. It is well explained by a saying of R. Akiba reported in '*Aboth* 3.17, worth citing for its affinity with the thought of this passage of the *Rule*: 'R. Akiba said, Jesting and levity lead a man to lewdness. The Massorah [oral tradition] is a fence to the Torah; tithes are a fence to riches; vows are a fence to abstinence; a fence to wisdom is silence' (trans. Singer, *op. cit.*, p. 195; Danby's numeration is 3.14, that of *AP* II, 3.18).

the righteousness of God The creation of an esoteric and privileged sect the author regards as a saving act of God no less than the others in history which he promised to recite. It is his correct response to this creative act of God to behave with the secrecy which God demands.

10.26. the measuring-line of the times See the note on 1.9. The reference is to the art of perceiving the message which a passage of Scripture has for a particular time, and ensuring appropriate action.

strengthening of hands for the fearful Isa. 35.3 f.

11.1. to instruct The verb is found at 4.22; 9.18, 9.20; 11.18 and the noun derived from it at 3.13; 9.12; 9.21, as well as at 1.1 if the reconstruction is correct. See the notes there and on 9.12, and p. 72.

to respond with humility Prov. 15.1; 25.15.

11.1–2. men of authority The vocabulary as far as **utter iniquity** is from Isa. 58.9, but does not correspond exactly to the MT nor to the text of 1QIsa (a), which read for the word here translated **authority** (literally 'staff') the word for yoke.

2. point the finger The oppressor is no doubt envisaged, as he singles out a victim for his attendants, probably soldiers, to seize. Wernberg-Møller rightly remarks that we cannot be certain of the meaning here 'because we do not know how our author interpreted Isa. 58.9'.

are zealous for wealth See on 10.19 (**wealth got through violence**). Here there seems a certain reference to the zealots; for even if at the time of the composition of the *Rule* the word was not yet a technical term, those who adopted violent measures on principle already prided themselves on their 'zeal'.

my judgment is with God   The lofty attitude here taken in view of persecution is typical of the Essenes as they are reported by Josephus, *BJ* 2.8.10 (for the passage see the note on 11.13 below), and of early Christians such as those who obeyed the counsel of, for example, I Peter 3.14, both resting upon the principle expressed in Isa. 8.12 f., cf. 49.4.

perfection of my way   1QH 4.30; Jer. 10.23; Prov. 13.6.

11.3. in his righteousness he will blot out   Wernberg-Møller points out that part of the vocabulary of this and of the preceding phrase is taken from Deut. 9.5; but the sense here is quite different. The **righteousness** of God which he has yet to perform is his action at the end of the age when he will accomplish the purification of **some from mankind** and **impart the wisdom of the sons of heaven to the perfect of way** (4.20 ff.). This purification will remove all blemishes from these elect and the author, believing himself to be among them, declares his faith that God will thus remove his **transgression** as though removing a stain by the use of water.

source of his knowledge   See on 10.12.

his light   The imagery is explained in the section on the Two Spirits where the concept of light in its relation to God is discussed (see esp. pp. 38 ff.). The notion here is of the privileged **illumination of** a single **heart** by God and the result—or the aspect of it emphasized here—is intellectual enlightenment. The author claims that **upon** God's **wonders** his own **eye** has **gazed.** The NT comes close to this only at a few points, esp. John 1.9 (see also the remarkable passage, Luke 11.33.; cf. Matt. 6.22 f.), for God dwells in unapproachable light (I Tim. 6.16) and he can be seen only in the incarnate Jesus (John 1.18; I John 1.1 f.).

11.3–4. in the secret of what shall be . . .   The phrase reminds us that for all the philosophical, even mystical flavour of the passage, its genre is apocalyptic. The revelation vouchsafed is of history. The thought is very close to that of 1QH 1.9 ff.; 4.13; 7.31 f. Enoch 'whose eyes were opened by God' (*I Enoch* 1.2) 'understood' . . . 'for a remote' generation. Thus, too, Dan. 2.28 f., 45 declares that God reveals the future by special means and John is to be shown the future in Rev. 4.1.

11.4. a strong rock . . .   Pss. 40.2 (Hebrew 40.3); 73–23; 85.13 (Hebrew 85.14).

shall not be shaken   Accepting the emendation of Guilbert and

Wernberg-Møller. For the verb whose *hithpalpel* is here read cf. 8.8; 1QH 6.27; 7.9.

the truth of God Bo Reicke (in *NTS* 1, 1954–5, pp. 139 f.) urges that the 'source of his knowledge' 'is quite simply the Law and the Prophets'. It is no doubt in one sense the Law and the Prophets, but not quite simply. **The truth of God** is indeed in the Scriptures, but divine illumination is necessary to reveal it to a specially endowed mind. See the note on 1.3 (**his servants the prophets**). Again, apocalyptic implies a special revelation by an angel or some such intermediary (see the full discussion on pp. 63 ff.).

11.5. the source of his righteousness See on 10.12.

decrees of light See on line 3 **his light.**

from his marvellous secrets These are the secrets in the Scriptures which the author is specially endowed to interpret. See the note on **the truth of God** above. It is a special feature of this claim that the endowment is peculiar to the author who thus possesses **wisdom . . . hidden from man**, who indeed, according to 1QH 7.32; 10.3 ff.; 12.27 f.; 13.13 f., cannot unaided attain to such wisdom.

11.7. from the assembly of flesh Supply before this phrase **hidden**, from the two previous phrases in line 6. On the phrase see below on line 9.

he has given them i.e. the gifts just mentioned, wisdom, knowledge etc.

an eternal possession There is one other occurrence in the scrolls of the word here translated **possession**, but the context is lost: CD 16.16. In Gen. 17.8; 48.4; Lev. 25.34, for example, it is the land which Israel is to inherit. The sect is to receive instead divine illumination and teaching. Cf. the phrase **their inheritance** at the end of the line.

11.7–8. the lot of the holy ones For **lot** in the sense of a class to which one may belong see on 2.2 **lot of God. The holy ones** are angels, as in Zech. 4.5; Ps. 89 (LXX 88).6; I Thess. 3.13; II Thess. 1.10; *I Enoch* 1.9; *Did.* 16.7. The members of the sect are to share the life of angels, and they are united with them in one community. Cf. 1QSa 2.3 ff.; 1QSb *passim*, esp. 4.25 ff.; 4QFl 1.3 ff.; 1QH 3.21 ff.; 6.13; DSW 7.6; 12.1 ff., and see B. Gärtner, *The Temple and the Community in Qumran and the New Testament*, pp. 63 ff., 88 ff., 92 ff. See also following note.

11.8. the sons of the heavens A periphrasis for 'sons of God' and again meaning angels. Cf. Gen. 6.2, 4; Job 1.6; 2.1; 38.7; Pss. 29.1; 89.7 (note the parallelism with 'holy ones' in the previous verse).

he has united their assembly   See note on **the holy ones** (7–8) above for the belief that God intended to unite the sect at the end of the age with the great company of his angels: it is no accident that the Pharisees believed in both resurrection and angels (Acts 23.8), for the one implied the other, as Jesus' teaching at Mark 12.25; Luke 20.36; Matt. 22.30 clearly shows. This idea of men and angels sharing a community is reflected outside the NT at *I Enoch* 104.6; *II Bar.* 51.5, 10, 12; as well as in the scrolls. Paul does not mention the term angels in connexion with the resurrection, but knows that flesh and blood must be transformed for it (I Cor. 15.44 ff., esp. 50); for him the final action of God which accompanies this transformation is 'the revelation of the sons of God' (i.e. of the angels) in Rom. 8.21. In the *Rule* it will be effected by God's purification of some of mankind (4.20 ff.); in the NT the great meeting of human and of heavenly beings is eloquently described at Heb. 12.23.

a house of holiness   See on 8.5, **a house of holiness for Israel**. There the word is *beth*, here *mabnith* as at 1QH 7.4, 9.

a planting for eternity   See 8.5, **an eternal planting**.

11.9. I belong   For all his confidence in God as his righteousness the author feels that even he belongs in some important sense to the other, sinful division of mankind (cf. 4.23 f.). Here is a remarkable parallel to Paul's famous, equally autobiographically styled, passage, Rom. 7.7–8.11, esp. 7.25.

The Adam of wickedness   4.23; 5.17; 11.6, 10, 15, 16, 20; CD 3.16; 9.1; 10.8; 11.16; 12.4, 16; 14.11; 19.25; DSW 10.14; 11.12; 1QH 1.21 ff.; 3.24 f.; 4.29 ff.; 12.32–34; 13.15 f., etc.; *II Bar.* 54.19; IV Ezra 3.21 f.; 4.30; Rom. 5.12–21; I Cor. 15.22, 45; Eph. 4.22; II Peter 1.4.

At 4.23 Adam is certainly the correct translation, but at 5.17 it is translated 'man', as it might well be here; but the transliteration is adopted to illustrate the fact that the term is used often in Jewish literature in this collective and corporate sense. It is significant that besides the frequent use in 1QH it is thus used eight times in CD, twice in DSW, but in the *Rule* only at 5.17 in this way other than the six times all concentrated in this column, where the thought is so closely parallel to that of 1QH. The meaning is partly determined by the parallel phrase **assembly of evil flesh** (equivalent to **men** of the lot of Belial 2.5), but partly by the conception which sees man himself as divided into two 'inclinations' (see the discussion on pp. 42 f.).

evil flesh   11.7, 12; DSW 4.3; 12.12; 1QH 4.29; 10.23; 13.13; 15.12, 21; 17.25; 18.21, 23, etc; Gen. 6.3, 12; Isa. 31.3; 40.6; Jer. 17.5; Job 10.4; Pss. 56.4; 78.39; Mark 14.38; John 1.13; 3.6; 6.63; 8.15; Rom. 6.19; 7.5, 18, 25; 8.3–13; 13.14; I Cor. 5.5; 15.50; II Cor. 10.2; Gal. 4.23; 5.16–24; Eph. 2.3; Phil. 3.3; Col. 2.11; I Peter 1.24 (cf. Isa. 40.6); II Peter 2.10, 18; I John 2.16; Jude 23; *'Aboth* 2.7; *Sotah* 5a. Kuhn ('Temptation, Sin and Flesh' in *The Scrolls and the New Testament,* p. 101) writes with careful precision: 'In the Qumran texts the word "flesh" is contrasted not only to the spirit of *God* but to the "spirit of truth", which the believer possesses, in accordance with his predestination. Therefore, man as "flesh" is unworthy of God and prone to do evil, or rather, prone to succumb to the Evil One. . . . Thus "flesh" becomes a contrast to the "spirit" which rules the pious man and determines his good actions, and dwells within him; consequently "flesh" becomes the area of weakness through the natural inclinations of man; it becomes almost synonymous with evil.' This is true: it should be emphasized that throughout the Hebraic tradition flesh is not evil in itself but rather the morally and spiritually weak, mortal, this-worldly element in man, the element in which sin and indeed all kinds of evil can find a hold and dwelling-place. Man is the riddle of the world, his being composed of flesh and spirit renders him an enigma, a paradox. The psalmist asks 'What is man?' and affirms his belief that God has made him lower than gods (who are not flesh but spirit) only to crown him with glory and honour (Ps. 8.5 f.), a prophecy about man which in the NT is applied to Christ, who alone, in Christian belief, has fulfilled this destiny (Heb. 2.5–9).

The author of this hymn rejoices that he, though flesh or dust, is granted revelation by God as though he were spirit (e.g. lines 20–21 below; cf. the frequent parallels in 1QH). The same sort of wonder at God's loving-kindness to undeserving man is found throughout the NT although the express contrast between flesh and spirit is not always present, as it is in so many of the passages whose references are given above. Later gnostic thought went beyond the orthodox wonder that God was willing to communicate with man, who is a mixture of flesh and spirit, and taught that he could communicate only with man's spirit, expressing surprise, even incredulity that spirit could be at home in the flesh. Thus the *Gospel of Thomas* logion 29: 'Jesus said: if the flesh has come into existence because of the spirit, it is a marvel; but if the spirit (has come into existence) because of the body, it is a marvel of marvels. But I marvel at how this great wealth has made its home in this poverty.'

my iniquities, my transgressions, my sins See on 1.24 **confess.**

11.10. assembly of worms 11.21; Isa. 14.11; (66.24); Job 7.5; 17.14; 21.26; 24.20; 25.6 (esp. the last, where man is compared to a worm); (Ecclus. 7.17); (Judith 16.17); Mark 9.48. The bracketed references are to another but synonymous Hebrew word. Probably the author thinks of flesh as belonging to the dominion of worms because of the common sight of this activity in putrefying meat; but it is possible that they are typical of those who live in darkness.

walk in darkness 3.21; 4.11; Isa. 9.2; Eccles. 6.4.

no way of his own Jer. 10.23. Brownlee and Wernberg-Møller are surely right to insist that the line is a clear case of haplography, the word *l(o)'* (not) having fallen out before *l'* at the beginning of *l'adam.*

11.11. by his knowledge shall everything happen Ecclus. 39.18–20; 1QH 1.20; 7.32; 10.2, 9. This line is a firm and lucid statement of the sovereignty and omnipotence of God. The language is accidentally like John 1.3, but there is no *logos* doctrine here, the statements being straightforward assertions of God's creative power. There is a very close parallel in 1QH 10.2, 9.

11.12. the mercies of God are my salvation for ever The assertion, using the vocabulary of Ps. 13.5, and indeed words which are indispensable to any summary of OT theology, expresses the faith of all monotheism, couched as it is in various forms. **Mercies** translates the plural of the key word *chesed*, loving-kindness or covenant love, the forgiving love of God by virtue of which he adheres to the covenant though Israel be faithless. For the Christian, God's mercies are epitomized and made active in Christ, the doctrine being summarized in many passages in the NT, e.g. Rom. 3.23–25; Gal. 2.16; Col. 1.13 f.; Heb. 9.11 f.; I John 2.1 f. The writer here as elsewhere (especially if he is the author also of 1QH) shows a strong conviction of personal vocation by God which gives him the assurance that God will forgive and remove his sins.

11.13. if my affliction should begin Like the early Christian

Church, the men of Qumran were destined to experience trial ('temptation') in two main forms, temptation to sin and testing by persecution, the latter being in itself a temptation to sin—that of denying God (or Christ).

he will deliver my life   Perhaps rather 'my soul': the vocabulary is that of Ps. 116.8 and the sentiment, originally a thanksgiving for the preservation of life when the psalmist was in mortal danger, is used even for a situation in which the delivered one loses his life in this world. Cf. II Macc. 7.9, 11, 14, 23. Paul makes this expectation integral to his outlook: Gal. 6.14, 17 (cf. Luke 14.27); II Cor. 4.10 f.; Phil. 1.20 f.; 3.8–10, and expresses it in moving terms in the face of death, II Tim. 4.18. In the Gospels it becomes a well-known corner-stone of teaching, as in Mark 8.35; Matt. 10.39; 16.25; Luke 9.24; 17.33; John 12.25. Josephus testifies of tortured Essenes in *BJ* 2.8.10, 'Smiling in their agony and gently mocking those who put them on the rack, they resigned their souls in the joyous certainty that they would receive them back.'

will make my steps firm   See on 11.10 above and cf. Pss. 37.23; 40.2 (Hebrew 40.3).

he has drawn me near   Cf. the idea in lines 16 f. below that God's chosen receives the special boon of being before God's face for ever. The idea of God drawing a person near to him is not common in biblical literature if we are restricted to this actual metaphor, but it is found in the following important passages: John 6.44; 12.32; cf. 6.37, 65; 17.6–8. A perhaps kindred metaphor is used in Acts 16.14. The underlying idea that God causes a man to turn to him in the spiritual sense is too common to need illustration. See also next note.

11.13–14. in his mercies he will bring in my judgment   Job 14.3; Eccles. 11.9; 12.14. The phrase suggests that the previous clause may be a forensic metaphor. God has drawn his servant near to judgment (cf., for example, Job 9.32; 14.3), but his judgment is an act of mercy.

11.14. he will cover   God's act of judgment, that is of mercy, includes this action expressed by the same verb which is used of atonement; but the idea that God has himself provided the atonement sacrifice for all mankind (Rom. 3.25) is entirely absent. For the atonement doctrine in the *Rule* see on 2.8 (**forgive by covering thine iniquities**).

he will purify me   See 4.20 ff.

R.Q.M.—R

11.15b. Blessed art thou   This formula for the beginning of a *berakah* (or benediction) does not appear in this exact form in the Bible. The formula 'Blessed be the LORD' is too common to require illustration from the OT, but the presence of *berakoth* in the NT is not always recognized. See Luke 1.68; Rom. 1.25; 9.5; II Cor. 1.3; 11.31; Eph. 1.3; I Peter 1.3; cf. I Tim. 1.11; 6.15 (this last being apparently an adaptation of an elaborate and self-conscious *berakah*). The formula was already so standard by the time of the composition of the first tractate of the Mishnah (*Berakoth*) that Benedictions are economically quoted there without it, the words being left to be automatically supplied (*Ber.* 6.1 ff.).

O my God   This exact address is uncommon in the Bible. See Pss. 22.2; 25.2; 102.24; Neh. 6.14. Cf. Pss. 7.1, 3; 63.1; 118.28; 140.6; Neh. 4.4.

who openest for knowledge   An Isaianic theme. Cf. Isa. 50.5 where God *opens* the ear of his servant (cf. 1QH 16.18; Ps. 116.16); **knowledge** is given for comfort in 9.18 (see note *ad loc.*).

11.16. the son of thy handmaid   Ex. 23.12; Pss. 86.16; 116.16.

the chosen among mankind   The sect's conception of themselves as the remnant to be established at the end of the age was no doubt shared with the zealots, as it certainly was with the early Church. Rom. 8.28 f.; 11.3 ff.; Gal. 4.28; Phil. 3.3; cf. Luke 2.34; Matt. 21.42; I Peter 2.8 ff.; Rev. 2.9.

11.16–17. to present himself before thy face for ever   The radical meaning of this highly significant prayer may be approached by way of examining the occurrence of the concept in the cult and in the consciousness of biblical writers. According to a very primitive code, each male must present himself three times in the year (at the great festivals) before God (Ex. 34.23; cf. 23.17; Deut. 16.16), and it was expected that he would bring a sacrifice, and not appear 'empty' (Ex. 23.15; Deut. 16.16). Closely connected is the ordinance to present every male firstborn to God, a softening of the original command to give (i.e. sacrifice) him to God, Ex. 13.2, 12, 15; Luke 2.22. In Deut. 31.11 all Israel is to appear before God (cf. Ps. 84.7).

The ceremonial observance is expressive of a feeling much more profound than is apparent: to come to appear before God was, perhaps is, at once the deepest desire and the deepest dread. The psalmist longs for the day (Ps. 42.2), the unknown prophet asks with great force by what sacrifice (since he must not appear 'empty') he ought to come before God (Micah 6.6–8). The classical Christian expression of the whole matter and of the answer to the prophet's question is found in Heb. 10.19–22. It is in the assurance of this final coming into the presence of God that Paul exhorts his readers to present their bodies (i.e. themselves) to God as a living sacrifice, Rom. 12.1; cf. 6.13, 19; and the author of Ephesians exhorts to valiant conduct in the time of persecution in order to be able finally 'to stand' (i.e. before God) on the evil day (of temptation or judgment), Eph. 6.13.

Our author prays for the final and eternal self-presentation before God, the privilege which Rev. 7.15 accords to the martyrs. Cf. 1QH 2.22–25.

11.17. without thy will nothing shall be brought to pass See on line 11 above. It will be observed that the last part of the hymn repeats a great deal of what has gone before in only slightly different words.

11.18. there is none other like thee 1QH 7.32; 10.9; II Sam. 7.22; I Chron. 17.20.

to give instruction Cf. Ecclus. 42.21; Wisd. 9.13.

11.19. understanding in all thy marvellous works Job 37.14.

11.19–20. power of thy might 1QH 4.32; 18.8; frgt. 15.4; cf. I Chron. 29.12; II Chron. 20.6.

11.20. comprehend thy glory Ecclus. 42.17; cf. 18.1–14; IV Ezra 8.21.

man among thy wondrous deeds 1QH 7.32 f.; 10.11; 11.4; Pss. 8.4 (Hebrew 8.5); 105.2; 144.3; Job 37.14. The deeds are the miraculous events wrought by God in history; among them is counted his creation of the various constituent parts of the world (Gen. 1.1–2.1).

11.21. born of woman 1QH 13.14; 18.12 f., 16, 23 f.; Job 14.1; 15.14; 25.4; Ecclus. 10.18. All these passages emphasize the finitude of man and his membership of the order of this world with which is contrasted that of the new age, sometimes thought of as already existing and removed from this world not by time but by space (e.g. Matt. 6.10; 18.10). Thus angels live in the other heavenly order; but when the fulness of time comes it will be possible for finite mortal men, whose origin and life exists so far only on the biological level, to attain to the other order of life. This is stated in John 1.12 f. In Matt. 11.11; Luke 7.28 it is not clear whether the two orders of existence are contrasted spatially or temporally. In all these passages emphasis falls on natural origin as implying inevitable limitation (John the Baptist is not blamed for his inferior status) and the means by which the ideal of John 1.13 can be fulfilled, that is by which some can attain sonship—the status of 'sons of God' or angels—is by unity with him whom God has sent to enter into their own mortality, finitude and subjection. Thus Jesus is **born of a woman** 'that we may receive sonship' (Gal. 4.4).

dwell in thy presence   *mah* is here taken as meaning *how?*—as often in the OT, e.g. Prov. 20.24 where the thought is similar. There is no need to emend to *mah yi'hasheb* ('how shall he be accounted?'); 1QS reads clearly *m-h-y-sh-b*. Dots above and below these letters have been taken to indicate error and so to justify emendation; but the scribe usually writes his corrections above the incorrect word. The facsimile shows the dots above and below the small space between the *he* and the *yodh*, i.e. between *mah* and *yesheb* on our interpretation. It seems then that the scribe was merely indicating that he should have left a bigger space in order to make clear that he intended two words.

from dust   1QH 3.21; 10.4 f.; 10.12, etc; DSW 14.14 (already noticed as akin to 10.1 ff.); Gen. 2.7; 3.19; 18.27; Ps. 103.14; Eccles. 12.7; I Cor. 15.47.

his forming   The word does not appear in biblical or Mishnaic Hebrew, but the root, one of whose meanings is to create or fashion, is common. The translation therefore follows Wernberg-Møller, who comments that the Peshitta of Gen. 2.7 uses the root *gbl*.

the food of worms is his dwelling   See on 11.10. Earth (the food of worms) is what man occupies: he inhabits the earth and he occupies a body formed from it. The whole passage is reminiscent of Job 4.19. Milik (*RB* 67) remarks that 4QSj supports 1QS here with *mdoro*; that this is the true reading of 1QS seems clear from the facsimile (although *mem* and *samech* are not easily distinguishable) and the transcription seems to be wrong in reading *s-d-u-r-u*, i.e. *sidduro*, his order (sc. of being). Both words are Mishnaic.

ejected spittle   The word or words—it appears to be only one—at the end of line 21 comprises the letters *m-ṣ-u-r-u-q* or *m-ṣ-u-r-r-q*, the penultimate letter being slightly smudged and uncertain. Habermann reads the ms. in the latter fashion, but prints *miṣṣur[uq]*. His note shows doubt about both reading and interpretation: (1) Isa. 51.1 suggests that *ṣur* (rock) may be used metaphorically of source or origin and that therefore we might read and point *miṣṣur* 'from a source', followed by *rq*, i.e. *req*, 'empty' or 'vain'. The attraction of this suggestion is that it accounts for all the letters in the ms. without alteration, *rq* appearing in this *scriptio defectiva* as an adjective at 10.24 and CD 10.18, and in five other places in the scrolls as an adverb; its disadvantage is that even in poetic language it seems strained to speak of a man arising from an empty or vain rock. (See below for the conjecture of Brownlee based on *ṣur* as a verb.) (2) *mṣydduq* can be paralleled from 1QH 12.32, where the phrase is *mṣydduq yṣr chmr*, upon which Licht comments that the sense, derived from the context, appears to be that a certain righteousness has been granted to 'a creation of clay' which enables him to utter words of praise. The vocabulary of the two passages certainly already has affinities which this emendation would increase, but Habermann rightly observes that the meaning in the 1QH passage also is obscure. Guilbert refers further to 1QH frgt. 2.8, 16, but gives up the problem in despair. It may be noted that 1QH frgt. 2.16 might support the reading *mṣydduq*. (3) *mh yṣdq* would mean 'What shall justify?' But this is too easy and too far from the ms.

Brownlee reads *m-ṣ-ṣ-u-r* as a noun otherwise unknown, derived from *ṣur*, a known root meaning 'to fashion, delineate' (cf. Ex. 32.4; I Kings 7.15). He does not discuss *rq*, but translates 'something shaped' (cf. Vermès 'but a shape').

Wernberg-Møller has an informative note for both this phrase and the following: he reads here *mṣy roq*. *Mṣy* he takes as a noun meaning 'something squeezed out, emitted', from the verb *mṣh*. (Is this the correct reading at 1QH frgt. 2.8? Licht reads *mṣu* [*thkhh*], but see Kuhn, *Konkordanz*, p. 74, s.v. *ḥmr*.) *Roq* means spittle, sometimes used (as *Niddah* 16b) for semen. Behind this rendering lies the conviction that the author is here depreciating man as formed from water, i.e. semen called 'a putrid drop' in *'Aboth* 3.1, whose thought and vocabulary are like that of this passage. This is the interpretation adopted in the translation.

11.22. clay nipped off 1QH 1.21; 3.24, 30; 4.29; 10.4 (where perhaps *mḥmr* could be restored before *qurṣ*); 11.3; 12.24, 26, 32; 18.12; frgts. 1.8; 2.8; 11.7; Gen. 2.7; Job 4.19; 10.9; 33.6; Pss. 8.4; 144.3; Isa. 45.9. The meaning here is quite clear. Mansoor in his note on 1QH 10.4 gives references to show that the phrase is part of 'Hebrew ceramic vocabulary'. Man is clay and because any individual man's body is derived from that of another man he is a piece of clay broken off from clay. The word used in Job 33.6 for 'nipping off' is found in the Gilgamesh Epic. It is tempting to compare Burke's remark about the younger Pitt as 'a chip of the old block', but the notion expressed in the *Rule* that man is clay is not intended as a metaphor, since the author believes that man really is made of dust and water. Of the passages referred to, 1QH 10.3 ff. and 12.24 ff. show such remarkable parallels that it is tempting to conclude an identity of authorship between those *Psalms of Thanksgiving* and this hymn. See also on 11.11.

for dust is his desire   Gen. 3.16. The word recurs in the scrolls at DSW 13.12; 15.10; 17.4. In the context of a passage like the present, emphasizing the humiliating character of man's origin, the reading (which is clear) is no doubt correct, although 1QH 10.4 (cf. 12.26) tempts to the emendation *tshubhtho*, 'his return' (cf. Gen. 3.19).

formed by hand   Continuing the theme of clay, but here introducing a metaphorical element, as though to be made of clay meant to be literally moulded by hand. This poetic licence seems the more likely explanation than to take **hand** as a euphemism for the *membrum virile* as at 7.13.

BIBLIOGRAPHY

TEXTS AND TRANSLATIONS OF THE SCROLLS
(normally cited by editor's or translator's name only)

BROWNLEE, W. H., *The Dead Sea Manual of Discipline, Translation and Notes* (Bulletin of the American Schools of Oriental Research, Supplementary Studies Nos. 10–12), American Schools of Oriental Research, New Haven, 1951

BURROWS, M., TREVER, J. C., and BROWNLEE, W. H., *The Dead Sea Scrolls of St Mark's Monastery*, The American Schools of Oriental Research, New Haven: Vol. I, *The Isaiah Manuscript and the Habakkuk Commentary*, 1950; Vol. II, Fasc. 2, *Plates and Transcription of the Manual of Discipline*, 1951

CARMIGNAC, J., and GUILBERT, P., *Les Textes de Qumran traduits et annotés*, Letouzey et Ané, Paris, 1961 (cited as Guilbert)

DUPONT-SOMMER, A., *The Essene Writings from Qumran*, Eng. trans. by G. Vermès, Blackwell, Oxford, 1961

GASTER, T. H., *The Scriptures of the Dead Sea Sect*, Secker and Warburg, London, 1957

HABERMANN, A. M., *Megilloth Midbar Yehuda* [The Scrolls from the Judean Desert], 2nd ed., Machberoth Lesifruth, Tel-Aviv, 1959 (Hebrew)

LICHT, J., *The Thanksgiving Scroll, Text, Introduction, Commentary and Glossary*, Bialik Institute, Jerusalem, 1957 (Hebrew)

MAIER, J., *Die Texte vom Toten Meer*: Vol. I, *Übersetzung;* Vol. II, *Anmerkungen*, Reinhardt, Munich and Basel, 1960

MANSOOR, M., *The Thanksgiving Hymns*, Translated and annotated with an Introduction, Brill, Leiden, 1961

RABIN, C., *The Zadokite Documents*, Clarendon Press, Oxford, 1954

VERMÈS, G., *The Dead Sea Scrolls in English*, Penguin Books, Harmondsworth, 1962

WERNBERG-MØLLER, P., *The Manual of Discipline*, Translated and annotated with an Introduction, Brill, Leiden, 1957

YADIN, Y., *The Scroll of the War of the Sons of Light against the Sons of Darkness*, Eng. trans. by Batya and Chaim Rabin, OUP, 1962

OTHER BOOKS AND ARTICLES

AALEN, S., *Die Begriffe 'Licht' und 'Finsternis' im alten Testament, im Spätjudentum und im Rabbinismus*, Norske Videnskaps Akademi, Oslo, 1951

' "Reign" and "House" in the Kingdom of God in the Gospels' in *NTS* 8.3 (April 1962), pp. 215 ff.

ABBOTT, E. A., *Notes on New Testament Criticism*, A. and C. Black, London, 1907

ALLEGRO, J. M., 'An Astrological Cryptic Document from Qumran' in *JSS* 9.2 (Autumn 1964), pp. 291 ff.

AUDET, L. P., 'Affinités littéraires et doctrinales du Manuel de Discipline' in *RB* 59 (1952), pp. 219 ff. and 60 (1953), pp. 41 ff.

BETZ, O., 'Donnersöhne, Menschenfischer und der Davidische Messias' in *RQ* 3.1 (Feb. 1961), pp. 41 ff.
Offenbarung und Schriftforschung in der Qumransekte, Mohr, Tübingen, 1960
Der Paraklet: Fürsprecher im häretischen Spätjudentum, im Johannes-Evangelium und in den neugefundenen gnostichen Schriften, Brill, Leiden, 1963

BEVAN, E., *Jerusalem under the High-Priests*, Arnold, London, 1904

BLACK, M., *The Scrolls and Christian Origins*, Nelson, Edinburgh, 1961

BRONGERS, H. A., *De Gedragsregels*, Proost en Brandt N.V., Amsterdam, 1958

BROWNLEE, W. H., *The Meaning of the Qumran Scrolls for the Bible*, OUP, New York, 1964

BRUCE, F. F., *Biblical Exegesis in the Qumran Texts*, Tyndale Press, London, 1960

BURROWS, M., *The Dead Sea Scrolls*, Secker and Warburg, London, 1956
More Light on the Dead Sea Scrolls, Secker and Warburg, London, 1958

BUTLER, B. C., 'The "Two Ways" in the Didache' in *JTS* (NS) 12.1 (April 1961), pp. 27 ff.

CARMIGNAC, J., 'Les rapports entre l'Ecclésiastique et Qumrân' in *RQ* 3.2 (May 1961), pp. 209 ff.

CHARLES, R. H., *The Book of Jubilees*, Translated from the Editor's Ethiopic Text, with Introduction and Notes, A. and C. Black, London, 1902

CROSS, F. M., *The Ancient Library of Qumran*, Duckworth, London, 1958

DANBY, H., *The Mishnah translated from the Hebrew with Introduction and Brief Explanatory Notes*, Clarendon Press, Oxford, 1933

DAVIES, J. G., *He Ascended into Heaven*, Bampton Lectures 1958, Lutterworth, London, 1958

DAVIES, W. D., *Paul and Rabbinic Judaism*, SPCK, London, 1955
Christian Origins and Judaism, Darton, Longman and Todd, London, 1962
The Setting of the Sermon on the Mount, CUP, 1964

DE VAUX, R., *L'Archéologie et les manuscrits de la mer morte* (Schweich Lectures for 1959), OUP, London, 1961

DIELS, H., and KRANZ, W., *Die Fragmente der Vorsokratiker*, 3 vols., Widmannsche Buchhandlung, Berlin, 1922

DODD, C. H., *The Interpretation of the Fourth Gospel*, CUP, 1953

DODDS, E. R., *Plato: Gorgias*, Clarendon Press, 1959

DUPONT-SOMMER, A., *The Jewish Sect of Qumran and the Essenes*, Eng. trans. by R. D. Barnett, Valentine Mitchell, London, 1954

EDERSHEIM, A., *The Life and Times of Jesus the Messiah*, Two Volumes in One, Longmans, Green, London, 1906

Encyclopaedia of Religion and Ethics (ed. J. Hastings), T. and T. Clark, Edinburgh, 1908–1926
   (Articles: 'The Ages of the World'
        'The Essenes'
        'Pythagoras and Pythagoreanism')

FINEGAN, J., *Handbook of Biblical Chronology*, Princeton U.P., Princeton, New Jersey, 1964

FLUSSER, D., 'The Baptism of John and the Dead Sea Sect' in *Essays on the Dead Sea Scrolls*, ed. C. Rabin and Y. Yadin (q.v.)

FOERSTER, W., 'Der heilige Geist im Spätjudentum' in *NTS* 8.2 (Jan. 1962), pp. 117 ff.

GÄRTNER, B., *The Temple and the Community in Qumran and the New Testament*, CUP, 1965
   The Theology of the Gospel of Thomas, Eng. trans. by E. J. Sharpe, Collins, London, 1961

GERHARDSSON, B., *Memory and Manuscript*, Gleerup, Uppsala, 1961

GERTNER, M., 'The Masorah and the Levites' in *Vetus Testamentum* 10.3 (1960), pp. 241–72

GLASSON, T. F., *Greek Influence in Jewish Eschatology*, SPCK Biblical Monographs, London, 1961

GONDOEVER, J. VAN, *Biblical Calendars*, Brill, Leiden, 1959

GUILBERT, P., 'Le plan de la *Règle de la Communauté*' in *RQ* 1.3 (Feb. 1959), pp. 323 ff.

HANSON, R. P. C., *Tradition in the Early Church*, SCM Press, London, 1962

HENGEL, M., *Die Zeloten*, Brill, Leyden, 1961

HIPPOLYTUS, *Apostolic Tradition*, ed. B. S. Easton, CUP, 1934

HOOKE, S. H., *The Siege Perilous*, SCM Press, London, 1956

JAUBERT, A., *La Date de la Cène*, Gabalda, Paris, 1957

Jewish Encyclopedia, ed. I. Singer, 12 vols., Funk and Wagnalls, New York, 1901

JONGE, M. DE, *The Testaments of the Twelve Patriarchs*, A Study of their Text, Composition and Origin, Van Gorcum, Assen, 1953

JOSEPHUS, *Flavii Josephi Opera* recognovit Benedictus Niese, 2 vols., Weidmann, Berlin, 1888
   The Works of Flavius Josephus, trans. by W. Whiston, Brown and Nelson, Edinburgh, 1835
   The Jewish War, trans. by G. A. Williamson, Penguin Books, Harmondsworth, 1959

KAHLE, P. E., *The Cairo Geniza*, 2nd ed., Blackwell, Oxford, 1959

KIRK, G. S., and RAVEN, J. E., *The Presocratic Philosophers*, CUP, 1957

KUHN, K. G., 'Der Epheserbrief im Lichte der Qumrantext' in *NTS* 7.4 (July 1961), pp. 334 ff.
Konkordanz zu den Qumrantexten, Vandenhoeck and Ruprecht, Göttingen, 1960
'The Lord's Supper and the Communal Meal at Qumran' in *The Scrolls and the New Testament*, ed. K. Stendahl (q.v.), pp. 65 ff.
'New Light on Temptation, Sin and Flesh in the New Testament' in *The Scrolls and the New Testament*, ed. K. Stendahl (q.v.), pp. 94 ff.
'The Two Messiahs of Aaron and Israel' in *The Scrolls and the New Testament*, ed. K. Stendahl (q.v.), pp. 54 ff.

LEHMANN, M. R., 'Ben Sira and the Qumran Literature' in *RQ* 3.1 Feb. 1961), pp. 103 ff.
' "Yom Kippur" in Qumran' in *RQ* 3.1 (Feb. 1961), pp. 117 ff.

LIGHTFOOT, J. B., *The Epistles of St Paul; Colossians and Philemon*, Macmillan and Co., 8th ed., 1886 (pp. 347–417, 'The Essenes')

LINDARS, B., *New Testament Apologetic*, SCM Press, London, 1961

LOWTHER CLARKE, W. K., *Divine Humanity*, SPCK, London, 1936

MAUSER, U. W., *Christ in the Wilderness*, SCM Press, London, 1963

MILIK, J. T., *Ten Years of Discovery in the Wilderness of Judaea*, Eng. trans. by J. Strugnell, SCM Press, 1959
Review of Wernberg-Møller's commentary in *RB* 67 (1960), pp. 410 ff.

MONTEFIORE, C. E., and LOEWE, H., *A Rabbinic Anthology*, Macmillan, London, 1938

MORGENSTERN, J., 'The Gates of Righteousness' in *HUCA* 6 (1929), pp. 1 ff.

NEUSNER, J., *A Life of Rabban Yohannan ben Zakkai*, Brill, Leiden, 1962

NOACK, BENT, 'The Day of Pentecost' in the *Annual of the Swedish Theological Institute* I (ed. H. Kosmala), Brill, Leiden, 1963, pp. 73 ff.

NOCK, A. D., and FESTUGIÈRE, A. J., *Corpus Hermeticum*, Paris, 1945

PHILO, ed. with an English translation by F. H. Colson and G. H. Whittaker, Loeb Classical Library, 10 vols., Heinemann, London, 1929–52

PRIEST, J. F., 'Mebaqqer, Paqid and the Messiah' in *JBL* 81 (1962), pp. 55 ff.

RABBINOWITZ, J., *Mishnah Megillah*, OUP, 1931

RABIN, C., *Qumran Studies*, OUP, 1957
'The Literary Structure of the War Scroll' in *Essays on the Dead Sea Scrolls*, ed. C. Rabin and Y. Yadin (q.v.)

RABIN, C., and Yadin, Y. (edd.), *Essays on the Dead Sea Scrolls in Memory of E. L. Sukenik*, Hekhal Ha-Sefer, Jerusalem, 1961 (Hebrew)

REICKE, Bo, 'Official and pietistic elements of Jewish apocalypticism' in *JBL* 79 (1960), pp. 137 ff.
'Traces of Gnosticism in the Dead Sea Scrolls?' in *NTS* 1.2 (Nov. 1954), pp. 137 ff.

ROMANIUK, K., 'La crainte de Dieu à Qumrân et dans le Nouveau Testament' in *RQ* 4.1 (Jan. 1963), pp. 29 ff.

RUSSELL, D. S., *The Method and Message of Jewish Apocalyptic*, SCM Press, London, 1964

SANDERS, J. A., *Suffering as Divine Discipline in the Old Testament and Post-Biblical Judaism* (Colgate Rochester Divinity School Bulletin, Vol. 28, special issue), 1955

SCHECHTER, J., *Mabo' la-Siddur*, Debir, Tel-Aviv, 1958 (Hebrew)

SCHECHTER, S., *Some Aspects of Rabbinic Theology*, A. and C. Black, 1909

SCHOLEM, G. G., *Jewish Gnosticism, Merkabah Mysticism and Talmudic Tradition*, Jewish Theological Seminary of America, New York, 1960
Major Trends in Jewish Mysticism, Thames and Hudson, London, 3rd edition, 1955

Scripta Hierosolymitana IV, ed. C. Rabin and Y. Yadin, Magnes Press, Jerusalem, 1958
    (Articles: J. Licht, 'An Analysis of the Treatise of the Two Spirits in DSD'
             S. Talmon, 'The Calendar Reckoning of the Sect from the Judaean Desert'
             D. Flusser, 'The Dead Sea Sect and Pre-Pauline Christianity')

SEITZ, O. J. F., 'Two Spirits in Man: an Essay in Biblical Exegesis' in *NTS* 6.1 (Oct. 1959), pp. 82 ff.

SIMON, U., *Heaven in the Christian Tradition*, Rockliff, London, 1958

SINGER, S., *The Authorised Daily Prayer Book*, 24th ed., Eyre and Spottiswoode, London, 1956

SMITH, MORTON, 'The Dead Sea Sect in Relation to Ancient Judaism' in *NTS* 7.4 (July 1961), pp. 347 ff.

SNAITH, N. H., *The New Year Festival*, SPCK, London, 1947

STARCKY, J., 'Les quatre étapes du messianisme à Qumrân' in *RB* 70.4 (Oct. 1963), pp. 481 ff.

STENDAHL, K. (ed.), *The Scrolls and the New Testament*, SCM Press, London, 1958

STEWART, R. A., *Rabbinic Theology*, Oliver and Boyd, Edinburgh, 1961

STRACK, H. L., and BILLERBECK, P., *Kommentar zum Neuen Testament aus Talmud und Midrasch*, Beck, Munich, 1928

SUTCLIFFE, E. F., 'Sacred Meals at Qumran?' in *Heythrop Journal* 1.1 (Jan. 1960), pp. 48 ff.
The Monks of Qumran, Burns and Oates, London, 1960

TARN, W., and GRIFFITH, G. T., *Hellenistic Civilization*, by Sir William Tarn, 3rd ed., revised by the Author and G. T. Griffith, Arnold, London, 1952

TALMON, S., 'The Calendar Reckoning of the Sect from the Judaean Desert' in *Scripta Hierosolymitana* IV (q.v.), pp. 165 ff.
'The "Manual of Benedictions" of the Sect of the Judaean Desert' in *RQ* 2.4 (Nov. 1960), pp. 475 ff.

TESTUZ, M., *Les Idées religieuses du Livre des Jubilés*, Droz and Minaud, Paris, 1960

THOMSON, G., 'The Greek Calendar' in *Journal of Hellenic Studies* 63 (1943), pp. 52 ff.
'From Religion to Philosophy' in *Journal of Hellenic Studies* 73 (1953), pp. 77 ff.

TOULMIN, S., and GOODFIELD, J., *The Fabric of the Heavens*, Hutchinson, London, 1961

VERMÈS, G., *Scripture and Tradition in Judaism*, Brill, Leiden, 1961

WALLENSTEIN, M., *The Nezer and the Submission in Suffering Hymn from the Dead Sea Scrolls*, Nederlands Historisch-Archaeologisch Instituut in het Nabije Oosten, Istanbul, 1957

WEINGREEN, J., 'Exposition in the Old Testament and in Rabbinical Literature' in *Promise and Fulfilment: Essays presented to S. H. Hooke on his Ninetieth Birthday*, ed. F. F. Bruce, T. and T. Clark, Edinburgh, 1963

WEISE, M., *Kultzeiten und Kultischer Bundesschluss in der 'Ordensregel' vom Toten Meer*, Brill, Leiden, 1961

WHITTAKER, M., *Die Apostolischen Väter* I: *Der Hirt des Hermas*, Akademie-Verlag, Berlin, 1956

WIESENBERG, E., 'The Jubilee of Jubilees' in *RQ* 3.1 (Feb. 1961), pp. 3 ff.

WILLIAMSON, G. A., *Josephus, the Jewish War*, trans. G. A. Williamson, Penguin Classics, Harmondsworth, 1959

WOUDE, A. S. VAN DER, *Die messianischen Vorstellungen der Gemeinde von Qumran*, Assen, 1957

INDEX OF SUBJECTS

Booths, Feast of, date, 24
Bul, 23

Cairo Damascus Document, see *Damascus Document*
Calendars, Babylonian, 20 ff.; Essene, 62; Israelite, 22, **23** ff., 39, 60, 79, **80** ff., **86** ff., 90, **95** ff., **101** ff., 148; of worship, 113, 237 ff.; Qumran, 25 f., 41, 60, 68, 79, **80** ff., **86** ff., **92** ff., **101** ff., 120, 140, 148, 230, 237 ff., 241 ff.
Camp Overseer, 189, 195
Canaan, influence on Israelite calendar, 23, 25
Celibacy, among the Essenes, 31 f., 113; among the Therapeutae, 32; at Qumran, 32, 211
Chaburah, 106 f., 162 f., 180 f., 194
　see also *Ma'amad*
Chaldeans, 87
Chaos, 80
Chesed, 256
Chief Priest (high priest), 127; office hereditary to sons of Zadok, 91
Christ, appoints the Twelve, 213; as intercessor, 133; coming to end Era of the Law, 103; condemns blasphemy, 202; crowned with glory, 255; epitome of God's mercies, 256; focus of doctrine of atonement, 214; incarnation, 259 f.; in Johannine Literature, 50; is divine righteousness, 246; light of life, 143; prophecy of his coming, 225; Qumran expectations, of, 182; rejection, 219; resurrection on third day, 98 ff.; reveals God's light, 252; sacrifice of, 219; teaching: on baptism, 140, on love, 121, 204 ff., on resurrection, 254, on the Spirit, 50, 53, on the state, 206; victory over the devil, 103, 126; withdrawal to the wilderness, 164
　see also Spirit, The Holy; Messiah
Christianity, concept of appearing before God in, 259; influences of Judaism on, 49 f.
　see also Church, The early; Judaism; New Testament; Paul
Chronicler, The, affinities with Ezra-Nehemiah and Ezekiel, 90; records

sectarian movements in Judaism, 92, 163
　see also Chronicles, Books of
Chronicles, Books of, affinities with Pentateuch, 90; evaluation of priests and Levites, 69 ff., 92; *midrash* of rewritten Kings, 74
Chronology, 83
　see also Calendars
Church, The, bride of Christ, 219
Church, The early, attitude to persecution, 252; bishops in, 189; conception of the new age, 103, 258; dating of Resurrection, Ascension and Pentecost, 98 ff.; Messianic hopes, 182; ordination of presbyters, 188; practice of mutual rebuke, 179; sharing of property, 122; use of Scripture, 222
　see also Baptism; New Testament; Paul
Circumcision, 167
Clay, man is, 261 f.
Cleanness, see Defilement; Holiness; Purification; Sin
Commandments, see Decalogue; Love
Commonwealth, Second, 70
Communism, see Wealth, Sharing of
Community, Titles of the, 136, 172 f., 180, 231
　see also Council of the Community; Holiness, Community of; Qumran community
Confession, 113, 128 f., 256
Constellations, see Astronomy; Universe
Conversion, 130
Corner-stone, 215 f., 218 f.
Council, of the community, 112, 120, 136, 166, 168 f., 172 f., 180, 182, 186 f., 189–91, 193, **211**, **212**, 214, 219; of the Many (the assembly): as judgment court, 169, 180, as court for interpretation of the Law, 166, as legislature, 169; power to examine and admit candidates, 191; priest to preside over, 182; rules for speaking in, 190
Counsel, member's to be at service of community, 197, 199, 208; of God, 35, 120, 123, 136, 139, 142; spirit of, in the New Testament, 120; in the Qumran community, 35, 120, 136, 139, 142

War, Eschatological, 33, 43, 214, 216, 218, 233, 249
War Scroll, 54, 69, 74, 93, 113, 127 f., 178, 237
Water, symbolism of, 215, 219
 see also Wells; Purification
Way, of God in the wilderness, **222** f.; of man, 142 f.; of the Lord, 231; of the righteous, 149
Wealth, sect's attitude to sharing of, 121–3, 164, 196, 199; to that got by violence, 249, 251
 see also Money
Weeks, Feast of (Pentecost); assembly of sect held annually on, 135; association with Law and Covenant, **99** ff.; date, 24 f., 94, 95 ff., 102; feast for renewal of the covenant, 95 ff., **104** ff., 140; origins as agricultural festival, 25, 100
Well, of darkness, 37, 47, 247; of holiness, 247; of knowledge, 196; of light, 246; of power, 196; of righteousness, 196, 246
Wicked, The, wickedness, 131, 135, 147, 154, 156, 158 f., 172, 217 f., 249; Adam of, 254
 see also Defilement; Evil; Iniquity; Purification; Sin; Transgression; and Index of Proper Names: Belial; Satan
Wilderness (desert), The; Way of God in, 222; withdrawal to, 139, 164, 212, 216, 220–2, 231 f.
Wisdom, and apocalyptic, **57** ff., 74; and the Law, 45 ff., 58; the secrets of God, 252 f.; equated with heavenly light, 45, with the Torah, 45, gift of

God, 36, 49, 60, 86, 160, 252 f.; moral character of, 58; of Solomon, 57
Wisdom of Solomon, Book of, 30; Greek influence on, 60; part of Wisdom literature, 57
Woes, Messianic, 215
Women, 32; see also Celibacy
Women, Court of, 76
Words, The, 199 f.
Work, 173, 180, 232
Worship, calendar of, **237** ff.; system of, based on structure of the universe, 88, 148; maintained by priests, 70; through praise, 224 f., 237, 248

Yeṣer haraᶜ, 153, 167
 see also Man, good and evil in
Yeṣer zenuth, 153
Yissurim, 137–9, 201
 see also, Fire, Refining; Order; Punishment
Yom kippur, 104
Yom kippur Prayers, 140

Zadok, Sons of, Zadokites; adherence to solar calendar, 92 ff.; at Qumran, 33, 90, 162, 171, 180, 231; authority of Zadokite priesthood, **91** ff., **165** ff., 177, 214, 225
Zeal, 151, 232 f., 248 f., 251
Zealots, comparison with men of Qumran, 33; condemned by author *Rule*, 249, 251; remnant to be established at end of the age, 258
Zeqenim, see Elders
Zif, 23
Zodiac, 19 ff., 81

INDEX OF NAMES

INDEX OF REFERENCES

BIBLICAL PASSAGES

OLD TESTAMENT

APOCRYPHA

NEW TESTAMENT

PSEUDEPIGRAPHIC LITERATURE

SCROLLS PASSAGES

RABBINIC PASSAGES

OTHER LITERATURE